ROUTLEDGE LIBRARY EDITIONS:
HISTORIOGRAPHY

Volume 29

INTERPRETATIONS OF HISTORY

INTERPRETATIONS OF HISTORY
Confucius to Toynbee

ALBAN G. WIDGERY

LONDON AND NEW YORK

First published in 1961 by George Allen & Unwin Ltd

This edition first published in 2016
by Routledge
2 Park Square, Milton Park, Abingdon, Oxon OX14 4RN

and by Routledge
711 Third Avenue, New York, NY 10017

Routledge is an imprint of the Taylor & Francis Group, an informa business

© 1961 Alban G. Widgery

All rights reserved. No part of this book may be reprinted or reproduced or utilised in any form or by any electronic, mechanical, or other means, now known or hereafter invented, including photocopying and recording, or in any information storage or retrieval system, without permission in writing from the publishers.

Trademark notice: Product or corporate names may be trademarks or registered trademarks, and are used only for identification and explanation without intent to infringe.

British Library Cataloguing in Publication Data
A catalogue record for this book is available from the British Library

ISBN: 978-1-138-99958-9 (Set)
ISBN: 978-1-315-63745-7 (Set) (ebk)
ISBN: 978-1-138-19261-4 (Volume 29) (hbk)
ISBN: 978-1-138-19263-8 (Volume 29) (pbk)
ISBN: 978-1-315-63982-6 (Volume 29) (ebk)

Publisher's Note
The publisher has gone to great lengths to ensure the quality of this reprint but points out that some imperfections in the original copies may be apparent.

Disclaimer
The publisher has made every effort to trace copyright holders and would welcome correspondence from those they have been unable to trace.

INTERPRETATIONS OF HISTORY
CONFUCIUS TO TOYNBEE

ALBAN G. WIDGERY

LONDON
GEORGE ALLEN & UNWIN LTD
RUSKIN HOUSE   MUSEUM STREET

FIRST PUBLISHED IN 1961

This book is copyright under the Berne Convention. Apart from any fair dealing for the purpose of private study, research, criticism or review, as permitted under the Copyright Act, 1956, no portion may be reproduced by any process without written permission. Enquiry should be made to the publisher.

© *Alban G. Widgery*, 1961

PRINTED IN GREAT BRITAIN
in 11 *on* 12 *pt. Janson*
BY SIMSON SHAND LTD
LONDON, HERTFORD AND HARLOW

To the Memory of
JAMES WARD
*Late Professor of Mental Philosophy
in the University of Cambridge*

PREFACE

What is the nature of human history? What meaning or meanings has it, if any?

Consideration of those questions has occupied me for a great part of a long life. Many answers have been given to them in the course of history. Some, implied in the great religions and in forms of civilization, have been and are still widely held. Others have been maintained by individual thinkers and particular groups, especially in the Occident. In the present volume I give an account of the chief of these as illustrative of some of the possible answers. My exposition is only incidentally critical. In a later volume I hope to present my own conclusions as to them.

Whatever erudition there may be in or behind this work, it is not meant primarily for scholars, though some may find it useful to have together what I have assembled in it. The questions concern everyone, and the intelligent may be expected to be interested in answers already proposed to them. Young historians and philosophers might learn much from this account. With one exception, detailed references have not been given. They might be distracting. The exception is for Arnold J. Toynbee's *The Study of History*, inserted because of the wide range over ten volumes. Any who need other references should have no difficulty in tracing them. A few recent works on the subject have not been described, either because they are well enough known or because I am not convinced of their significance.

Even with its limitations, the scope of this book is still wide. Friends have read chapters in particular fields in which they are specialists: Chapter I, Dr Wing-Tsit Chan, Professor of Chinese Culture, Dartmouth College; II and IV, the late Dr J. T. Manry, Professor of Philosophy, Forman College, Lahore, Pakistan; III, Dr H. M. Poteat, Professor of Latin, Wake Forest College; V, Dr Waldo Beach, Professor of Christian Ethics, Duke University; VI, Dr E. W. Nelson, Professor of History, Duke University; VII, Dr W. E. Hocking, Professor (emeritus) of Philosophy, Harvard University; VIII, Dr Vergilius Ferm, Professor of Philosophy, The College of Wooster. Dr Arnold J. Toynbee read the section on his work in Chapter IX. I express my thanks to these for their comments and suggestions. They are not to be regarded as necessarily accepting the views presented.

It was the late James Ward, Professor of Mental Philosophy

in the University of Cambridge, who, more than forty years ago, first aroused me to take a historical view of experience, and I dedicate this book to his memory. The volume contains the first part of a series of lectures delivered on the Reynolds Foundation at Amherst College. I have to thank Duke University for financial aid for several years through its Research Council for its production.

ALBAN G. WIDGERY

CONTENTS

PREFACE 9

PART ONE. GENERAL CONCEPTIONS OF HISTORY—Oriental and Occidental

I *Quietist and Social Attitudes to History in China* 15

II *Metaphysical and Individualist Views of History in India* 43

III *Conceptions of History in Ancient Greece and Rome* 65

IV *Theistic Conceptions of History: I. Zoroastrian, Jewish, Islamic* 90

V *Theistic Conceptions of History: II. Christian* 114

PART TWO. PARTICULAR THEORIES OF HISTORY—Occidental

VI *Some Independent Reflections on History from the Renaissance to the Nineteenth Century* 143

VII *Idealist Treatments of History in the Nineteenth Century and After* 178

VIII *Naturalist Treatments of History in the Nineteenth Century and After* 203

IX *Attitudes of Historians and the Approach to Philosophy of History* 231

INDEX 258

PART ONE

GENERAL CONCEPTIONS OF HISTORY
Oriental and Occidental

CHAPTER I

QUIETIST AND SOCIAL ATTITUDES TO HISTORY IN CHINA

I

FROM early times there was a considerable amount of written history in China. From what remains, it appears to have been mainly 'annals' with reference mostly to individuals of the ruling classes, the events of their lives, civil conflicts, and the rise and fortunes of successive dynasties. There was little reflection on the nature and meaning of history. There was no continued effort to find significance in historical processes and events in any remote goal. Attention was on the present and the past. The cultured of the occident have been fascinated and tremendously impressed by Chinese works of art, paintings, carvings of ivory, jade, and wood, and by the palaces of Peiping. But the amount of such art, however large it may seem independently considered, is comparatively little when thought of with reference to the long history and the teeming millions of the people of China. Throughout their history the masses of Chinese have been occupied with agriculture and handicrafts. Their lives have been essentially simple and it is from this standpoint that we may understand their attitudes to history. Even the philosophies of China have arisen in relation with this simplicity and they are largely imbued with its spirit.

There has been far more philosophical reflection and writing in the history of China than is usually supposed by occidentals. In this regard the Chinese may be placed along with some peoples of India, with the ancient Greeks and the Germans of the nineteenth century. Though Chinese philosophy has little *specific* consideration of the nature and meaning of history it is wrong to suppose that it has no implications with regard to them. Chinese philosophies have involved particular attitudes to history which might have led to theoretical expression and defence of definite philosophies of history. Those philosophies developed in relation with ideas formed in and largely shared by social groups. Some of these were widely accepted before being taken up in philosophical thought. The philosophies were often the expression of widespread beliefs; sometimes, at least in part, they diverged from them. To understand the Chinese attitude to history attention must be given to the chief of these early ideas and beliefs.

The most frequently used term in the philosophies was *Tao*, but it was known long before them. Though now usually translated: 'the Way', its early implications were probably wider. Nearest to the notion of 'the Way' is the meaning of regularity, especially in the processes of Nature as men leading a life of agriculture were concerned with it, the sequence of the seasons, the order in the growth, fruition, and decay of vegetation, the uniform repetition of the movements of the astronomical bodies. There were also some regularities, however simple, in the organized life of the social community. Men felt themselves to be part of Nature, with the immediate impression of spatial continuity as including all. *Tao* may have signified the vast whole of things experienced physically. *Tao*, as the whole, dominated all within It. As it was futile to strive against It, there was a widespread attitude of passive acceptance of the course of things. But the Chinese regarded neither the parts nor the whole of Nature as inanimate. However vaguely conceived, everything was treated and responded to as having an inner life such as men themselves felt. What Western scholars have called Animism was prevalent. The early Chinese talked of the 'spirits' of the rivers and trees and of most other things. The highest spirit was *Shang-ti*, 'the Lord of Heaven'. There was a 'commerce' between men and these non-human spirits, carried on in agricultural and domestic rites and in religious ritual. Eventually the supreme ruler of China came to be described as 'the Son of Heaven'. The early Chinese did not come to intellectual conceptions of themselves or of the Lord of Heaven as 'personal' in the modern occidental sense of that term. Nevertheless, their attitudes were 'as if' the spirits, including *Shang-ti*, were like themselves in practical response. Their histories were *not* lived as constituted simply of the relations of men to one another and to an inanimate physical world.

There was a general recognition of dualistic aspects of existence, expressed by the terms *Yin* and *Yang*. *Yin* stood for the receptive and relatively passive; *Yang* for the projective and active. One is complementary to the other, and life is a rhythm of the dominance of the one and then of the other. The history of the individual is a sequence of the rhythm of relative passivity and of dynamic striving. The history of social groups is analogous with that. *Yin* and *Yang* are two differentiated conditions within the *Tao* as the whole; and *Tao*, as regularity and order is manifested in them. The masses preserved an equanimity, resting in the whole and submissive to the universal rhythm of *Yin* and *Yang*.

Throughout their history the Chinese have almost universally practised ancestor worship. It suggests the belief that the spirits of those who had died still lived on with human needs. Only with such a belief are the forms of sacrifices, the visits to the tombs, and the domestic ancestral rites intelligible. The idea of personal immortality seems to be implied. But, curiously, there is little evidence of any general concern with that idea in such a manner as to affect this life or as involved in the meaning of history. The Chinese have not *indigenously* treated this life as preparatory to another in another world or as a stage to perfection to be attained in a series of lives. Most of those who adopted any such views accepted forms of Buddhism imported into China. Neither Taoist nor Confucian thinkers embarked on serious discussion of personal immortality or sought any meaning in history in that idea. The independent thinker Mo-Ti championed the belief but his influence was neither wide nor prolonged.

The lives of the majority of Chinese, though simple, were of course, not of unalloyed happiness. Even with the regularity of the *Tao* of Nature there were occasions of the failure and the destructions of crops through adverse weather conditions and other sufferings from storms and disease. In the *Odes* there are evidences of social inequalities and of maltreatment of the poor. Wars and banditry have been very frequent in the history of China. The adversities do not seem to have been met by any ardent looking forward to the future. There was rather a looking back to what was represented as a happy past, and with this an advocacy of return to its mode of life. Chinese thinkers often regarded history as teaching moral lessons, showing vice to be always punished and virtue always rewarded. Such results of conduct were not always or immediately apparent. Imperial power might be attained by the wicked; but it was urged that they could not keep it. Even though the wicked might appear fortunate in externals, inwardly they were miserable. War should be undertaken for defence with the conviction that the righteous will eventually win.

Consideration of the Chinese attitude to history must take into account a trait of character almost universal amongst them: their temperament of equanimity. Their imperturbability has been (and is) more general and conspicuous even than that of peoples of India. Individuals are not often very greatly disturbed by evils in their own histories; and they are rarely deeply moved by calamities in their social history as a people. This state of mind has persisted through Chinese history, shared to some extent by all, whatever the particular forms of thought they have professed. Their experience of history has been with resignation rather than with joy.

In the third century B.C. Tsou Yen formulated a cyclic view of history, analogous with the recurrence in natural processes. In the ancient *Book of Rites* there is a conception of three ages of the world. The Han commentators regarded that idea as implied in the *Annals of Spring and Autumn*. Very little attention was paid to this conception throughout Chinese history. It was, however, revived by K'ang Yu-wei (1858-1927 A.D.).

In consideration of the state of mind to which we have referred, the Chinese attitude to history may be called Quietist, and this with justification from much in their philosophies. The philosophies have indeed differed in the extent and manner in which in relation to the quietist state of mind they have urged practical activity and effort. It is appropriate to treat first of the philosophy of Taoism, although its ancient writings may have come to us from later periods than some of those of Confucianism. According to a long tradition, the founder of Taoism was Laotze. His historicity has been questioned, but there can be no scientific settlement of any doubt concerning it. What concerns us are the implications of Taoism regarding the interpretation of history and the attitudes to be adopted with relation to it. But through its long history there have been different forms of Taoism with some variations relative to history.

II

The earliest stage of specific Taoism has been regarded as that of a number of recluses who endeavoured to enjoy equanimity in an egoistic manner by isolating themselves from society. Legends of Laotze have depicted him as wandering off alone as though he adopted this method at least for a time. From this standpoint the meaning of history was sought essentially in one's inner peace and one's freedom from external obligations and influences. The *Tao Te Ching*, which may be considered the basic text of Taoism, gives expression more to what has been called its second stage. It presents a more formulated philosophy, going far beyond the mere beginnings of reflection. It passes from the changing aspects of things to the *Tao* as permanent, the real basis for equanimity in face of the instability of the transient. But the transitory being accepted as resting in the *Tao*, there is no emphasis on any deliberate abstention from the simple relations of social life, and the participation so far in social history. However, convinced Taoists avoided becoming entangled in official positions in government. The implication is 'the less government the better'. Taoism, while admitting social relations, is definitely concerned with history as it is for the inner life of individuals. Its interest in political government is little, and that incidental. It has no philosophy of history with reference to a continuity, regression or advance, of nations or of what may be called civilization in general. Yet though individualistic, Taoism as expressed in the *Tao Te Ching* is not in any narrow sense *egoistic*. For as the equanimity of the individual rests on the *Tao*, the fundamental attitude is to be described as *cosmic*, which includes relations with other individuals. In the *Tao Te Ching* the quietist attitude is given a philosophical justification in a consciously developed metaphysics. For it '*Tao*' is the central and ultimate conception. Its significance is not the whole as naïvely and immediately felt as implied by its earlier connotation, but a deeper underlying reality. The *Tao* as ultimate reality is beyond description. Though signified by the term '*Tao*', it cannot be 'named', that is as though a member of a class. Otherwise put, it cannot be defined. The *Tao* is eternal; it goes on for ever, the invisible unchanging source of the visible and the changing. It is infinite: though without form, it is 'all complete', 'flooding in every direction'. It functions without any specific efforts. The *Tao* is the ultimate reality of the cosmic whole. Understanding that and one's place in it, the individual may achieve equanimity. With this central concept, the *idea* of the individual has little place in the formulated Taoism of this period. Indeed, any of the particulars, persons or events, of history are as such of little significance. Thought goes beyond anything specifically individual or social to the cosmic. All history is simply a manifestation of the ultimate whole, and its particular events are all relative.

Such an attitude and such a philosophy is taken to include recognition of the social. For 'in your self you see other selves; in your family you see other families, in your district you see other districts; in your country you see other countries, in your society as a whole you see the Great Society of man'. It is only in the light of the *Tao* that one comprehends the Great Society. Such a passage suggests that the Taoists might have come to look at history from the standpoint of a cosmopolitanism or universalism such as that of later Stoicism or of Christianity, but they reached no precise expressions of this kind. There is no arousing of ardent enthusiasm or strenuous effort for the general welfare of mankind. The impression is rather simply of the avoidance of harm to others. The welfare of each in history is or will be achieved, as far as it may, by allowing all without external interference to realize their own natures. It is his own 'nature' which the *Tao* accords the individual, and in it his true satisfaction consists. The *true* welfare of mankind is that the *Tao* should be fostered in each *individual*. What is usually thought of as the *general* welfare, as supposed attained by political organization and activity, is of only transitory externals.

The recognition of one fundamental characteristic of events leads to an avoidance of any great perturbation with any series of them: they are in a process of recurrence. Those that lead in one way will be followed by those that lead in the contrary direction. The empirical is a flux as of 'forward and backward' or 'up and down'. 'All things were made by one process, and as our eyes demonstrate to us, they all turn back.' 'They may flourish abundantly, but each turns and goes back to the root, home. Home to the root. Home, I affirm, to stillness. This means, to turn back is destiny; and the destiny of turning back, I affirm, can never be changed.' One who 'knows' the *Tao*, the never-changing, has the capacity to treat the events of this flux of history impartially. He is freed from temporary egoistic desires, as from all anxiety as to social happenings. He may enjoy quietude and equanimity.

After the *Tao Te Ching*, the next most important exposition of Taoism was the *Book of Chuangtze*. Though regarded by scholars as not entirely by Chuangtze (369-286 B.C.), it may be considered as containing much by him. Even what was not by him is in the main of the same type of thought. Though of diverse authorship, it presents a more systematic philosophy than the *Tao Te Ching*. It might be said to expound a form of spiritualism or idealism. Something of the Berkeleyan or the Hindu attitude is suggested in the oft-quoted passage: 'Once Chuangtze dreamt he was a butterfly, fluttering here and there just as if he were a butterfly, conscious of following its inclinations. It did not know that it was Chuangtze. Suddenly he awoke; and then demonstrably he was Chuangtze. But he does not know now whether he is Chuangtze who dreamt he was a butterfly, or a butterfly dreaming he is Chuangtze.' A type of Idealist conception is expressedly stated: There is a great awakening and then we shall know that all this (present experience) is a great dream. Fools, however, regard themselves as awake now—so personal is their knowledge. It may be as a prince, or it may be as a herdsman, but so sure of themselves. Both the Master (Confucius) and you are dreaming, and when I describe you as dreaming I am also dreaming. And these words of mine are paradoxical: that is the name for them. And a myriad generations will pass before we meet a sage who can explain this, and when we meet him it will be the end of our little day.' With the idea of life as a dream and of each having his little day, there could be no great concern of seeking meaning in history in the broad sense.

The relative insignificance of history is implied in many ways by Chuangtze. The real is eternal: therefore 'Take no heed of time. . . . Passing into the realm of the Infinite, take your final rest therein.' The action of the *Tao* being one of reversion and recurrence, Chuangtze a ked: 'Then what should one do, or what should one not do?' and answered: 'Let the changes go on by themselves.' A true view of things shows that they are fundamentally in harmony, thus if men strive 'to make a unity of them' they simply wear out their 'spirit and intelligence'. In the perpetual flux of the processes of the *Tao* the particulars of history are relatively indifferent. Chuangtze himself avoided entangling himself in political life. 'All this governing of the Great Society is like trying to wade through the sea, or to bore a hole through a river, or to set a mosquito to work on carrying a mountain.' It is not by social organization that equanimity is to be attained. 'The control exercised by the sages was outside political controlling.' The relativity of all within the flow of history was emphasized by Chuangtze. 'After all, now there is life, now death, now life. What is possible at one time is impossible at another, and what is impossible at one time is possible at another. Being linked to the right is being linked to the wrong, and being linked to the wrong is being linked to the right.' Truthfulness, efficiency in business, orderly government, companionship in human-heartedness, and such like, may be recognized if they arise spontaneously and not by enforced effort. Their real significance is 'within' and not in externals. The use of force is deprecated. 'Force is not of the *Tao*.' 'Violence is not of the *Tao*.' What is obtained by force 'quickly perishes'. Empirical history is only husk: 'The really grown man concentrates on the core of things, the eternal *Tao.*' The Taoist attitude is not a striving for empirical progress, but holding 'fast the stability of stillness'.

In its extreme form Taoism is thus a philosophy of a thoroughgoing quietist attitude to history. 'Passivity, calm, mellowness and inaction, characterize the things of the universe at peace and represent the height of the development of *Tao* and character.' 'The business of the *Tao*' is 'one of day by day dealing with less; yes, dealing with less and less until you arrive at inaction'. The contemporary Chinese thinker, Lin Yutang, rightly says: 'The doctrine of inaction is usually difficult to understand.' He suggests that its meaning 'in the light of science' is to make 'use of natural forces to achieve one's object with the greatest economy'. But this is not as helpful a suggestion as it may at first seem, for the question arises as to the nature of 'one's object'. The mechanical methods of modern civilization achieve objects with the greatest economy known at the time. Would Taoism imply that men should concern themselves with such objects? They are constituents of a type of civilization which is in contrast with the simple life which empirical history seems to have been for Taoists. Much in the *Tao Te Ching* describes aspects of what is called civilization as bringing (moral) confusion, rivalry, malice, robbery, and so on. 'The more weapons men have, the more will the darkness of evil be over state and family; the more forms of skill men have, the more monstrous inventions there will be.' If rare merchandise is not prized, theft will be stopped. But the position of Chuangtze was sometimes different: one is to accept things as they come. He admitted 'the necessity of living in this world as we find it', though keeping one's mind centrally on the invisible reality of the *Tao.* Even Chuangtze says that he would leave 'the gold in the mountains' and 'the pearls in the sea'. Living in the world as one finds it, Taoist quietism is opposed to any anxious efforts to change it, that is, to strive for progress in history. 'It is equally out of the question to infer either that there is progress or that there is not.' One is to take as one's pattern 'the true man of antiquity' who 'was not conscious of loving life and hating death. As life opened out he did not long for joy. As he entered (the shadow of death) he did not hang back. Like a bird he flew away, just as like a bird he had come: that was all.'

The earliest Chinese attitude may be said to have been practically Naturalistic, though not metaphysically Materialism. The *Tao* was in one sense the whole as immediately experienced. Yet in the *Book of Chuangtze* one has arrived at a metaphysical view for which the *Tao* is the invisible eternal behind the visibly mutable. Quietude is thus represented fundamentally as dependent on a grasp, an intuitive awareness of this ultimate. No flight 'from the world' is advocated, but a relative indifference towards it. Among the thinkers of the third and fourth centuries A.D., whom Dr Fung Yu-lan calls Neo-Taoists, there appears to have been a change suggestive of a return to a position similar to the earlier Naturalism. Their statement that the *Tao* is literally 'nothing' is a rejection of an invisible metaphysical transcendent. For them the real *Tao* is the immediate totality of things. 'Everything produces itself.' There was an insistence at one and the same time both on the whole, the one, and the particulars, the many. Though everything 'exists for its own sake', it 'needs every other thing'. The attitude advocated by the Neo-Taoists was thus both individualistic and cosmic. The historical is thereby once more brought into view. Its adequate consideration involves the acknowledgment of the distinctive nature, place and experience of each with all his relations to all else that is. Each is what he or it is. What we are not, we cannot be. What we are we cannot but be. What we do not do, we cannot do. What we do, we cannot but do. Though there is perpetual flux, the process is not of free spontaneity but determined. The practical exhortation as to the attitude to adopt in and towards history is thus expressed: 'Let everything be what it is, then there will be peace.' Commenting on a statement of Chuangtze that the world is disturbed by the thinkers, Kuo Hsiang said: 'The current of history, combined with present circumstances, is responsible for the present crisis. It is not due to any certain individuals. The activity of the sages does not disturb the world. It is due to the world at large, but the world itself has become disorderly.' The historical is entirely relative. Everything in it is to be regarded simply with reference to its own circumstances of time and place, and not from the standpoint of any absolute principles or values or any goal to be reached. Notwithstanding the differences of Neo-Taoism from the earlier forms of Taoism, the attitude to life and history was essentially the same: follow nature, with no anxious and strenuous struggles against it. Some Neo-Taoists considered this to be achieved by living in accordance with reason; others by acquiescing in impulse and sentiment. This spontaneity was contrasted with the artificial life of conventional morals and institutions of Confucianism. The passive aspect of Taoism sometimes came to extreme expression. The sage is so to suppress desire that he has not even 'a desire for no desires'. He must take history as it comes. With no desires he would do nothing to influence it.

Chuangtze's and the general Taoist insistence on the impermanence of the events of history did not involve feelings of pessimism. Rather it meant a freedom from anxiety as to the future. Joy is found in living in the present as an expression of the *Tao*. In the book of Chuangtze, it is said: 'To be cast in this human form is to be already a source of joy. How much greater joy beyond our conception to know that that which is now in human form may undergo countless transitions with only the infinite to look forward to? Therefore it is that the sage rejoices in that which can never be lost, but endures always. For if we emulate those who can accept graciously long age or short life and the vicissitudes of events, how much more that which informs all creation, on which all changing phenomena depend?' That, indeed, implies faith in continuity, but also an entire lack of perturbation concerning or any suggestion of strenuous striving for the future. Lin Yu-tang has admirably summed up his view of Taoism as a philosophy: 'It is a philosophy of the essential unity of the universe, of reversion, polarization and eternal cycles, of the levelling of all differences, the relativity of all standards, and the return of all to the Primeval One, the divine intelligence, the source of all things.' Such a philosophy was a basis for humility and meekness and involved abstention from strife and fighting for selfish advantage. It was well adapted to the thinkers not engrossed in political life and to the mass of the Chinese people. But the wars in Chinese history are evidence that there were enough of those who did not follow Taoism to cause almost continuous turmoil in one part of China or another. It was partly against these conditions that Confucianism was first directed.

III

Officially and among the literati Confucianism achieved far greater practical prominence in the history of China than did Taoism. Yet the quietism underlying Taoism was shared by Confucianism. Some later Taoists even claimed that Confucius (551-479 B.C.) had been a disciple of Laotze. It may be insisted that the influence of his personality on his disciples was a prime factor in the origin of the movement associated with him. In later ages he was progressively idealized. His name was used for many sayings taken to be in his spirit, that were first put forward in ages after his own. The *Analects* were traditionally accepted as authentically of Confucius. Modern scholars maintain that only about half can be regarded as probably by him. By themselves these sayings are inadequate to account for his influence. They must be supplemented by tradition. He sought high political office to which he considered his teachings relevant. Whether he attained such is disputed. He declared that he was simply trying to present the meanings of ancient traditions and to express their true spirit. His teachings were certainly in harmony with the traits of Chinese temperament. Their practical difference from Taoism was chiefly in the emphasis on the moral in its personal and social aspects and in the challenge to effort as contrasted with the more passive Taoist attitude.

Confucius was perturbed by conditions of wars between the feudal states and the prevalent forms of bad government. He ardently desired changes in the present. For ideas as to what should be done he professed to learn from the age of the Sage-Kings of the past. He appears to have had no conception of a goal of history to be reached through progressive stages. In the parts of the *Analects* now credited to Confucius, he is represented as teaching 'goodness' as the truly significant in life and history. He attempted no definition of goodness and was disinclined to regard any individual as fully worthy of the title. His attitude was predominantly ethical. Goodness for Confucius was not quietist in the passive sense. It was a condition of equanimity while pursuing the aims and duties of the social position in which the individual found himself. He was prepared to acknowledge that 'all'—'seek wealth and rank and detest poverty and obscurity'. By this 'all' Confucius surely meant no more than those of his own and allied upper classes. That the majority of the people of China sought wealth and rank or were perturbed by obscurity is not to be supposed: that they detested poverty may be admitted.

'Is goodness indeed so far away?' asked Confucius, and continued: 'If we really wanted goodness, we should find that it was at our very side.' Goodness is rooted in inner sincerity. Conduct, however socially right, done under external compulsion could not make for equanimity. Externals are to be treated as definitely secondary. Whatever the external consequences one should abide by goodness. Feelings of affection or of enmity should not be the motives of conduct. Yet Confucius acknowledged the place of feelings in the meaning of life, talking of 'Pleasure not carried to the point of debauch; grief not carried to the point of self-injury.' Cheerfulness is to be maintained whatever the external circumstances. Describing Hui as 'incomparable', he said: 'A handful of rice to eat, a gourdful of water to drink, living in a mean street—others would have found it unendurably depressing—but to Hui's cheerfulness it made no difference.' So, also, a humble origin cannot be a right basis for discrimination. Goodness shows itself in personal manner: the 'true gentleman' is calm and at ease; the 'small man' is fretful and ill at ease. The 'gentleman' is free from 'all traces of violence or arrogance'. His looks betoken good faith, his speech is devoid of coarseness and impropriety. Goodness goes beyond individual character to social feelings and beneficence. 'Moral force never dwells in solitude; it will always find neighbours.'

On account of the uncertainties as to what parts of the *Analects* may be definitely ascribed to Confucius, there has been some doubt as to whether he emphasized 'filial piety' in his teaching.[1] That doubt might well be overcome in consideration of the important place it has had in Chinese history. The opinion has been expressed that the ideas of Confucius have been misrepresented, that he actually stood for a kind of political and social equality analogous with that of modern democracy. But Confucius may rather have supported a feudal hierarchical system of society. Orthodox Confucianism in all periods has involved a view of morality as of the duties of the different classes. In Confucius's own time there was some breakdown of the earlier feudal system. In pointing to the past as containing the ideal he may have wished the feudal system in its best form to be renewed. His many references to the 'gentleman' suggest that he was thinking, perhaps most often, of the ruling classes. The 'gentleman' is not in need of practical skills. The common people may be made to know the Way (*Tao*) but they cannot be made to understand it. Confucius was devoted to learning and urged others to continuous effort in it. That could hardly have been an exhortation to the common people who could not understand the *Tao*. The social attitude he advocated was paternal rather than one of democratic justice. 'A gentleman helps the necessitous: he does not make the rich richer still.' 'In dealing with the aged' one is 'to be of comfort to them'. One is to be of good faith with friends, and cherish the young. These relations are all personal. Confucius insisted on the performance of traditional ritual: the manners conducive to ease and harmony of intercourse, and the ancestral rites. The former were probably of the more refined life of the members of the upper classes, and the latter in preserving family tradition would help to maintain social distinctions.

One gets the impression that Confucius had great appreciation of music. The Succession Dance with its music seemed to

[1] Dr Chan rightly comments that the doctrine is 'very important' in the *Analects*. I agree, as is suggested by my discounting the doubt mentioned. The doubt is implied in Mr Arthur Waley's edition of *The Analects of Confucius*, Allen & Unwin, 1938. He writes (p. 38) that by far the larger number of references to filial piety are 'in Books I and II which do not, I think, belong to the earliest strata of the work'. Mr Waley goes on to say: 'But it seems clear that during the fourth century B.C. a place of extreme importance had already been allotted by the Confucians to *hsiao* (filial piety) in its extended sense of piety towards living parents.'

him of 'perfect beauty and perfect goodness'; the War Dance 'of perfect beauty but not perfect goodness'. That he considered music an instrument of education does not mean that he lacked enjoyment of it in itself. The *Book of Music*, included in the present *Book of Rites*, says: 'Music is the expression of joy.' It would seem that some of the significance of history should be in the enjoyment of music, yet, apparently, music has been one of the least developed arts in China.

Confucius may have had the conviction that history proceeds on a principle of justice: the good are happy, the evil miserable. 'He that is really good can never be unhappy. He that is really wise can never be perplexed. He that is really brave is never afraid. Man's very life is honesty, in that without it he will be lucky indeed if he escapes with his life.' Confucius generally avoided metaphysical discussions. If it was formulated at all in his time (which may be denied) he was not concerned with the philosophical Taoist doctrine of the *Tao* as the invisible ultimate. The term *Tao* had for him its sense of 'the Way', regularity, order, harmony. Life and history were for him the empirical experiences of ordinary existence. He did not deny actuality to the multiple spirits of the popular animism, but in practice ignored them. He rejected anthropomorphic ideas of God but nevertheless, under the term 'Heaven', acknowledged a power dominating men's lives. One is to submit to what Heaven determines. Further, 'He who has put himself in the wrong with Heaven has no means of expiation left'. Tzukung complained that Confucius would not tell anything at all of 'the ways of Heaven'. There is no suggestion that Confucius considered the meaning of history to be in a state reached beyond this life. The meaning is in it as it goes along. According to another part of the *Analects*, Confucius surveyed his life: 'At fifteen I set my heart on learning. At thirty, I had planted my feet firm upon the ground. At forty, I no longer suffered from perplexities. At fifty, I knew what were the biddings of Heaven. At sixty I heard them with docile ear. At seventy, I could follow the dictates of my own heart, for what I desired no longer overstepped the boundaries of right.' He is also recorded as saying perhaps with thought of himself: 'This is the character of the man: so intent upon enlightening the eager that he forgets his hunger, and so happy in doing so, that he forgets the bitterness of his lot and does not realize that old age is at hand.' It is said that the four subjects of his teaching were culture, conduct of affairs, loyalty to superiors, and the keeping of promises.

The hierarchical, even feudal, character of early Confucianism may be inferred from the opposition of Mo-Ti (between ?500-396 B.C.). Rejecting the discriminations based on the natural relationships of the family and of traditional social classes, Mo-Ti maintained that the fundamental moral principle was that of 'universal love'. Further, positions in governmental administration or other important social functions should be solely on merit and the capacity to perform the offices well and in no case dependent on birth in a 'higher' social group. Mo-Ti made a protest against carrying on history in accordance with traditional social organization. In contrast with Confucius's vagueness concerning and general ignoring of 'Heaven', Mo-Ti insisted that it was 'Heaven' that required universal love to be shown amongst men, and that 'Heaven' would reward or punish individuals according to their conformity or non-conformity with it. In his teachings there appears to have been a challenge to the mode of life of the upper classes of society. The impression he may have had of the poverty of the masses may have caused him to emphasize the economic as concerned with physical well-being, and to force attention to the utilitarian in this sense by his derogatory attitude to music, rituals and everything non-utilitarian. That Mohism did not last for long in Chinese history is intelligible: those who dominated in China found their interests expressed in Confucianism. There were some proposals to burn the writings of opposing philosophies, and in any case their adherents were mostly kept from positions of public influence.

Apparently Mencius (371?-289? B.C.) did not gain much attention during his lifetime, and it was not until the Sung Dynasty that official recognition was given to his work, described as *The Book of Mencius*. By what may be called psychological analysis he endeavoured to show that Confucianism conformed with the constitution of the human mind. In this connection he took a definite position in a discussion of some significance as to the nature of history. He maintained that human nature is inherently, originally good. He defended this against three other views: i, that it is neither good nor bad; ii, that there are good and bad elements in it; and iii, that some men are by nature good and others bad. Mencius argued that *all* men have by nature a feeling of compassion for others; a feeling of shame which turns them from wickedness; a feeling of modesty that makes for courtesy; and a sense of the distinction of right and wrong. It is the possession of these that distinguishes men from infra-human beings. Minds agree in reason and righteousness. It is with these that there is a possibility of that good life which is the meaning of history. On the basis of his psychological analysis Mencius rejected Yang's egoism and Mo-Ti's teaching of undiscriminating universal love. The root of all responsibilities is the responsibility for one's self; and the root of all duties is the duty to one's parents. Mencius insisted that there is a basis in men's nature for the social distinctions of Confucianism. Men manifest different degrees of love and these are to no small extent according to blood and particular group relationships. Looked at from the standpoint of the nature of man as mental and moral, Mencius regarded the universe itself as fundamentally analogous with it: as Dr Fung Yu-lan puts it: 'The moral principles of men are also metaphysical principles of the universe.' That, however, was only to make explicit what was implicated in Confucius's own conception of the *Tao*. Thus, whatever the emphasis that may be given to social morality in Confucianism, it cannot rightly be taken to be merely relativist, a social product varying with time and place, as sometimes represented by modern occidental sociological theories. Mencius gave recognition to something of the mystical, and that may have been one reason for the attention the Neo-Confucians paid to him. But in his extant writings this mysticism is not developed. He wrote: 'All things are complete within us. There is no greater delight than to realize this through self-cultivation.' For him Confucianism was not merely a social morality but an experience of one's self as in unity and harmony with the cosmic whole. There are two statements in the *Book of Mencius* referring directly to history.

One asserts an oscillation in history: 'Now there is order; now there is confusion.' The other has some suggestion of the traditional idea of Sage-Kings: 'Every five hundred years a king arises.'

With the early neglect of Mencius, Hsun Tze (320-235 B.C.) came to be regarded as the moulder of ancient Confucianism. He rejected the passivist teachings of philosophical Taoism. 'To carry to completion by actionless activity, to accomplish without trying to, is to be described as Heaven's function. Deep though that function is, great though it is, and of vital import, the man of consummate understanding nevertheless does not consider it to any extent, nor does he get additional ability through it, nor does he probe into it.' Hsun Tze thus kept to the experience of ordinary life, like Confucius not denying the metaphysical but disregarding it. 'Although the Way of Heaven is deep, this man will not put deep thought on it; although it is great, he will not use his ability for its investigation; although it is mysterious he will not scrutinize it.' His attitude was essentially ethical. He tried to show how human ills may be overcome. In contrast with Mencius he contended that the congenital nature of man is evil; goodness is acquired. Men seek their own gain, and in consequence there is strife with social discord. Man's desire to be good comes from his original nature being evil. Man needs government because he is by nature evil. However, Hsun Tze definitely acknowledged human freedom by which one is able to acquire. 'The mind is the ruler of the body and the master of the spirit ... It itself makes choices; it itself causes action; it itself stops action.' There are natural consequences of one's actions, and these cannot be escaped. 'The mind must bear what it chooses. It cannot prevent the results of its action appearing in themselves.' With this freedom it is open to all to reach the ideal of 'the superior man'. Those who do not attain to it do not *will* to do so. Any man may become good by following the rules of proper conduct which Confucianism teaches on the basis of the principles of the Sage-Kings. The good life is not to be expected as a gift from Nature or God. Hsun Tze described it as though simply of terrestrial existence: 'Birth is the beginning of man; death is the end of man.' If the whole of life is beautiful, 'the way of man is complete'. It is the 'superior man' who experiences the real meanings in history. He is governed by principles and being dignified and contented, orderly and of strong will, he has self-respect. Good men are a joy to him; and the evil cause him grief. He is benevolent and just. He gives attention to the satisfaction of all sides of life, endeavouring to keep all in harmony. He satisfies his desires and passions under the control of principles. He gives due recognition to cause and effect in Nature; strives for intellectual knowledge, and for the moral use of power.

Confucianism, as Hsun Tze presented it, sets no goal for history in a remote future, and it makes no attempt to find the meaning in history by reference to anything 'transcendent', anything 'eternal' or 'beyond' history. Confucianism stands for a mode of life with peace of mind and social harmony in the here and now. Though Nature has made men more or less alike, there are differences between them by which they occupy specific positions and perform varied functions in society. It is man's capacity for social organization that differentiates him from other animals. Men cannot get every desire satisfied, but they may obtain what is possible for them in their own social status. 'The young serve the old; the inferior serve the noble; the degenerate serve the worthy—this is the pervading rule of the universe.' 'If people leave their positions and do not serve each other, there will be poverty; if the masses are without social divisions, there will be strife.' Hsun Tze emphasized the social aspects of Confucianism. *The Great Learning*, thought to have been composed in the middle of the 4th century B.C., while insisting on the social, teaches that 'The bringing of the individual self to flower is to be taken as the root.' *The Mean in Action*, of approximately the same period, emphasizes that a man must 'be true and real in himself'. Further, although there was no technical discussion of 'freedom of the will', all forms of Confucianism acknowledge the necessity of the individual's own attitude and action.

Early Taoists, Confucians and even Mohists pointed to alleged Sage-Kings and to ideal conditions of the past. Their view of history was thus backward turning rather than forward looking. Opposition to that attitude was one of the characteristics of the Legalist School of Han Fei Tze (d. 233 B.C.). Against the view that for happiness it was necessary to return to modes of life of the past, Han Fei Tze, on the basis of a doctrine of relativity, insisted that the different circumstances of different times called for different ideas and actions. Dr Fung Yu-lan says: 'This conception of history as a process of change ... was revolutionary against the prevailing theories of the other Schools of ancient China.' With a hedonist view of men's aim in history, yet motivated by social considerations, the Legalist School advocated making men conform with social requirements by rigidly enforced laws, offering opportunities for pleasures to the obedient and ensuring pain for the others. Though the teachings of the Legalist School appealed to some rulers and administrators, they were not widely nor long enough accepted to undermine the traditional Confucianism.

The Confucianism with which the Chinese have been most familiar since the tenth century has been the Neo-Confucianism formulated and elaborated chiefly in the Sung Dynasty. This has a greater scope and more philosophical conceptions than the earlier Confucianism. There is an acceptance within it of fundamentals of Taoism, and some definite influence by Buddhism. Neither Taoism nor Buddhism was satisfied with personal and social concern with the phenomenal humanistic experiences of the 'here and now'. They recognized something more than apparent individual personalities in terrestrial social relations. For both the relationship of the apparent individual to the ultimate was essentially mystical. That relationship was a fundamental in the individual's life or history. In Neo-Confucianism this was also admitted, and indeed, central for it was its concept of 'the Great Ultimate'. However, this was not taken to involve any withdrawal from the affairs of individual and social life as they were conceived in earlier Confucianism, no separation from political activities for peace in contemplation of the Tao, no abandoning of ordinary life for the monastery. The practical aspects of earlier Confucianism were retained: they were envisaged from the standpoint of the immanent and transcendental ultimate that was now acknowledged and emphasized. The continuity with earlier Confucianism is seen in the authoritative position given to what were called 'the Four Books': *The Analects of Confucius*; *The Mean in Action*; *The Great Learning*; and *The Book of Mencius*. Neo-Confucianism provided for the metaphysical and mystical needs which early Confucianism had neglected. There is something more in history than the merely phenomenal, yet this something more is to be realized in life as it proceeds: it is not presented as a goal to be reached in another life by progressive attainment. One of the chief Neo-Confucian criticisms of Buddhism was its too frequent advocacy of withdrawal from the ordinary affairs of social life.

Neo-Confucianism may be the highest and richest expression of Chinese philosophical thought. Of its many great thinkers, to judge by his later influence, the most eminent was Chu Hsi (1130-1200 A.D.). It is to some aspects of his thought as illustrative of Neo-Confucianism that this account must be limited. Though it would appear not to be correct to describe his system as Idealist in the occidental sense of that term, he undoubtedly emphasized the *dominance* of mind. He described the capacities of mind as contrasted with the limitations of the body. 'So fine is it that it penetrates the very point of a hair or the smallest blade of grass and I become conscious of them. So great is it that there is not a single place from nadir to zenith, or within the four points of the compass, where it is not present. Back through the countless ages of the past, or forward through the unknown periods of future time, my thought reaches to the end of them the very moment it proceeds from my mind. It is unfathomable in its spiritual intelligence, most intangible, most . . . marvellous in its orderliness.' He agreed with Mencius that inherently the mind as spiritual is originally good. Evil may arise in 'the natural mind', that is the mind as simply concerned with the world of sense and common mundane affairs apart from thought of its inner spiritual principles. The failure to attain spiritual equanimity is due mainly to egoistic concern with and exaggeration of the worth of the physical. Though there is no one who does not possess mind, 'most men know only the desire for gain till the mind becomes completely submerged in it. At home or abroad, all that they seek is pleasure and self-indulgence; their every thought, the moment it is born, is of these things'.

Neo-Confucianism was metaphysical with the basic concept, that of 'the Great Ultimate'. It seems to me that this is a rendering of what previously I have regarded as an early meaning of *Tao*, and essentially the same as the unnameable *Tao* of early Taoist philosophy. But the emphasis in Neo-Confucianism was probably on the ethical, and its greatest influence ethical. Its use of the term *Tao* is definitely ethical. The meaning of history is known from the fundamentally moral character of mind as experienced inwardly by the individual and by the recognition of the universal applicability of its principles. Basic is 'the good' or '*jen*'; and allied with this are righteousness or justice, reverence, wisdom and sincerity. It is pre-eminently in the realization of these in life here and now that there is equanimity and the worth of the historical process. Dr Chan says that from the Neo-Confucian standpoint, the universe, as due to the eternal oscillation of the *yin* and *yang* of the Great Ultimate, is 'a progressively evolved and co-ordinated system'. Harmony 'is its unalterable law'. Each of the multiplicity of particulars of experience is unique. However, as the same Reason is in all, they are to be accepted within the whole. Thus, 'All people are brothers and sisters and all things are my companions.' There may be some suggestion of a satisfaction gained in a mystical relation with the Great Ultimate even in its manifesting Itself in Nature and in human society. Chu Hsi, in opposition to the teachings of the Buddhist monks who had spread over much of China, vigorously rejected the theory of transmigration.

The essential meaning of history for Wang Yang-ming (1472-1529 A.D.) is implied in his statement that the only occupation worth while is to strive to become a sage, that is, to realize the moral personality and the social conduct involved in the Confucian ideal. This is not a life of contemplation (such as he considered Buddhists to teach) but of activity in the position in which one finds one's self. Yet Wang Yang-ming did not seek the meaning of history in progressive social movements to a future goal. 'The highest virtues are innate to the mind.' It is more important to investigate the nature of the mind than the externals of sense experience and social intercourse. But he did not try to turn men from ordinary experiences to a mystical relation to an 'eternal', as though the goal of history is in something transcending time. He did sometimes refer to immortality and to transmigration, but the occasions were few and incidental, and it may be doubted that he sought any of the significance of history in them. Goodness in all forms may be experienced in this life, for its basis is in the inner nature of the mind. In the varying conditions of existence there need not be, and should not be, any loss of inner equanimity through failure or success. For the virtuous man, or sage, 'failure or success, premature death or long life' are 'the decrees of Heaven, and therefore do not excite or disturb the mind'. Wang Yang-ming challenged the idea that the methods of government used in the past were necessarily to be adopted. His view of the study of history was pragmatic. 'The Five Classics are merely history—history for the purpose of explaining good and evil and for the sake of instruction and warning. The good may well be used for instruction. Time has left its footprint in order to exhibit precepts. The evil may well serve as a warning.'

At the end of the nineteenth century and the beginning of the twentieth K'ang Yu-wei (1858-1927 A.D.) endeavoured to revive neglected aspects of early Confucianism with an emphasis on religious implications. Of significance with regard to history was his attempt to bring back attention to the idea, previously mentioned as contained in the *Book of Rites* and in the Han commentaries on the Annals of *Spring and Autumn* that there are three ages in history. According to Dr Chan, K'ang Yu-wei, whom he describes as 'the last of the great Confucianists', declared that this idea was taught by Confucius. If so, it is strange that it should have been so little regarded during the long period of Chinese history. K'ang took the first period, the Age of Disorder, to be that of Confucius, and apparently most of the time since. He considered that with the political and social reforms in Europe and America and the increase of communications between the east and the west, the second period, the Age of Righteousness was beginning.

The third period, the Age of Great Peace, would come with the universal adherence to *jen*, human-heartedness.

IV

Buddhism has had a long history in China. Its early form, indigenous to India, will be treated in the next chapter. In China it was developed in a distinctive manner so that it has been maintained that one should talk of 'Chinese Buddhism'. For a period the Buddhist monastic life became so widely adopted that there was a suppression of it as detrimental to general social welfare. That the idea was suggested that Gautama had been a disciple of Laotze indicates that the attitude of Buddhism was considered as resembling that of Taoism. Chinese Buddhism was essentially quietest and so in conformity with the Chinese temperament. The doctrine of perpetual flux and the impermanence of all that constitutes historical processes encouraged the attitude of taking things as they come, with a feeling of non-attachment to worldly concerns and so of no anxiety or strenuous effort for them. But Wang Yang-ming maintained that it was the true Confucianists and not the Buddhists who really had equanimity. 'The claim of the Buddhists that they have no attachment to phenomena shows that they do have attachment to them. And the fact that we Confucianists do not claim to have no attachment to phenomena shows that we do not have attachment to them ... The Buddhists are afraid of the troubles involved in human relationships and therefore escape from them. They are forced to escape because they are already attached to them. There being the relationship between father and son, we respond to it with love. There being the relationship between sovereign and subject we respond to it with righteousness. And there being the relationship between husband and wife we regard it with mutual respect. We have no attachment to phenomena.' Chinese Buddhism was distinctively of inner contemplation as contrasted with the Confucian balanced expression of all sides of human life. There is little evidence that the Buddhist doctrine of transmigration with the goal of history the ultimate attainment of *Nirvāna* had any effect of radically changing the Chinese attitudes to history.

V

There may be some, both in and outside of China, who consider the indigenous philosophies of China as obsolete, as dying, if not indeed already dead, and that its thought and life must henceforth be on occidental lines. Large numbers of Chinese students have studied in Europe and America. Some Chinese thinkers have followed occidental forms of philosophizing, but rarely of Idealistic of Theistic types. The late John Dewey and Bertrand Russell lectured on philosophy in China, but the philosophy they expounded was Naturalistic. There was nothing in it to encourage belief that the significance of history is to be found in a future life or in a mystical relation to a Great Ultimate transcending time.

Within the acceptance of a hierarchical form of social organization, the Chinese were led to expect that with each doing his particular duty the welfare of all would be achieved. They had governments which rarely sought the general welfare. That the Nationalist Government of recent times was a dominance by a minority without genuine democratic representation may not have perturbed the great majority of Chinese. But in that it did not attend sufficiently to the general welfare, it was not given ardent widespread support in opposition to Communism. In their propaganda the Communists are proclaiming the welfare of the masses to be their aim. For their social ideal they can appeal to the traditional social feelings. The Dialectical Materialism of Communism suggests resemblances to forms of Chinese thought with no (or little) consideration of God or a future life. There has been much in the Chinese attitudes to history that may be described as Naturalistic. The essential nature of Communism is also Naturalistic. The Taoist in every Chinese may submit with a quietist attitude to Communist organization and government as has been done to other forms of government in the long history of China. The Chinese temperament makes for conformity in externals. But the individual Chinese is aware of an inner freedom that no one can take from him: that may be what is most significant in history for him.

In conclusion it is interesting to consider the main attitudes of a contemporary Chinese thinker free from the Communism of present-day China. Lin Yutang was the son of a Chinese Christian pastor and himself prepared for the Christian ministry. He has lived many years in the occident and studied its ways of thought and life. Though for recent years he has proclaimed his reversion again to Christianity his book *The Importance of Living* (1937) was significant partly for its statement of his reasons for rejecting Christianity at that time and for its criticisms of much in Western civilization. In his opening sentence he wrote: 'In what follows I am presenting the Chinese point of view . . . a view of life and things as the best and wisest Chinese minds have seen it and expressed in their folk wisdom and their literature.' Though he called his book 'a personal testimony' and himself 'a child of the East and the West', he supported his position as Chinese by frequent references to Chinese literature, with emphasis on the philosopher Chuangtze and the poet T'ao Yuan-ming.

Lin Yutang regarded the Chinese as little, if at all, concerned with belief in a future life for the individual. There is an interest in one's ancestors and in one's successors in the historical sequence of the family. The only idea of immortality implied is of the race and of one's work and influence. The meaning of history is primarily sought and found in the individual's terrestrial life. 'Deprived of immortality, the proposition of living becomes a simple proposition. It is this: that we human beings have a limited span of life on earth, rarely more than seventy years, and that therefore we have to arrange our lives so that we may live as happily as we can under a given set of circumstances.' 'The Chinese philosophers clutch at life itself and ask themselves the one and only eternal question: How are we to live?'

Though Lin Yutang on a number of occasions acknowledged that we are in a general 'stream of life', he insisted that the individual is basic. 'Philosophy not only begins with the individual, but also ends with the individual. For an individual is the final fact of life. He is an end in himself and not a means to other creations of the human mind.' He quoted Confucius: 'From the Emperor down to the common man, the cultivation of the personal life is the foundation of all.' However, the Chinese think of the individual as within the family. He is 'never thought of as greater or of more importance than the family because apart from the family he has no real existence'. Lin Yutang thought that the 'sense of family consciousness is probably the only form of team spirit or group consciousness in Chinese life'. Throughout his book there was no suggestion of general occupation with efforts for political advance and for the future progress of the state. 'Man is always thought of as greater and more important than the state.' 'An appointment three weeks ahead of time is a thing unknown in China.' With such an attitude the Chinese with a traditional type of mentality are not likely to give much thought or to make much effort for the future history of China. Lin Yutang presented no evidence of any.

The aim for this life should be the harmonious satisfaction of 'our given instincts', animal and spiritual. For this harmony the teachings of the Golden mean is fundamental. That doctrine is an expression of the 'sanest ideal of life ever discovered by the Chinese'. The so called 'philosophy of half and half' has the same implication. As far as concerns their attitudes all men are 'born half Taoists and half Confucianists'. Yet, though he is a hard worker, the carefree leisure of the Taoist had a special appeal for Lin Yutang. He contrasted the Chinese way of taking history, quietist, with the American way, activist. The value experiences are in history as it goes along. Men's lives are not determined: they manifest spontaneities that upset 'the calculations of the propounders of new theories and systems'. Nevertheless, he admitted that the experiences of these values are not completely satisfying: 'living in a real world man has yet . . . the wistful longing for an ideal'. Thus, though his position as so far described might then be called Humanistic, Lin Yutang recognized the need for something more than Humanism. 'No philosophy is complete, no conception of man's spiritual life is adequate, unless we bring ourselves into a satisfactory and harmonious relation with the life of the universe around us . . . Man lives in a magnificent universe, quite as wonderful as man himself, and he who ignores the greater world around him, its origin and destiny, cannot be said to have a truly satisfying life.' 'All Chinese pagans,' he wrote, 'believe in God,' for whom the most commonly met designation in Chinese literature is *chaowu*, the Creator of Things. Probably with thought of specific discussions of deity, especially with reference to religious attitudes, being almost non-existent in Chinese philosophies, he said: 'The Chinese pagan is honest enough to leave the Creator of Things in a halo of mystery, towards whom he feels a kind of awed piety and reverence . . . That feeling suffices for him.' The widespread equanimity among the Chinese is related with this kind of faith in God.

CHAPTER II

METAPHYSICAL AND INDIVIDUALIST VIEWS IN INDIA

I

Though the history of India goes back for thousands of years comparatively little record of it has so far been discovered. The most noteworthy literature of India has been religious and philosophical. In the great epics, the *Mahābhārata* and the *Rāmāyāna* and in the *Purānas* there are historical references, but even these writings are mostly mythological and of ethical and religious import. Through most of its history the learned men of India have been Brahmins whose interest was religious and not historical. During the Moghul empire there was more historical writing by Muslims, but it was undertaken by those associated with the princely and imperial courts and was largely of the lives of the rulers and of their conquests. Serious investigation of the history of India was pursued during the last century and since, at first mainly by British and then by native scholars. Here we are not primarily concerned with the history of the peoples of India but with their dominant attitudes to history as actual. What has been the implication of their lives and beliefs as to the nature of history? What meaning or meanings, if any, have they found in history?

In the *Mahābhārata* and the *Purānas* a cyclic conception of history is suggested. In each cycle there are four *yugas* or ages. In the first, *Krita*, the Golden Age, all is perfect; in the second, *Treta*, there is a decline of virtue; in the third, *Dvapara*, disease and sin are rife, external ceremonies increase and laws are formulated; in the fourth, *Kāli*, the lowest depth of the cycle, suffering predominates and religion is neglected. At its end all is absorbed into the Brahman, and the cycle begins all over again, and so on eternally. We are living in the *Kāli yuga* and times are predominantly bad.

Hindu mythology contains many stories of divine incarnations in human history. The chief of these have the idea that the incarnation has been to bring some kind of help to men: that the divine is concerned with the course of history. In the *Bhagavad Gītā*, the Lord says: 'To guard the righteous, to destroy evil doers, to establish the law, I come into birth age after age.' Hindu philosophers have treated the stories of divine incarnations as myths or legends, but have not suggested how the saying in the *Bhagavad Gītā* may be considered with reference to history. However, neither the cosmological conception of a cyclic process in four ages nor the idea of divine incarnations has had much effect on the attitudes of Hindus to history and no further discussion of them is necessary here.

That there has been comparatively little historical record in India has led some to say that Hindus have no 'historical sense'. They may not have had it in the occidental meaning of that phrase, but the statement may be misunderstood. That no writings are known that could be described as 'philosophy of history' does not involve that Hindus have had and have no philosophy of history. On the contrary it must be maintained that they have had and mostly still maintain definite attitudes to history to which expression is given in their philosophical and religious writings as in their practical religion and everyday life.

In the earliest age of which we have knowledge, the Vedic period, the people seem to have had a predominantly happy life with the simple experiences of their relation with the physical world, with one another, and their religious worship. There was a prospect of a continued existence in a good realm beyond that of this life. In this period an idea was conceived, expressed by the term *Rita*, corresponding with one meaning of the Chinese *Tao*. Its essential connotation is that of regularity and order. It had three references: (i) to the uniformities of the processes of the physical world, the sequence of the seasons, the germination, growth, fruition and decay of vegetation, the movements of the heavenly bodies; (ii) to the order of the social community, and thus to moral 'right'; (iii) to the 'ritual' of religion, the harmonious relations of men with the divine beings. One implication of the term *Rita* continued to be recognized in the widespread doctrine of the *law of karma*, to be discussed later.

II

By the time of the composition of the *Upanishads* there must have been considerable pessimism as to terrestrial life. No one has given satisfactory reasons for the change of feelings. History came to be regarded not as having intrinsic significance but as something to be escaped from. 'Sir,' asks a king who had abdicated in favour of his son, 'in this ill-smelling, unsubstantial body which is a conglomerate of bone, skin, muscle, marrow, flesh, semen, blood, mucus, tears, feces, urine, wind, bile and phlegm, what is the good of the enjoyment of desires? In this body which is affected with desire, anger, covetousness, delusion, fear, despondency, envy, separation from the desirable, union with the undesirable, hunger, thirst, senility, death, disease, sorrow and the like, what is the good of the enjoyment of desires?' 'In this *samsāra* (the flow of the transitory historical) what is the good of the enjoyment of desires?' 'In this *samsāra*, I am like a frog in a waterless well.' In the *Upanishads* there is a marked concern with death and what may come after it. Does the history of man cease with death? In the famous passage of the *Katha Upanishad*, Nacitketas's choice of three boons, he asked as the last and most important: 'This doubt that there is in regard to a man deceased: "He exists", say some; "He exists not", say others: this would I know.' Offered earthly goods instead of this knowledge, he rejected them as ephemeral. 'Even a whole life is slight indeed' compared with this knowledge. Eventually he got the answer. The *ignorant*, thinking 'This is the world', suffer repeated births and deaths in transmigration. The *wise* know that they are not born and do not die; they are immortal in the realization that they are spirit, eternal.

Empirical history is a realm of desires and its desires are to be abandoned. The true Brahmin has no desire for sons, or wealth. He even becomes 'disgusted with learning' and 'both with the non-ascetic state and the ascetic state'. 'The man who does not desire—he who is without desire, who is freed from desire, whose desire is satisfied, whose desire is the Soul —his breaths do not depart. Being very Brahma, he goes to Brahma.' 'When are liberated all the desires that lodge in one's heart, then a mortal becomes immortal.' History is temporal. 'Some sages discourse . . . of time . . . Deluded men!' Time 'is a form and formless too'. 'From Time flow forth created things. From Time too they advance to their growth. In Time too they disappear.' Significance is not in the temporal which is transient, but in the eternal which is permanent. Redemption is to be found not in history but in escape from it. The extent to which this pessimism concerning secular life has been shared by the peoples of India cannot be estimated. Only a very small minority were capable of or strove for a desireless state. To express such ideas of asceticism is one thing: to conform with them in practice is another. Nevertheless, it may be said that a dominant attention to religion in one form or another has been a characteristic of the history of the peoples of India.

Other ideas were promulgated with implications for the conditions of ordinary human life. In that of reincarnation (and so of transmigration) there is a definite expression of a fundamental characteristic of the Hindu attitude to history: its individualism. It is the particular self that has a series of lives. Whatever relation the individual may have during these lives to the external world and to other individuals the central purpose is his own attainment of an ultimate goal. Not attaining, and in most instances not ardently striving for desirelessness, many have found secondary meanings in their histories. Despite the pessimists the majority have certainly had some good experiences. Hinduism expressed another attitude to the historical with reference to social organization. The constitution of Hindu society in different castes involved specific duties of their members. By his performance of his duties an individual might hope to advance towards his own goal. Participation in social life was recognized as merely relative and transitory. Society as an organic whole was never considered as being the locus of the meaning of history.

No belief has been more widely or more firmly held in

METAPHYSICAL AND INDIVIDUALIST VIEWS IN INDIA

India than that in the *law of karma*. It has been accepted by all schools of Hindu philosophy and all Hindu religious sects as well as by Jains and Buddhists. It is implied also in the *Granth Saheb* of the Sikhs. Simply stated the *law of karma* is that a man reaps precisely what he sows. It has reference to particular individuals as such. The doctrine is an expression of the moral order of human life covered earlier by the term *Rita* in its second meaning. There is the conviction, despite any appearances to the contrary, that the history of human individuals proceeds in accordance with the principle of absolute justice. It is not to be seen to be fully realized within any particular history in any one incarnation. With reincarnations there is a continuity of consequences of conduct from one life to another. The *law of karma* involves an acknowledgment of the chain of causation in each individual's history. The concept of causation was not developed in India, as in the occident, predominantly with reference to the physical. But the *law of karma* does not involve mechanical determinism as occidental thinkers have not infrequently thought. For the Indian doctrine is definitely associated with the belief in the possibility of spiritual advance and eventual attainment of the goal. The individual has an inner freedom for his own spiritual history. If he sows differently, he reaps differently. The acts of sowing may be in conditions caused by previous sowing but are not themselves the effects of past acts. This spiritual freedom is fundamental. Its recognition has meant an appreciation of the individual's own dominant responsibility for his own history. Whether he experiences happiness or misery from his relations to the physical world and to other persons depends on himself.

For the peoples of the West, the term History usually suggests the past. Hindus are not much concerned with the past. History for them is essentially the living present of this incarnation with thought of continuance in the future. History is so regarded in the concept of the *asrāmas*, the sojourns (or 'dwellings') of human life. The individual of the higher castes is to consider his history in four periods. The first, *brahmachārya*, is of education and preparation for what is to follow. In it he has to care for his physical health and growth, for the attainment of knowledge and the cultivation of moral and religious attitudes. The second, *grihastha*, is the time for performance of social duties and the enjoyment of the values of social life and culture. The third, *vanaprastha*, of some liberation from social life and mundane desires, as of the 'forest dweller', is largely a preparation for the final *asrāma*. This, the fourth, *sannyāsa*, is of complete withdrawal from secular society for inner spiritual cultivation. The goal of his history cannot be reached by the Hindu without fulfilling the requirements of each and all of these periods, which besides leading to that goal have some worth in themselves. The periods may not be passed through all in one life. It is probable that most Hindus in the past did not reach the third. Most of those now living may get no further. If, however, the first two (or three) have been satisfied in previous lives an individual may embark on the third (or fourth) in his new life. The primary aim of the fourth period, *sannyāsa*, is individualistic, the person's own attainment of *moksha*, redemption and bliss.

The aims of human life are also described as *purushartha*, those of *pravritti* or pursuit and those of *nivritti* or renunciation. The former may be considered to be of the first two *asrāmas*, and include *dharma*, morality and the ritualistic practice of religion, and *kama*, the enjoyment of sex love and of the fine arts. The latter (*nivritti*) are those of the last two *asrāmas*, *vanaprastha* and *sannyāsa*. Individual and social history have other characteristics expressed in the terms *tamasik*, *rājasik* and *sattwik*. The *tamasik* is the uncontrolled impulsive nature of the individual and social discord. The *rājasik* is the control by force, as of the will of the individual or that of rulers and warriors in society. The *sattwik* is the perfect peace for the individual and universal harmony in society that come with spiritual attainment through right knowledge. History should show progress from the *tamasik* through the *rājasik* to the *sattwik*.

Though fundamentally individualistic, the Indian attitude to history is not egoistic. That is true for Hindus, Buddhists, Jains and Sikhs. The duties of the Hindu castes have social significance, although they have more importance in that their performance is a necessity for the individual's own spiritual

METAPHYSICAL AND INDIVIDUALIST VIEWS IN INDIA

advance. For that, general moral principles are to be adhered to and moral qualities cultivated, and these have social implications and effects. The feeling of kindliness or benevolence is of intrinsic worth to the individual himself and through its expression others may be accorded consequences for their own kindliness. The *law of karma* operates in part through social relations.

From Vedic times there has been a continuance of religious worship in India, in homes, before a multitude of small shrines and in temples. This worship has been and is a part of the meaning of history for Hindus. It is a *present* commerce with the divine, an experience of equanimity and joy. A distorted and in the main false view of the Hindu attitudes in and to history may be given by the all too frequent presentation of Hinduism as a type of philosophy. With acknowledgment of the place of religious worship one may well consider the three paths that may lead the individual to his goal. The order in which these paths are listed varies with the relative importance with which different persons regard them. Thinkers and contemplatives place *jnāna-marga*, the way of knowledge, first; the energetic, *karma marga*, the way of action; the emotional, *bhakti marga*, the way of devotion. An individual may, and generally should, try to follow all paths, though by his temperament and capacities he may inevitably place different emphases on them. Following these paths in advance to the goal is a meaning in history. The concepts, knowledge, action, devotion may be taken in a narrower or a wider sense. Too often in the history of India they have been taken in a narrow sense: by knowledge, the knowledge of Hindu doctrines; by action, the performance of caste duties; by devotion, the ritual practice of religion. The wider interpretations are much more profound and more in accord with the essence of Hinduism. The pursuit of knowledge in general brings an inner spiritual satisfaction, takes one's attention from trivialities and leads to equanimity. Occupation with all kinds of serious activities, as in agriculture, industry, commerce and in the fine arts, brings an emancipation from egoistic self-concern and makes life richer. Devotion to God in aesthetic modes of worship, love shown to all, leads to a deeply felt joy in which the individual self is united with all that is good. So understood, the three ways to the goal may include all that is significant in history.

Hindus have in general practised prayer to God, as individual spirits in communion with Him. That and the symbolism of images indicates the dominant Theistic character of Hindu religion as distinguished from some forms of Indian philosophy. The *law of karma* though itself considered as an impersonal process in history has nevertheless been regarded as divinely ordained. Prayer is a free act and has its effects on the one who prays. For his spiritual advance the individual may pray for divine grace, which as help from the deity is acknowledged in practical Hinduism. By grace the individual is aided to choose and perform those acts which will bring good consequences. It operates inwardly on the self. Through His grace, God may be a factor within the individual's history.

God, under many different names in different parts of India and in different periods of its history, has been thought to be the creator of the world. The process of creation was often conceived with the symbolism of the interaction of the feminine and the masculine, the *shakti* and the *shakta*, in some ways analogous with the *yin* and the *yang* of Chinese thought. There is something sacred in sex relations and sex symbols are found in or near many temples. The religious ceremony of marriage has associated it with the universal principle of generation. The joyousness of marriage has in its turn helped to promote the idea of the divine joy in creation: the *līlā*, the sport, the rich imagination, the glamour of the divine. The acceptance of this idea of the divine *līlā* counteracted the tendencies to pessimism. So eventually, as in the *Kāma-sutra* of Vatsyayana and other writings, the life of desire, of love and the fine arts, singing, instrumental music, painting, sculpture, architecture were given acknowledgment and a religious sanction. Some of the significance of human history, as intended by God, was seen to be in them.

That men are to acknowledge the divine dominance in history and endeavour to accord with His will are important teachings of the *Bhagavad Gītā*, which has had a more widespread and profound influence than anything else on Hindu life and thought. The *Bhagavad Gītā* indicates how a dilemma in Hindu ideas and teachings is to be met: the apparent conflict between the contention illustrated previously from the *Upanishads* that the goal is to be attained by desirelessness and on the other hand of participation in and enjoyment of God's creation in the experiences of mundane life. The goal of the history of the individual is a state of perfection in which he will cease to be reincarnated. There are no more consequences to reap. But good acts produce consequences no less than bad, and with their continuance transmigration would be prolonged. The state of desirelessness as expressed in some *Upanishads* would thus seem to suggest a cessation of all action. That would imply a negation of participation with God in the things of His creation and enjoyment of them. The *Bhagavad Gītā* solves this dilemma by its teaching of 'non-attachment'. This is not 'indifference' as it has sometimes been misrepresented by occidental writers. Acts leading to good consequences are to be performed but not with the egoistic desire for the fruits for one's self. They are to be done 'as unto God'. 'Whatever be thy work, thine eating, thy gift, thy mortification, make thou of it an offering unto Me.' All the striving for and experience of good in the details of history are to be regarded as a fulfilment of divine purpose. The *Bhagavad Gītā* opens with a description of two armies facing one another, and the question is raised as to whether one ought to fight. As the implication of the discussion the answer is: 'Therefore fight'. To fight is the duty of the warrior caste. Yet, the fighting is to be 'as unto God', that is, in a good cause. In fighting the soul is not killed. 'If the slayer thinks to slay; if the slain thinks himself slain, both these understand not. This one slays not, nor is slain.' The spirit, what is truly real in man, cannot be slain. As the warriors so all others are to perform good acts in the course of history, 'as unto God'.

III

Jains claim that their religion originated before Brahmanical Hinduism. Most of the Jain twenty-four Tirthankaras (or teachers) are alleged to have lived in the remote past. Occidental scholars consider the last two, Parsvanatha and Mahavira, to be historical. Though it flourished more widely in earlier times, for many centuries Jainism has been the faith of a comparatively small group. With its contention that the proper attitude to life, and thus to history, can be adopted only with *knowledge* of the actual nature of reality, it is fundamentally metaphysical. It is extraordinarily defective with respect to the empirical content of history. It gives no satisfactory account of the physical world as a system or of the regularity of its processes with relation to which men live their terrestrial history. The idea of God as creator of the world is rejected. Though the Jains have produced sculptures and architecture and gold and silver jewellery of the highest quality, they have neglected consideration of the cultural values of human history. They have not concerned themselves with general records of history. But it is not therefore to be concluded that Jainism has no implications as to the meaning of history. The Jain attitude is definitely individualistic. History is the lives of individuals, who are not considered simply as constituents of society in the continuance of which its significance may lie. The individual is described metaphysically as 'pure spirit', without origin and persisting for ever. In accordance with the *law of karma*, he reaps what he sows, and may go on from one incarnation to another until he reaches perfection. It is *karmic matter* which keeps the spirit in a state of limitation and discontent. History should be the stopping of the flow of *karmic matter* to the spirit and emancipation from that already accumulated. The goal of history is reached, presumably only through many terrestrial lives, when the individual reaches an unsullied awareness of himself as 'pure spirit'. Within history the Jain must conform to the principle of *ahimsa*, non-killing, taken positively as universal kindness. The ardent adept of Jainism becomes a monk or nun involving dissociation from the concerns of ordinary history. The goal of Jainism is thus an escape from history.

The original exposition and the early spread of Buddhism in India suggest a recrudescence of the kind of pessimism that in a previous age had been expressed in the *Upanishads*. Suffering was a central concern of Gautama, the Buddha. Those who wholeheartedly followed his teaching became monks and nuns. The Buddha (563-483 B.C.), in what has been called his first sermon, declared: 'Birth is painful; old age is painful; sickness is painful; death is painful; sorrow, lamentation, dejection and despair are painful. Contact with unpleasant things is painful, not getting what one wishes is painful.' After a concentration on the ills of life, he considered their cause and expounded the way to emancipation from them. They are caused by a 'craving' that leads to rebirths in a series of lives. There is a 'finding pleasure here and there, namely the craving for passion, the craving for existence, the craving for non-existence'. Pain may be eliminated 'with the cessation without a remainder of that craving, abandonment, forsaking, release, non-attachment'. Though the state sought is one of perfect equanimity, the Buddha did not teach a quietist, inactive, attitude to history. This is seen in his description of the Noble Eight-fold Path: 'Right views, right intention, right speech, right action, right mindfulness, right concentration.' But there has been a difference in the manner of their acceptance of his teachings by laymen on the one hand and the monks and nuns on the other. Gautama referred to his teaching as that of the Middle Way, between the life of the passions, 'low, vulgar, common, ignoble and useless', and that of ascetic self-torture, 'painful, ignoble, useless'. The formula of the Eight-fold Path could be interpreted, as the laymen did, with the implication of participation in ordinary history, with as great equanimity as possible and effort for the good on all sides of life. Nevertheless, the Buddha himself pointed to 'a going forth from the world'. An order of monks gathered around him, and he eventually permitted an order of nuns. Monasticism has been a feature of Buddhism throughout its history. The ultimate goal of the individual *may* therefore be said to be escape from history. However, in a later Mahayana Buddhist school of thought it was suggested that *saṃsāra* (the realm of the transient, i.e, history) is identical with *nirvāna*, with the implication that *nirvāna* may be found only within history.

The Buddhist attitude, like that of Hinduism and Jainism, is individualistic. History is of individuals in their series of lives until they reach the goal of release from the wearisome round of births and deaths. The doctrine of the 'chain of causation' expounded by the Buddha conforms with the *law of karma*. There is no possibility of escape from the consequences of wrong doing. Yet the individual has the inner capacity or freedom to change the course of his history. Without this the whole preaching of the doctrine would appear futile. Indeed, the individual's attainment of his goal was said by the Buddha to be dependent solely on himself. In what has been called 'A Sublime Discourse', he declared: 'Be ye a refuge to yourselves. Betake yourself to no external refuge.' It is superficial to argue that Buddhism could not be individualist because it did not accept a real soul. The non-soul doctrine was widely taught in early Buddhism. But though there are some passages accredited to the Buddha in its support, his position seems rather to have been that for the purpose of his teaching it was not necessary to affirm or to deny the reality of the individual soul in the sense it was affirmed by some previous and contemporary philosophies. To affirm or to deny it might lead to misunderstandings. He contended that the problem of suffering arises within the flow of experience and has to be dealt with there. Throughout the history of Buddhism, monks, nuns and laymen were all treated as individuals, and even adherents to the non-soul theory had to use terms that can be translated only by a word such as 'self'. It is the task of the individual selves to seek redemption, to attain *nirvāna*. The importance accorded to the *sangha* (community) is not in contradiction with this individualism. Admitted to the community, the novice declared: 'I take my refuge in the Buddha; I take my refuge in the *dhamma* (doctrine); I take my refuge in the *sangha* (community).' The Buddha, the doctrine and the community are three aids. In the *sangha*, one monk helps another by teaching, advice, etc, but there is no idea that the purpose of the individuals is to further a 'higher' good of the community. The association in the community is instrumental.

The earlier Buddhism has been called *Hināyāna*; and a distinctive later development, spread in non-Indian regions of the Far East, *Mahāyāna*. Many fundamentals are obviously common to both, but two aspects of the latter have their own bearing on history. While in the former attention was directed overwhelmingly on the monks and nuns, in the latter Buddhism became far more a kind of religion for the masses. It meant for

METAPHYSICAL AND INDIVIDUALIST VIEWS IN INDIA

their histories the experiences of devotional worship. It found objects of worship in the Buddhas and Bodhisattvas who came to be regarded like the deities of Hinduism. Secondly, Mahayana Buddhism gave emphasis to the idea of the salvation of others. This was expressed in the concept of the *Bodhisattvas*, whose ideal was the saving of all creatures. Thus Santideva, a seventh century A.D. adherent to Mahayana Buddhism, wrote that he was 'filled with the thought that he must strive through unnumbered births to acquire the virtues through which, in the presence of the Buddhas, he prays to become a tranquillizer of all the pains of all beings'. With this attitude the original individualism of Buddhism was transcended. This was the ideal of the 'great career', the *Māhāyāna*, contrasted with the 'low career', the *Hināyāna*.

Buddhism has no consideration of the character of the physical world with its regularity of processes upon which history to so large an extent depends. In its concentration on human suffering and escape from it, no adequate attention was paid to the idea of God as creator of that world. With its 'going forth from the world', it neglected consideration of the values of culture that are possible in that world. The idea of a 'chain of causation' was applied, not to the world as a whole, but to the experiences of individuals as such. Buddhism did promote some forms of art, as painting, sculpture and architecture, but always in the service of Buddhism as a religion. Buddhists have manifested interest in the legendary (or other) history of the Buddha and of great promoters of the faith, but very little in general history. The past is gone. The history of real significance is in the now and the future so far as concerned with the attainment of *nirvāna*.

Though Buddhism contained a *dhamma* or doctrine and forms of philosophy were developed in its history, it was a mode of life rather than of belief. This is evidenced by the elaboration of detailed practical rules before the advance of philosophical reflection. The rules were for a mode of life dissociated from ordinary history. Though its goal was individualistic, the method for its attainment was the opposite of egoism. It required universal love, of human and infra-human beings. One may maintain that it was a felt need in Buddhism as a religion that in the *Mahāyāna* a conception of the Enlightened One came to be accepted 'which made him indistinguishable from the highest conceptions of Hindu deity'. With this, *nirvāna*—often taken by early occidental students of Buddhism to mean complete extinction—was anticipated not merely as freedom from rebirth but also as a state of bliss. Most could not expect to reach the goal until they had gone through many lives: nevertheless, it is repeatedly maintained in Buddhist scriptures that it is possible of attainment in the present life. The goal may not be in a distant historical future, but here and now.

For almost a thousand years Buddhism thrived in India: then, apparently in a brief time, it mostly disappeared. The causes for this rapid decline have never become clearly known. The general social life may have become so disorganized through the 'going forth from the world' of so many that, with an economic breakdown, they could no longer be supported as monks and nuns. The demands of ordinary history had to be met: in the world men cannot get entirely from them. There may have been a revulsion from the aspects of pessimism in Buddhism. Some adherents to the Hindu conception of castes may have insisted on their full recognition in contrast with the Buddhist ignoring of them. There was a revival of worship in Hindu temples and a return to definite acceptance of the idea of God as creator and as concerned with the history of individuals in conferring His grace. Some religious emotions, long starved, were aroused again.

IV

Another cause of the decline was probably the definite development of systematic Hindu philosophical thought. In the period of Buddhist decline in India there was much criticism of Buddhist metaphysics by Hindu thinkers who also expounded their opposing Hindu systems. Among these thinkers, Sankaracharya formulated and defended the philosophy of Advaita Vedānta which since his own day, right up to and including the present, has had wide acceptance amongst thoughtful Hindus. Sankara and his followers received support from Hindu rulers, with whose help they established *maths* or monasteries in strategic places throughout the country. The accounts of Hinduism usually given by Hindu swamis in Europe and America is from the standpoint and in the phraseology of Sankara's Advaita Vedānta. It seems to be in relation with this form of thought that one finds the dominant contemporary Hindu ideas as to the nature of history.

The fundamental principle of Advaita Vedānta is that reality is 'One without a second', that is, is 'non-dualistic'. Only the Brahman, the Absolute, is truly real and It is eternal. But two conceptions of the Brahman are presented: that of *nirguna* or qualityless, Brahman, and that of *saguna* Brahman, with all qualities. Though some attention must be given to the first of these conceptions, it will be seen that it is the latter that provides for significance in history.

With the concept of *nirguna Brahman* attention is concentrated on the reality of the Brahman and on the unreality of all that might be thought to constitute empirical history. The physical world, the multiplicity of particular individuals—all such is *māyā*, illusory. The interrelated lives of individuals are like a dream, and as such of no fundamental significance. The aim, like that of the desireless of the *Upanishads*, is to escape from it. To take the physical world as real and to believe that ultimate satisfaction can come in relation with it is one of the greatest of errors. But the difficulties of this side of Sankara's Advaitism are many and serious. How is the knowledge of Brahman as *nirguna* attained? It cannot be through the immediacies of sense experience, for what is thus known is not real. Nor can it be through the discursive intellect, for the data for that is from the realm of illusion and the intellect can arrive only at abstract ideas. The *nirguna Brahman* can be known only by an immediate intuition of one's own identity with It, in what might be called a 'super-conscious trance state' to be reached by the practice of *yoga*. To the extent to which individuals give themselves up to this, they may be said to be endeavouring to escape from history. With the concept of *nirguna Brahman* there is no possibility of passing to a meaning or meanings in history.

If the physical world, the particular individuals, and the experiences of history are *māyā*, illusory, the question must be asked: Who suffers the illusion? For Sankara's Advaitism there can be only one answer: the Brahman. But as the *nirguna* Brahman has not even the 'quality' of suffering illusion, the illusion would seem itself truly to be nothing. That involves the negation of all that we might call the empirical. However, it is also said that there is illusion because there is *avidya*, ignorance. The question then arises: Who is the subject of ignorance? The Brahman: for there is no second to It. Yet by intuitive awareness of the Brahman ignorance is overcome. The Brahman, the only subject of ignorance, must be entirely free of ignorance. The Advaitist line of thought appears to be that the Brahman is not affected, for ignorance itself is nothing. Thus, ignorance treated positively as though the basis for taking the world and the facts of history as real, is then itself negated. With these difficulties the idea of *nirguna Brahman* is usually neglected by those engaged in history though it may remain at the back of their thoughts to be reflected on in times of meditation.

Advaitist preachers exhort their hearers as individuals just as do those of Hindu sects opposed to Advaita Vedāntism. Still maintaining the doctrine of 'One without a second', they think of all as within the One. Brahman is *saguna*, with all qualities. What with the concept of *nirguna Brahman* was treated as *māyā*, illusion, is then regarded as divine creation, the *līlā* or 'sport' of the divine spirit. This involves human history. With this conception there is a difficulty which its adherents rarely face. Both sides of conflicts of all sorts must be within the Brahman, as parts of Its infinite perfection. The aggressors and the defenders in wars are alike Its manifestations. In contradictions it is It that affirms both sides: it is It that negates. The Advaitist might possibly urge that through creation and destruction the Brahman is 'proceeding to' a goal giving meaning or meanings to history as the occidental usually conceives of them. It seems to be with the concept of *saguna Brahman* that the Advaita Vedāntists in India today concern themselves with what the occidental calls civilization. But what is the relation between *nirguna Brahman* and *saguna Brahman*? If men are achieving something in the world and in history, as suggested by the latter concept, how is this to be reconciled with emancipation from the illusion of the world and history, in accord with the former concept?

The demands of contemporary life, and probably some effects of associations with occidental peoples, have led some exponents of Advaita Vedāntism to turn from the avowal of the essential individualist attitude of Hindus to history and to present Hinduism as distinctly social. Their argument is that each being ultimately the Brahman is identical with every other; that in loving others the individual is loving himself, that the ideal is therefore universally social. This emphasis on the social is a valuable and important aspect of current history in India. But on the basis of Advaitism an equally cogent argument could be developed for the utmost egoism. For, if I am identical with the Brahman, all enjoyment and suffering (if there really is any) must be experienced by the Brahman that is the real I. It may then be said in purely egoistic fashion: 'If all others are myself, simply in loving myself I am loving all others.' Advaita Vedānta cannot show that the significance of history for Hindus is in a social goal, however valuable social morality may be in the individual's advance to his own redemption.

From soon after Sankara's exposition of it, there were definite criticisms[1] of his Advaitism in India itself, especially by Rāmānuja and his followers of the school of *Vishistādvaita* (modified non-dualism) and by Madhvāchārya and the school of *Dvaita* (dualism). Advaitism has been expounded primarily by the monks of the Sankara monasteries, from the standpoint that the way of knowledge is the most important path to the goal. Vishistādvaitists and Dvaitists have been more concerned with the way of devotion and (secondarily) of action. Their criticisms of Advaitism were motivated by their emphasis on a practical as contrasted with a contemplative mode of life. The former were advaitists in their belief that there are not two kinds of reality, but only one, spirit, they meant to discard the idea of God as *nirguna Brahman*. They considered individual souls as real in a manner Advaitism rejected. There is an

---

These criticisms should be studied in the classical work of S. N. DasGupta: *History of Indian Philosophy*. Cambridge—I, 1922; II, 1932; III, 1940; IV, 1949.

external world (though it is not ultimately material) and there are individual souls. They have had a far less pessimistic attitude to history. The participation in worship, here and now, is a joyful association with the divine. They conceived the distant goal more as a condition of communion with God than as identity with Him. No more than Advaitists have they supposed that men can obtain complete satisfaction in earthly conditions. They have a fervent belief in and hope for divine grace. God is in history in what may well be described as a personal relationship with His worshippers. For the individual Vishistādvaitist ritualistic and emotional religion has been a present meaning in his history. He conforms with the requirements of the castes. Of the *purushārtha* he attends more to those of pursuit than to those of renunciation. His attitude has been essentially individualistic, the effort for continuity of advance to his own goal of final bliss. However, through the Vaishnavite forms of worship there has been a more definite cultivation of social feelings than among Advaitists. Thus the implications of the Vishistādvaita as to history are in many ways similar to those of non-Indian theistic religions discussed in the following chapter.

The Dvaitists asserted the reality of matter as a substance other than minds or spirits. Individuals are real, and even with the attainment of the final goal of release from transmigration they retain their distinctions. In this latter belief they may not differ essentially from Vishistādvaitists, but they are more definite. Their attitude to history also resembles that of Vishistādvaitists. Of the many other schools of thought in Hindu India, none had wide influence. The *Carvakas* (materialists) are known almost solely from criticisms by others. It may be inferred that the meaning of history for them is simply in the experiences of living as a physical organism. But Materialism never thrived in India. The different forms of *Sankhya* philosophy generally acknowledged a distinction between the physical and the spiritual and a plurality of spirits. Their implications as to history are like those of the schools discussed, other than Sankara's *Advaita Vedānta*.

That in India there has been a large amount of pessimism as to man's historical life on earth is indisputable, but Hinduism,

METAPHYSICAL AND INDIVIDUALIST VIEWS IN INDIA

Buddhism, Jainism and Sikhism have not been finally pessimistic. For they all have taught the possibility of reaching equanimity and perfection. The goal is not one of terrestrial history. For Hindus, it is not merely emancipation from illusion and ignorance and redemption from suffering: it is also *sat, chit,* and *ānand*, reality, beatific vision and bliss. For Buddhists it is the attainment of the peace and joy of *nirvāna*. For Jains it is the experience of perfect spirituality, and for Sikhs the ecstasy of the love of God. Hinduism, with the concept of *līlā* gives recognition of participation in the empirical goods of ordinary history. The Sikhs, though aware of the danger of predominant occupation with the mundane, have discouraged asceticism.

V

The views concerning and the attitudes to history among the peoples of India have been to some extent, though not radically, changed by influences coming from outside of India. The Muslim rulers, especially the great Moghul emperors, were motivated by Muslim conceptions, and with these guided the lives of the many, who through conversion and otherwise, came to form a large part (though still a minority) of the population. The Zoroastrians (Parsis) who had originally come from Persia had a definitely non-ascetic attitude. They were among the first in India to develop commerce and industry along occidental lines and by their success turned the attention of Hindus and Muslims to the benefits of an occidental type of civilization. Their leaders were also among the first to champion Western political ideas. Though conversion to Christianity has been comparatively rare among educated Hindus, it has been preached for some centuries in India with important practical effects. Missionary colleges have done much to introduce Western knowledge, as, even more so, have the provincial universities inaugurated by the British administrators in their parts of the country. During British rule there was much that was occidental in the form of government. There was a long period of peace with the promotion of a very large amount of trade with Europe. All these influences and factors have led Hindu leaders to changes of attitude towards history. In these changes they have had the support of young Hindus who in increasing numbers have studied in Europe and America. Many Hindus today think of history in terms of individual and social advance along the lines of general civilization. It would, however, be false to suppose that Hindus in general have abandoned their traditional ideas of history. Even the occidentally educated leaders find ways of fitting their concern with progressive civilization into their Hindu mode of thought.

That is exemplified in some of the published works of S. Radhakrishnan, eminent for some decades in India and in Europe. Radhakrishnan has made a thorough study of European philosophy and presents his views of Hinduism with the consideration of fundamental problems of world-wide contemporary life. Dispensing with critical discussion of his interpretations of Hindu philosophies, for our purpose it is sufficient to indicate his views relative to history as stated in his *The Hindu View of Life*. Incidentally, it should be remarked that in this book he has avoided discussion of the conception of Brahman as *nirguna*; and in our opinion his exposition is obscured by an ambiguous use of the term 'God'. Hinduism is a way of life more than a specific form of thought. It is 'a movement, not a position; a process, not a result; a growing tradition, not a fixed revelation'. From the nature of the past he has confidence that Hinduism will be able to meet any emergency in the future 'whether on the field of thought or of history'. Hinduism is comprehensive and synthetic. It 'regards the endless variety of the visible and temporal world as sustained and supported by the invisible and eternal spirit'. With this conception, Radhakrishnan can encourage effort for all the goods of human civilization.

The variety of existence is found in individuals and in social groups. 'Every human being, every group and every nation has an individuality worthy of reverence.' Progressive reforms are to preserve such individuality and a continuity with the past. Those who attempt to reform the world in one generation in accordance with their own programmes meet defeat. 'The mills of God grind slowly in the making of history,' and 'Hinduism does not believe in forcing the pace of development.' With the recognition that every historical group is unique, with an ultimate value of its own, we 'must work for a world in which all races can blend and mingle, each retaining its special characteristics and developing what is best in it'. 'The political ideal of the world is not so much a single empire with a homogeneous civilization and a single communal will, but a brotherhood of free nations differing profoundly in life and mind, habits and institutions, existing side by side in peace and order, harmony and co-operation, and each contributing to the world its own unique and specific best, which is irreducible to the terms of the others.' In this passage and in much else in the book there is an insistence on the social aspects of human life. But, true to his Hinduism, Radhakrishnan rejects any merely sociological view of history. 'The stature of man is not to be reduced to the requirements of the society. Man is much more than the custodian of its culture or the protector of his country or producer of its wealth. His social efficiency is not the measure of his spiritual manhood.' The fundamental aim is the perfection of the individual as spirit, who in the temporal is to see the manifestation of the eternal and to find his pathway to It. For this he has spiritual freedom. Radhakrishnan emphasizes that though according to the doctrine of *karma* the past sets conditions for the present, the individual's present conduct is of free choice among possible alternatives.

As described above, Radhakrishnan's view of Hinduism implies a comprehensive appreciation of the values of human history. But the aspects of Advaita Vedānta in his exposition must be noted. 'Activity is a characteristic of the historical process.' As, however, the perfect lacks nothing, it can have nothing to be active for: thus it cannot be historical. The ultimate goal is an emancipation from history. 'If the historical process is not all, if we are not perpetually doomed to the pursuit of an unattainable ideal, then we must reach perfection at some point of the historical process and that will be the transforming of our historical individuality, of our escape from birth and death, or *saṃsāra*. History is the working out of a purpose, and we are getting nearer and nearer to its fulfilment. *Moksha* is the realization of the purpose of each individual. On the attainment of perfection, the historical existences terminates.' 'When the whole universe reaches its consummation, the liberated individuals lapse into the stillness of the Absolute.' Then in semblance of the cyclic view to which reference was made in the second paragraph of this chapter, he says: 'The world fulfils itself by self-destruction.' Then, 'Another drama may commence and go on for ages.'

CHAPTER III

CONCEPTIONS OF HISTORY IN ANCIENT GREECE AND ROME

I

EARLY Greek life was a simple one in relation with Nature, parts of which were considered as having an inner being such as men were conscious of in themselves. The Greeks conceived of their lives as involved in part in a commerce with these 'spirits', the greater of whom may be called 'gods'. Religion was a bond of social life and an expression of men's relations with the divine. The Homeric epics give evidence of an early belief in a future existence, but the dominant conception of life after death was one of gloom. Though there were some ideas of happy realms for the souls of heroes, even the ghost of Achilles is represented as saying: 'Rather would I live upon the soil as the hireling of another, with a landless man who had no great livelihood, than bear sway among the dead that are no more.' The Greeks had a love of life on earth. The thought of this life as in any way preparatory to another and better existence, or that it was to be transcended in an experience of an 'eternal One', was of individual thinkers and minority groups.

The Epics and much of Greek religion through the ages give evidence of the belief that men's histories were in large measure under the control of the gods. Sometimes both gods and men appeared to be dominated by an impersonal fate. There were definite limitations to the scope of human activity. By prayer men could speak with the gods and by oracles receive communications from them. The leading heroes of the race were sometimes regarded as partly of divine origin, suggesting recognition of the importance of outstanding individuals in history. The relations with the gods were essentially external. Alienation from them was in practical conduct. Their favour was accorded in particular external benefits. The early Greeks had little sense of inner spiritual guilt. Greek drama depicts crimes as forms of conduct and the punishment as experiences of suffering and misery. The feeling of horror of death was from the thought of the loss of earthly joys rather than from fear of what might come after. In the funeral speech put into the mouth of Pericles, nothing was said of a future life, but consolation was suggested in the remembrance of the happiness of 'the greater part of the days' and the brevity of those of sorrow. The Greeks in general (as distinguished from individual thinkers and small groups) devoted 'themselves freely and fully to the art of living, unhampered by scruples and doubts as to the nature of life'. They had an appreciation of music, realized high standards in poetry and drama, and in architecture and sculpture reached an excellence comparable with any in human history. They cared for the human body, their recognition of the beauty of which is evidenced in their friezes. They discussed and took active interest in social and political organization. In the course of time they turned to the study of Nature, history and philosophy. That the Greeks were pre-eminently concerned with history as 'this life' is manifested in their whole civilization and culture. The aspects of thought and life contrary to this were relatively incidental and at most only characteristic of minorities.

In the *Works and Days* of Hesiod (?8th c. B.C.) there is a conception of five ages of mankind. The first, the Golden Age, was ruled by Kronos. In it, men dwelt with the gods, in good health and without toil or pain. In the second, the Silver Age, ruled by Zeus, men became insolent with their fellows and neglected the gods. The third, the Age of Bronze, was a period of savagery and barbarism. But out of this arose the fourth, the Heroic Age, of valiant and great men. Thence followed the fifth, the Age of Iron, in which Hesiod thought he himself was living, one of selfish individualism. 'Now in these latter days is the Race of Iron. Never by day shall they rest from travail and sorrow, and never by night from the hand of the spoiler; and cruel are the cares which the gods shall give them. . . . Right shall rest in the might of hand. . . . All the sons of sorrowful man shall have strife for their helpmate—harsh-voiced strife of hateful countenance, rejoicing in evil.' Though he did not explicitly state a view of cyclic process, he may have implied it. 'Would that I were not living in the fifth age of men, but that I had either died *before* or been born *later*' (italics A.G.W.). With reference to evil, Hesiod related the ancient myths of Prometheus and Pandora. They implied that evil in history rests ultimately on opposition to and disobedience of the divine.

Hesiod stressed the importance of work. Poverty is due to lack of industry; riches and honour can be won only by it. Misfortunes are relieved by constant toil. Men reap the consequences of their work or idleness, though they may be slow in coming. 'The man who worketh evil to another worketh evil to himself.' History goes on in accordance with a principle of justice. 'Justice prevaileth over insolence in the end; even the fool knoweth that from experience.' 'Finally, Zeus imposes requital for the wicked man's unjust deeds.' The emphasis on justice is conspicuous. The awareness of their capacity for justice distinguishes men from the lower animals. A basic social concern in history, it is intrinsically divine, for it is 'the daughter of Zeus'. Later, Sophocles also expressed the widely held conviction that the laws of morality were 'begotten of Heaven'.

Some early Greek thinkers definitely expressed a view of the processes of existence as cyclic. Heraclitus may have meant it: 'All things are passing, both human and divine, upwards and downwards by exchanges.' Parmenides, looking on history as constituted of transient changes in the One Reality, said: 'It is all one to me when I begin, for I shall come back again there.' Empedocles, symbolizing the two active principles of reality as love and strife, maintained that 'they prevail in turn as the circle comes around, and pass into another and grow great in their appointed turn.' 'In so far as they never cease changing continually, so far are they evermore continuous in the circle.' Among the Etruscans the idea was held that each race had its Great Year in which it arose, flourished, decayed and died.

The correctness of our description of the general Greek

attitude to history may perhaps be challenged by reference to the Orphics and Pythagoreans. But there is no certainty as to where and when Orphism originated, and no evidence that it was accepted by more than a minority. Though its ideas affected some later Greek thought, they did not change the fundamental Greek attitudes. Orphism insisted on a radical distinction of the soul as spiritual and the body as earthly. In terrestrial life the soul is imprisoned in the body. The true significance of history is to be found in the soul gaining its emancipation from the physical. The soul may have had previous and may have future incarnations. Some of the evils of any particular life may be due to pre-natal sin. Between different incarnations the soul may have periods in hell. For the Orphics there was a change of focus of vision from this world to a spiritual world beyond, and with this an advocacy of an asceticism alien to the Greek attitude of moderation in a harmonious psycho-physical life. In contrast with the popular polytheism Orphism was pantheistic: 'One Zeus, . . . one god in all.' The ultimate goal may have been believed to be one with the retention of spiritual reality and not a simple absorption into the infinite divine. The Pythagoreans may have adopted the idea of transmigration and some forms of practical discipline from the Orphics. In contrast with Orphic emotionalism, they cultivated the intellectual. The Eleusinian mysteries also turned the attention of some Greeks to a life after death, the initiates being promised that death would lead to good.

Of Greek historians, Herodotus (484-425 B.C.) and Thucydides (451-400 B.C.) should be considered here. The work of Herodotus has had so great an appeal partly because of its wide geographical range and his interest in the diverse forms of organizations and customs of different peoples. Conscious of their variety, he remarked that most peoples regarded their own way of living as the best. Yet, along with diversities he saw that men as men have everywhere some identical principles of conduct, 'laws all men hold in common'. This idea anticipated the conception of 'natural law' of the Roman Stoics and of Medieval Scholasticism. Herodotus wrote that Pindar was right when he said that 'Law is king over all'. He thought it worth while to record frequent resort to oracles, especially at Delphi, with implications that human history was affected by the gods. In a speech put into the mouth of Xerxes he said that God guides us and if we follow His guidance we prosper greatly. However, he seemed to accept the idea of an ultimate fate: it is 'not possible even for a god to escape the decree of destiny'. The principle of justice was to be satisfied in history, but not necessarily with reference simply to an individual himself. His descendants might reap consequences of his conduct, whether good or ill. Individuals shared in the responsibilities, the joys and the sufferings of the social group in its continuity. This idea differs from the oriental conception of the *law of karma* in that its implications are not individualist. Herodotus commented on the shortness of man's life, but with no suggestion of consolation in faith in a good future life. He declared that though men may be happy in general there have been none who have not many times wished they were dead.

The range of Thucydides's work was much narrower than that of Herodotus. It was not only more systematic: it also manifested differences of attitude regarding history and of ideas as to the forces in it. Though he did not explicitly rule out all influences of God (or the gods), he did not concern himself with them. He said that 'When visible grounds of confidence forsake them, (some) have recourse to the invisible, to prophecies, oracles, and the like.' These, he added, 'ruin men by the hopes they inspire in them'. As Dr Godolphin wrote: 'For Thucydides a plurality of causes related to problems of economic wants and political power must replace the Herodotean Nemesis.' The natural causes are there even though we fail to recognize them. Yet history is not a plain, straightforward affair of determined processes. 'The movement of events is often as wayward and incomprehensible as the course of human thought,' and that is why we ascribe to chance what belies our calculations. Thucydides acknowledged the human will as a cause in history, but insisted that the extent of its power is limited. Hermocrates is made to say: 'Nor am I so obstinate and foolish as to imagine that because I am master of my own will, I can control fortune of which I am not master.' There is nothing in Thucydides's work to suggest that the meaning of history is to be sought in something transcendental and eternal, or in a progressive movement to a higher civilization. In the course of history 'all things have their times of growth and decay'. In a speech put into the mouth of Pericles, we may have some of Thucydides's own views of the values in history as it goes along. The Athenians were 'lovers of the beautiful'. They cultivated their minds without loss of manliness. They had equal justice for all. Much of the meaning of history was in its variety. 'The individual Athenian in his own person seems to have the power of adapting himself to the most varied forms of actions with the utmost versatility and grace.' Though giving recognition to environmental causes, Thucydides found the chief bases for historical variety in the minds of men. 'The diversity of men's minds makes the difference in their action.' In the many speeches he introduced in his *History* he indicated differences of ideas as to the ends to be sought and the means to be adopted for them. But he gave no definite statement as to any conception of his own as to a purpose or purposes in or of history.

II

The relation of the Sophists to Greek attitudes to history may not have been appreciated in most discussions of them. They did not represent a 'school' of thought but rather shared in a sceptical criticism of those who professed to present knowledge beyond that of ordinary experience. They were in the main defenders of the 'this world' Greek attitude to life. That some of the principles they propounded were open to philosophical objection is obvious in the Platonic *Dialogues*, but that is no proof that their humanism and pragmatism were not in closer accord with Greek life than the philosophical views developed in opposition to them. Though they concerned themselves with historical life as immediately experienced, they did not adequately appreciate religious values as among its meanings. That may have been one reason for hostility to them, leading to the banishment of Protagoras and the burning of his books.

More people have read the *Dialogues* of Plato than any other literature of ancient Greece. In consequence there has been some misrepresentation of the Greek attitude to history through its being taken to be, in accord with some ideas in the *Dialogues*, a seeking redemption from the world in contemplation of the eternal. The term Platonism has been used for various systems of thought distilled from the *Dialogues*. But Plato's systematic philosophy may have been presented to those with capacity for it in his lectures in the Academy. The *Dialogues* may have been occasional writings for those outside the Academy, unsystematic discussions of diverse aspects of Greek thought. The literary form of the *Dialogues* has had much to do with their wide appeal. With reference to some serious problems raised in them, Plato resorted to mythology and to poetic phraseology, both pleasantly distracting to many minds. The Platonism of the *Dialogues* should be treated in its proper proportions in any survey of Greek thought: hence our account is brief.

Though there is no systematic treatment of the nature and significance of history in the *Dialogues*, there are many implications as to them. They contain some suggestions that the whole cosmic process is cyclic as, for example, in the myth of the 'year of the world'. There is, however, so much obscurity as to this idea that no more than its mention is worth while here. Further, it is not clear what is meant by the term 'idea' as supertemporal and the only ultimate reality. Is the supreme idea purely static? Is the supreme idea, the Good, the same as God? Or is God an active mind influencing history? Is the individual soul only a temporary manifestation of an eternal idea of soul? The *Dialogues* include arguments for the immortality of the soul as though something different from an eternal idea—for if it be an eternal idea no such arguments would be needed. Is reminiscence—in which history must in one sense consist—a function of beings with a reality other than the ideas they remember? These and many other questions that may be raised indicate difficulties involved in any attempt to get an intelligible conception of history from the Platonic writings.

The *Dialogues* present conflicting views of the temporal, especially of the physical, involving on the one hand an acceptance of and on the other an escape from the world. The *Theaetetus* states: 'There are two patterns eternally set before' men 'the one blessed and divine, the other godless and wretched.' In the *Timaeus* it is declared that God formed the world because He is good, implying that the world is good. In the *Philebus*, pleasure as experienced in the temporal, though not the highest good, is admitted to be a concomitant of it, or as a constituent of the complete good. In the *Phaedrus* there is a prayer to Pan and other gods: 'Give me beauty in the inner soul and may the outer and the inner man be one. May I reckon the wise to be wealthy and may I have such a quantity of gold as a temperate man and he only can bear and carry.' In the *Symposium*, love is said to run through all, from the lowest plants and animals up to the highest visions of truth attainable by rational beings. We may rise to the highest through the sensible world. Though love, beauty and truth as perfect and complete exist eternally unmixed with the finite and the material, they are realized in history in 'beautiful souls', 'beautiful shapes' and 'beautiful sciences'. 'The true order of passing ... to the things of love is to begin from the beauties of earth and mount upwards for the sake of that other beauty, using them as steps only.' In all this there is a positive view of history in essential agreement with general Greek attitudes. In a good world formed by God, men may realize the values of the good, the true, and the beautiful, and obtain pleasurable satisfaction.

But in the *Dialogues* and other writings of Plato, quite different implications as to history may be found. Time, in which the experiences of history occur, is the enemy of man. The body is the prison house of the soul. Instead of rising to the highest through the sensible world, using it as steps, every effort must be made to escape from it. In the *Republic* we are told that only one who has learned the renunciation of things sensuous is capable of philosophic cognition. According to the *Phaedo* the true philosopher despises the so-called pleasures of the body, 'his soul runs away from the body', desires 'to be alone and by itself'—presumably free from social affairs of history. Eyes and ears and 'so to speak the whole body' are distracting factors hindering the soul from truth. If death is the end of all for men, they would be 'happily quit of their bodies'. The *Apology* says that if one supposes there is no consciousness after death 'but a sleep like the sleep of him who is undisturbed by dreams, death will be an unspeakable gain'. This second attitude to history is in accord with the statement in the *Theaetetus*: 'Evils, Theodorus, can never pass away, for there must always remain something which is antagonistic to good. Having no place among the gods in heaven, of necessity they hover around the mortal nature and this earthly sphere. Wherefore we ought to fly away from earth to heaven as quickly as we can, and to fly away is to become like God, as far as this is possible, and to become like Him, to become holy, just and wise.'

Aristotle left Plato's Academy and established his own Lyceum. Though some modern scholars have emphasized similarities in the philosophies of these two thinkers, the age-long recognition of the distinctions between them is of more importance. For practical life Aristotle maintained the 'this worldly' general attitude of the Greeks. With apparent reference to the Platonic 'Idea' of 'the Good', he wrote: 'Even if there is some one good which is universally predictable of goods or is capable of separate and independent existence, clearly it could not be achieved or attained by man; but we are now seeking something attainable.' He insisted on the particularity of goods. The doctor, for example, is not concerned with 'good in itself' but with 'the health of man', 'rather the health of a particular man: it is individuals that he is healing'. Aristotle considered characteristics of man as an animal, but insisted that he differs from the infra-human by his possession of reason. Human happiness involves the satisfaction both of the animal and the rational nature. His doctrine of the four causes may be applied to history. He recognized the activity of will as an efficient cause. The 'final cause' or essential purpose of any being is the realization of its own distinctive nature. For man the purpose of history is his satisfaction as a psycho-physical being, more especially of his reason. He emphasized the attitude of moderation, commonly acknowledged by the Greeks, but insisted that 'the mean between extremes' must be relative to the individual and the prevailing circumstances. As man is by nature 'a social animal', his history has come to include political organization.

Aristotle surveyed the forms of political government that could be or had been actual in history. He considered which would be most conducive to the full satisfaction of man's nature. The *Politics*, as we have it, is incomplete. His view may have been that the best is that in which each and all with capacities for participation in it should have such participation in accordance with their capacities. He considered some, as slaves, as having no such capacities. Though he may have regarded the use of reason in philosophical contemplation as the highest value for man, he did not stress it to the exclusion of any other values. Admitting metaphysically that reason, the universal element in man, persisted after the death of the body, he did not teach a doctrine of personal immortality in such fashion as to make a future life the motive for conduct in this one. After Aristotle a number of different philosophies were expounded in Greece, of which Epicureanism, Stoicism, and Neo-Platonism are considered later in this chapter.

III

The Romans were a practical rather than an intellectual people. From the latter half of the second century B.C. a few concerned themselves with philosophy under influences from Greece. From early times they had a high regard for family life for which the domestic religious ritual was of continued significance. They were also closely knit as a community. Both the family and the community were felt to be affected by super-human or divine powers. These divine powers were not conceived in the modern sense of that term.[1] The Romans were not given to mythological story making about the gods. However, they were very much interested in historical records. Of the many histories relating to them, the one with most relevance to our purpose was by a Greek, Polybius (204-122 B.C.).

[1] This view accords with that of W. Warde Fowler: *Roman Ideas of Deity*, London, 1914, p. 92: 'The Roman deities were not personal ones, but functional forces of nature, with a tendency to form abstractions.' Dr Poteat is inclined to think this incorrect. His doubt may be justified, for the Romans may have responded to their deities as though beings like themselves in conscious willing.

CONCEPTIONS IN ANCIENT GREECE AND ROME

Polybius undertook the writing of what to him at that time was a 'universal history'. He insisted that for a true view of history it is essential to survey the whole in all its related parts. He was especially interested in investigating how the Romans had subjected 'nearly the whole inhabited world to their sole government'. He treated historical record as of pragmatic worth. 'There is no more ready corrective of conduct than knowledge of the past.' He himself wrote from the standpoint of common sense, disregarding or dismissing superstitions. His references to fortune were not to the goddess Fortuna in whom some Romans believed. Fortune was 'the nature of things', the actual circumstances of any particular time and place. They could be favourable or unfavourable. If the latter they could be opposed and sometimes counteracted by men. It is evident that Polybius held that what was most important in history was due to men's characters and their thought, or lack of it. Only a few exceptions to this may be credited to 'good luck or chance'. He did not consider the universal Roman dominion as a 'destiny' determined by God. It was due to their 'schooling themselves' in 'vast and perilous enterprises'. He referred more than once to the Roman taking of oaths and the fidelity with which they abided by them. He associated this with their religious attitude. 'The quality in which the Roman commonwealth is most distinctly superior is in my opinion the nature of their religious convictions.' But he himself regarded the mythology and ritual of religion as for the 'common people', influenced by pageantry and 'invisible terrors'. Religion would not have been necessary if it 'had been possible to form a state composed of wise men'. He wished for a simply causal explanation of events in history. 'We must seek for a cause, for every event whether probable or improbable must have some cause.' He endeavoured to show sequences from remote causes to the latest consequences. Polybius had surveyed the rise of Roman dominion, but with a conviction of a cyclic process in history he anticipated its end. 'Such is the cycle of political revolution, the course appointed by nature in which constitutions change, disappear, and finally return to the point from which they started. Anyone who clearly perceives this may indeed in speaking of the future of any state be wrong in the estimate of the time the process will take, but if his judgment is not tainted by animosity or jealousy, he will very seldom be mistaken as to the form into which it will change. And especially in the case of the Roman state will this method enable us to arrive at a knowledge of its formation, growth and greatest perfection and likewise of the change for the worse which is sure to follow some day. For, as I said, this state, more than any other, has been formed and has grown naturally and will undergo a natural decline and change to its contrary.'

A later writer, of wider influence than Polybius, the poet Virgil (70-19 B.C.), inspired by the greatness of Rome, did not entertain the idea of its decline and fall. He did not regard its history as simply natural in Polybius's sense. Rome was divinely originated and had an eternal destiny. In the *Aeneid* he wrote of its mission to the world. Warde Fowler says that to the Romans of its time the *Aeneid* expressed the conviction that 'Providence, Divine Will, the Reason of the Stoics, or in the poetical setting of the poem, Jupiter, the great protecting Roman deity, with the Fates behind Him somewhat vaguely conceived, had guided the State to greatness and empire from its infancy onwards and the citizens of the State must be worthy of that destiny if they were to carry out the great work. This mighty theme pervades the whole poem.' Man's destiny is controlled in part by powers other than himself. Yet some element of freedom is acknowledged. Dido, 'maddened by destiny', was dying 'not in the course of fate but the victim of a sudden frenzy'. The Father of the Gods, addressing a council on Olympus, declared: 'I have forbidden that Italy should meet the Teucrians in the shock of war: what strife is this in defiance of my law?' The poem maintained that the greatness of Rome had been due, along with the aid of Providence, to Roman *virtus* and *pietas*. Conformity with divine principles of morality was necessary for success in history. Jupiter was 'king alike to all' and He 'held aloft His scales (of justice) poised and level'. 'Each man's own endeavours shall yield him the harvest of labour or fortune.' Aeneas's journey to Hades was for the cleansing and strengthening of his character, and suggested questions as to what follows death.

According to Warde Fowler it was an expression of 'a yearning in the soul of man to hope for a life beyond this and to make of this life a meet preparation for that other'. However the last six books of the *Aeneid* are concerned with the terrestrial future of the Roman people with the destiny of enduring domination of the world.

Rome did undergo a decline and fall. The causes have been much discussed by historians. One of them may have been the adoption of a life of ease and luxury by the patricians who should have maintained its power. An incentive to that kind of life may have been the Epicureanism which was one of the first forms of philosophy to be introduced from Greece. Though from earlier times there had been expressions of similar attitudes to life, it was Epicurus (341-270 B.C.) who gave them a philosophical defence. Whether Epicureanism was accepted in Greece beyond a small minority of the well-to-do may be doubted. It may have been more widely adopted among the Romans whose political successes had provided the means of enjoyment. The Epicurean implications as to history may be simply stated. Man was conceived as entirely physical: what is called consciousness ceased at death. The history that had real value for any man was his own during the period of his life. Though Epicurus curiously admitted belief in the existence of the gods, he considered them to be far off and as having no concern with the history of men. Two great fears, supposed to be the chief hindrances to human happiness, were thus taken to be baseless: the fear of what may follow death, and the fear of the anger of the gods. For there is no conscious future life after death and the gods are indifferent to men. A fragment ascribed to Epicurus says: 'While we are, death is not: and when death has come, we are not.' Such release from fear was an implication of the *De rerum natura* of Lucretius (99-55 B.C.).

Many of the Romans, as others in later history, may have misunderstood the teaching of Epicurus, regarding it as implying sensuous indulgence. But excess in that direction might lead to pain, to be avoided as much as pleasure is sought. The Epicurean ideal was rather one of simple contentment with abstention from multifarious desires. There was no advocacy of asceticism, but the keeping of desires in check for a life of repose. Men may avoid pains better by virtuous conduct. They get pleasure in kindness to others. Considering history to be a 'natural' set of processes, they looked on historical record pragmatically, as illustrating what led to an equable pleasant life and what to suffering. They had no serious concern for the future history of the community and made no efforts towards a higher civilization to be enjoyed by later generations. The meaning of history was for each the attainment of a pleasurable equanimity for the period of his life. Lucretius's poem raises a significant question: Was there in his time among the Romans widespread fear of what might come after death? The Pythagoreans of south Italy with their distinction between the soul and the body pointed to the possibility of bliss for the soul in a future life.

The aim of equanimity was also put forward by the Cynic precursors of Stoicism, but they lacked the intellectual acumen of the propounders of Stoicism, which was formulated at the close of the fourth and the beginning of the third centry B.C. from the teachings of Zeno and Chrysippus. Though rationalistic, its motive was basically practical. It helped in the cultivation of Roman character in encouraging the exercise of power of will, guided by reason, in the control of impulses and passions. Stoicism concerned itself with history as immediately experienced, and did not urge escape from it, being thus in accord with the general Greek and Roman attitudes to life. That may be the chief reason why it was more widely accepted among thoughtful Romans than the world-renouncing doctrines suggested by some of the Platonic *Dialogues.*

The Stoics considered the uniformities of the physical world as a manifestation of reason. God was conceived as the universal reason immanent in the Whole. Though their language sometimes seemed to imply a personal supreme being such as the deity of theistic systems, Providence was this immanent reason. As universal reason Providence was concerned with the particular events of life, especially with regard to their relations within the Whole. From the standpoint of the conception of the Whole, all events would appear to be of 'necessity', that is, determined. However, the Stoics tried to give recognition to moral worth and responsibility with the implication of a 'rational freedom' of individuals. They had difficulty in bringing these views of necessity and freedom together. Cosmologically they held the conception of world cycles. The world as we know it has arisen, eventually it will end; then the cycle will begin again, go through its course, end, and so recur eternally. For most Stoics there was no thought of this life being a time for preparation for a future life in another world. The value of this life had to be found in this life.

Cicero (100-43 B.C.) devoted much of his writing to an exposition of Greek philosophical ideas. Of the conflicting theories he discussed in his *De natura deorum*, he thought Stoicism was nearest the truth. But what Cicero presents has more the character of theism than of Stoic pantheism. The world and human beings are due to a Mind, who as Providence cares for men in history. Religion, as the communion of men with the divine, is a continuing aspect of history. Some passages of his *De senectute* present an attitude to history similar to that of Marcus Aurelius. 'Boyhood has certain pursuits: does youth yearn for them? Early youth has its pursuits: does the matured or so-called middle stage of life need them? Maturity, too, has such as are not even sought in old age, and finally there are those suitable to old age. Therefore, as the pleasures and pursuits of the earlier periods of life fall away, so also do those of old age, and when that happens man has had his full of life and the time is ripe for him to go.' Significance is to be found in the individual's history as it goes along. 'Hours and months and years go by; the past returns no more, and what is to be we cannot know; but whatever the the time given us in which to live, we should therefore be content.' 'For even if the allotted space of life be short, it is long enough to live honourably and well.' Nevertheless, Cicero later came to feel that there must be something for men beyond this life. Towards the end of his *Tusculan Disputations*, he wrote: 'For not to blind hazard or accident is our birth and creation due, but assuredly there is a power to watch over mankind, and not one who would beget and maintain a race, which after exhausting the full burden of sorrow, should then fall into the everlasting evil of death: let us regard it rather as a haven and a place of refuge prepared for us.' But it is quite impossible to determine with certainty to what extent this view was shared even by educated Romans of his time.

The dominant interest of the Latin historians was the history of Rome: its origin, its internal conditions, the lives of its great leaders, the expansion of its power. In general, other peoples were referred to only as bearing on Roman history. Here we can treat briefly of only two of them, Livy (59 B.C.-17 A.D.) and Tacitus (c 54-c 117 A.D.). Livy's *History of Rome* was of a long period and detailed in its treatment. In his preface he wrote: 'This it is which is particularly salutary and profitable in the study of history, that you behold instances of every variety in a conspicuous movement; that from thence you may select for yourself and your country that which you may imitate; thence note what is shameful in the undertaking and shameful in the result, which you may avoid.' Convinced that it was the qualities of the Roman people that had made Rome great, he sought to indicate the virtues that had led to its successes and the vices that resulted in misfortunes. Nevertheless, throughout his work (as now extant) he described omens and prodigies as though involving supernatural influences. The Romans 'possess as much as the gods have been pleased to bestow'. Yet, ultimately, there is a necessity that 'even the gods themselves do not overcome'. At the outset of his work he declared: 'In my opinion, the origin of so great a city and the establishment of an empire next in power to that of the gods, was due to the fates.' Sometimes fortune may completely 'blind the minds of men'. But despite such statements Livy's account is of Roman history made essentially by the Roman people with the assistance of the gods.

Tacitus's writings were concerned with only a short period of Roman history, a time that was 'rich in disaster, frightful in its wars, torn by civil strife, and even in peace full of horrors'. Though occasionally he used phrases like 'the wrath of heaven', he did not seek any theological or religious interpretation of history. Though recording some instances taken as omens, he himself considered causes to be 'fortuitous or natural'. After referring to supposed omens on one occasion, he said 'the most portentous spectacle was Vitellius himself'. The interest of his *History* and of his *Annals* lies in his treatment of history as dependent predominantly on the personal qualities of men, their strength or weakness of character, their range of vision or their ignorance, their virtues or their vices. Along with the evils of the emperors and other leaders he described the fickleness and lack of discipline of the mob. He was an 'ethical' historian showing the results of conduct in history as it went along. He barely touched on problems of deeper philosophical import. 'I suspend my judgment of the question whether it is fate and unchangeable necessity which governs the revolutions of human affairs. Indeed, among the wisest of the ancients and among their disciples you will find many conflicting theories, many holding the conviction that heaven does not concern itself with the beginning or the end of our life, or in short, with mankind at all; and that therefore sorrows are continually the lot of the good, happiness of the wicked; while others, on the contrary, believe that though there is a harmony between fate and events, yet it is not dependent on wandering stars but on the primary elements and on a combination of natural causes. Still, they leave us the capacity of choosing our life, maintaining that, the choice once made, there is a fixed sequence of events. Good and evil are not what vulgar opinion counts them: many who seem to be struggling with adversity are happy; many amid great affluence are utterly miserable.' 'Possibly there is in all things a kind of cycle, and there may be moral revolutions just as there are changes of the seasons.' At the end of his *Life of Agricola*, he did refer to a future life—'a place of refuge for the souls of the virtuous'—but only as a possibility. His judgments of men were solely with reference to their earthly conditions. There is not the slightest suggestion in the works of Livy or Tacitus that Romans did or should regard the dominant purpose of men in history to be redemption from sin or that they were or should be concerned with any idea of escape from the world as transitory to an eternal transcendent realm.

INTERPRETATIONS OF HISTORY

IV

The emperor Domitian, probably fearing a stimulation of independence of thought among his subjects, in 94 A.D. issued an edict banishing philosophers from Rome. Among those who left was Epictetus, an emancipated slave. In his writings that have come down to us, he expressed a Stoic attitude to history. 'Remember that thou art an actor in a play, of such a part as it may please the director to assign thee; of a short part if he choose a short part; of a long one if he choose a long.' Whether in human terms short or long, it is really brief. 'For I am no Immortal, but a man, a part of the sum of things as an hour is of a day. Like the hour I must arrive and like the hour pass away.' Considering men as rational, as sharing universal reason, Epictetus urged that they should look on their histories as under the beneficent control of Providence. With this conviction they should participate in the joyful praise of God. 'If I were a nightingale, I would do after the nature of a nightingale; if a swan, after that of a swan. But I am a reasoning creature, and it behoves me to sing the praise of God: this is my task and this I do, nor, as long as it is granted me will I ever abandon this post. And you too, I summon to join me in the same song.'

The most impressive reflections by a Roman relevant to the nature and significance of history were those of Marcus Aurelius (121-180 A.D.) who as emperor for a time had a prominent part in Roman history. His *Meditations* expressed both his Roman temperament and his Roman interpretation of Stoic ideas. To judge by the number of the different 'books' in which he refers to it, he had a profound conviction that the universe as a whole is involved in a cyclic process. He applied that idea to history. 'The course of Nature has been the same from all eternity and everything comes around in a circle.' 'This world itself subsists by continual changes, not only of the elements, but of those things which are composed of those elements in a perpetual circle of successive generation and corruption.' In the changes of history there is always repetition. History is always the same in the nature of its contents. 'He that has viewed the present age has seen everything that has been or will be to all eternity. For things have always gone on and always will go on in the like uniform manner.' 'In general, if you reflect on what passes around you, you will find that all the events of the present age are what the histories of every age are full of. There is nothing new . . .' 'Take a view of the whole court of Hadrian, or Antonius, of Philip of Macedon, or Croesus, for you will find they exactly resemble your own, though the performers in the drama were different.' The length of life is thus really a matter of indifference, for 'whether we behold this same scene for one hundred or one hundred thousand years, it comes to much the same thing'. With such a belief the idea of a future life after death could have little appeal. It could not be used to give a ground for hope in face of ills of the present life, for a future life would only be a repetition of the experiences of this one. Marcus Aurelius did not absolutely deny the possibility of continued personal existence after death. Man is body and soul. At death the corporeal frame will be 'reduced to its original elements', the 'spiritual part either extinguished or translated to some other state of existence'. His dominant view seems to have been that 'all spiritual beings are soon resolved into the soul of the universe and the very memory of all things is, with the same speed, buried in the gulf of time'.

The significance of history is to be sought neither in a future terrestrial condition for which the present is to be treated as instrumental, nor as a preparation for a higher life after death. Each individual has his own period of time. 'The Supreme Being allots to every creature a due proportion of time.' It is thus in the 'now' of his own time that the meaning of history is to be found for each and every individual. Marcus Aurelius focused attention on the 'now'. 'All those advantages (that state of perfection and happiness) at which you wish to arrive by a long circuit of time and trouble, if you are not your own enemy you may obtain now. This you will accomplish, if, thinking no more of the time past and leaving the future to Providence, you employ the present time according to the dictates of piety and justice; of piety by submitting cheerfully to what is allotted to you, for that will conduce to your good in the end and you were destined to this allotment; of justice that with freedom and without prevarication you may speak the truth and act on all occasions according to the law of reason and according to the importance of the object.' The good of history as we live it is not hedonistic. The mind can and should be relatively indifferent to pleasure and pain. The basic essential for happiness is self-respect. 'Wrap up yourself in your own virtue and be independent. For a rational mind that acts always with justice and integrity is sufficient to its own happiness and will enjoy a perpetual calm.' Though this individualism was fundamental for Marcus Aurelius, he gave full recognition to man's social nature and duties. Each is to do diligently what he was 'born to do'—including that involved in his position in society. 'I am solicitous only that I myself may do nothing contrary to the nature of man, nor act, in any manner or on any occasion, unbecoming my duty or my station.' As we 'are fellow-citizens in the same commonwealth' 'the first and principal duty of man is to cultivate society'. Specifically he had a place as a Roman, but his outlook was cosmopolitan. 'For me, Antoninus, my city is Rome; but as a man it is the universe.'

Within itself the mind is 'invincible': it 'cannot be forced against its own will'. The mind is possessed 'of an exclusive sovereignty' in its own sphere. 'The power of living is most happily situated in your mind.' Marcus Aurelius admitted three possible views as to the ultimate causes of the events in history: that all is by chance; that all is determined by 'fatal necessity'; that all, apart from what is due to human freedom, is dependent on a kind, merciful, benevolent Providence. He adopted the third view. What is beyond one's control must be accepted with equanimity. The belief in Providence rules out a hedonistic conception of history. For with a hedonistic conception one would have to 'complain often of the dispensations of Providence, as distributing its favours to the wicked and to the virtuous without regard to their respective deserts, the wicked frequently abounding in pleasures and the means of procuring them, and the virtuous, on the contrary, being harassed with pain and other afflictive circumstances.' However belief in Providence implies that 'all things are administered with the utmost equity and impartiality'. This leads to the question of Marcus Aurelius's view as to evil in history.

His position is not clear. Though he declared that 'the whole universe is one harmonious system', he often referred to the wicked. As for the hardships and pains of life: 'nothing ever befalls anyone but what is in his power to bear'.

The final paragraph of the *Meditations* is an impressive statement as to man's life as a drama similar to the idea expressed by Epictetus. 'Oh, my friend, you have lived a citizen of this great commonwealth, the world; of what consequence is it to you that you have lived in it but a few years? ... Is it any hardship that you are sent out of the world, not by a tyrant, or an unjust judge, but by that Being which first introduced you, as the magistrate who engages an actor for the stage, dismisses him again at his pleasure?

'But I have performed only three acts of the play and not the whole five!

'Very true, but in life even three acts may complete the whole drama. He determines the action of the piece, who first caused it to be composed and now orders its conclusion. You are not accountable for either. Depart therefore with a good grace; for He who dismisses you is a gracious and benevolent being.'

v

During several centuries there was a breakdown in Roman political organization, and with much social chaos a disintegration of the ancient mode of life of the Romans, as there was also of that of the Greeks. In the conditions of disillusionment and much suffering many different doctrines of redemption and ways of salvation were advocated throughout the regions of the eastern Mediterranean, some from Egypt and Persia. Eventually Christianity became dominant. In the Italian Renaissance there was a return to some of the Greek attitudes to life. In their teachings Ambrose and Augustine carried over much that was good in Greek thought. The last impressive system of that thought was the Neo-Platonism of Plotinus which in the early centuries of the Christian era led to forms of (non-Christian) Gnosticism and to heresies among Christians.

W. R. Inge wrote that 'the speculations of seven hundred

years' were 'summed up' in Neo-Platonism. That view may be definitely challenged. Our account is based on his two-volume *The Philosophy of Plotinus*. Though Neo-Platonism was presented as a form of philosophy, its adherents did not regard it as a product of merely rational reflection. It was rather a symbolic expression of knowledge believed obtained in mystical experience. The ultimate Reality is the One, the all-embracing Absolute which is perfect. Though it was said that 'Spirit . . . is all that really exists,' the One is sometimes described as 'beyond Spirit'. Spirit is not to be identified with soul, for it is 'super-conscious'. Plotinus (207-270 A.D.) spoke of 'the Universal Spirit', of 'particular spirits'; the 'Universal Soul' and of 'individual souls'. The One is the ground of all as a hierarchy within Itself. It is not a cause in the sense of temporal production. For the One is eternal, and eternity is not a passing sequence from the past through the present to the future. It has rather the character of an all-inclusive now. Despite this description Inge made frequent use of the term 'create' in such manner as to imply time as involving a sequence of changes, and as an essential characteristic of history. Plotinus made no attempt to explain time away or to formulate any conceptual theory of it. He accepted it as a fact of experience. 'Time is natural.' There is some doubt as to his view of the relation of time to eternity. Inge considered it to be that time is 'the image of eternity'; time resembles eternity as much as it can. There is something of the eternal in all the temporal. That has a definite implication for human history. Inge inferred from it that there is something eternal in every worthy object of human activity. (One might ask: Why not also in every unworthy object?—for that also is in time.)

According to Plotinus, the universe is 'a living chain of being, an unbroken series of ascending and descending values and existences', which form the harmonious Whole. Creatures 'endowed with Soul' were sent into the world that they might be 'moulded a little nearer to the Divine image by yearning for the home they had left'. 'This aspiration, which slumbers even in unconscious beings, is the mainspring of the moral, intellectual, and aesthetic life of mankind.' Each soul has its time, place and task in the Whole. 'The history of the world consists in an infinite number of vast but finite schemes, which have each of them, a beginning, middle and end.' But there are ambiguities as to the nature of individual persons in such history. Inge says that Plotinus was 'anxious to preserve human individuality'. 'Each individual must be himself'; each is 'an original cause', though it is 'entirely its own master only when out of the body'. However, though the super-conscious in them has the reality of Spirit, particular persons as known in history are not truly real. There may be no self-conscious future for human souls and the goal of history is not to be sought in a future personal immortality. The meaning of history for them must be their participation in the values of the 'eternal now' in the particular periods of their terrestrial life.

In Neo-Platonism there are the same two conflicting views as to the attitudes men are to adopt with regard to the human body and the world that were previously indicated in the Platonism of the *Dialogues*. History, as we know it, has in part to do with matter. The Neo-Platonic account of matter is ambiguous: it is, and it is not. 'In denying reality to matter,' wrote Inge, 'we do not affirm that it is absolutely non-existent.' Matter is an inferior element of the Whole, lower in value and 'degree of reality' (whatever that may mean). Porphyry reported that Plotinus seemed to be ashamed of being 'in the body'. 'We must hasten to depart hence, to detach ourselves as much as we can from the body to which we are unhappily bound . . .' 'Our life in this world is but a falling away, an exile.' The soul 'must remove from itself good and evil and everything else that it may receive the One alone'. The descents and ascents of the soul are nevertheless declared to be 'necessary and integral parts of the universal harmony'.

At times Plotinus presented a different outlook, viewing the earth as 'a good copy of heaven'. 'How can this world . . . be separated from the spiritual world. Those who despise what is so nearly akin to the spiritual world prove that they know nothing of the spiritual world except its name.' The earthly, the temporal, are of positive significance and value: for they are constituents of the perfection of the eternal One. Inge endeavoured to meet the difficulty of reconciling the two different attitudes to the world that have been indicated. He wrote that we must remember that for Plotinus reality consists 'in the rich and glorious life of Spirit, in which, whatever we renounce in the world of sense, is given back transmuted and ennobled'. Of that statement, one may say that the meaning of 'transmuted and ennobled' is not evident. Admitting that the doctrine of reality as a kingdom of values is not explicit in the writings of Plotinus, Inge described the meaning of history for Neo-Platonism to be the experience of the eternal values of the True, the Good, and the Beautiful. 'Retire into thyself and examine thyself. If thou dost not yet find beauty there, do like the sculptor who chisels, planes, polishes, till he has adorned his statue with all the attributes of beauty. So do thou chisel away from thy Soul what is superfluous, straighten that which is crooked, purify and enlighten what is dark, and do not cease working at thy statue until virtue shines before thine eyes with its divine splendour, and thou seest temperance seated in thy bosom with its holy purity.'

Inge, a Christian priest, proclaimed himself 'a disciple' of Plotinus. His thought was essentially Neo-Platonist, but he avoided any statement of Christian doctrines in its terms. He presented Neo-Platonism as 'a living philosophy' to be considered in our own age. From its standpoint he was vigorously critical of the occidental idea of human progress. However, in the preface to the third edition of *The Philosophy of Plotinus*, he bemoaned the fact that 'the modern spirit' is 'out of sympathy' with Plotinus who was 'profoundly indifferent to worldly affairs and the problems of civilization'. With reference to Plotinus's conception of history as constituted of an infinite number of temporary finite schemes, he contended: 'This view is in every way far superior to the loose theories of perpetual progress which are so popular in Europe and America. An infinite purpose is a contradiction in terms. Such a purpose could never have been formed, and could never be accomplished. There may be a single purpose... in the present world-order taken as a whole; but only on condition of our admitting that the present world-order had a beginning and will have an end. Physical science is of course well aware of the fate in store for this planet. The achievements of humanity will one day be wiped off the slate... (Those) who, rejecting belief in a spiritual world, project their ideals into an unending terrestrial future, suffer shipwreck both in philosophy and science . . . Man must find consolation for the inevitable fate of his species either nowhere or in a heaven where all values are preserved eternally.'

CHAPTER IV

THEISTIC CONCEPTIONS OF HISTORY
I. ZOROASTRIAN, JEWISH, AND ISLAMIC

I

In the Occident, the name Zoroastrianism has been widely used for a form of religion and thought which originated in ancient Persia. Today there are comparatively few Zoroastrians in Persia itself. The leading communities of this faith are in India, to which their forefathers began to migrate about a thousand years ago. Though there were many similarities in the early religion of the Persians and that of the Hindu *Vedas*, the Zoroastrians in India have been a closed group and have preserved their religion and thought with very little, if indeed any, modification through influences of the surrounding Hinduism. Zoroastrianism has remained clearly distinguished from later forms of Hinduism. Zoroastrians in India, today generally called Parsis, include some of the most educated people of that country. They have been pioneers in the making of modern India, and this has been due basically to their views of and attitudes to history.

The date of Zarathustra, the founder of Zoroastrianism, is uncertain. Scholarly Parsis think he lived about 1000 B.C. but some occidentals have placed the date as late as the seventh century B.C. The *Gathas*, the earliest extant Zoroastrian literature, are taken to express his teaching, the main principles of which have been maintained throughout Zoroastrian history. Central in them was the idea of God. The name given to Him, Ahura Mazda, gives explicit recognition to the wisdom of the godhead. In accord with this is the emphasis that has been placed on mind rather than on the physical as the basis of existence. Ahura Mazda is perfect, eternal, all-dominant, all-seeing, and all-good. The physical world and human beings are His creation. He aids and judges men, being ever-present in human history.

One basic attitude of Zoroastrians to history is revealed in the Gathic description of the goodness of God's creation. He upholds the earth and the firmament from falling. He made the moon wax and wane and determined the paths of the sun and the stars. He yoked swiftness to the winds. He clothed the heavenly realms with light. He created 'joy-giving' cattle, plants, and 'the waters'. He created human beings, their spirits and their bodies, and endowed them with freedom of will. He inspired love between father and son; gave sleep and wakefulness, and many other blessings. The physical world is the stage for human history, which in His wisdom He ordained for them. For it, He established moral order in accord with the principles of which they are to live their history. With their freedom they may violate them. But the *Gathas* do not represent the individual's history as completed on earth. Zarathustra had a belief in immortality. He prayed for the goods of terrestrial life and eventually to share in the final condition of bliss when evil has been entirely eradicated.

Zarathustra was much concerned with the evils in human life. His urging of unceasing war against them led to a second basic attitude of Zoroastrians in history: the strenuous resistance to them in all forms. The *Gathas* refer to evil as Angra Mainyu, the evil one, the enemy. Evil is essentially *druj*, 'the lie', 'deceit', in contrast with the wisdom of God. Zarathustra and his followers have made no attempts to explain evil away as illusory. He and they have never advocated an escape from ordinary life, 'a going forth from the world'. He concentrated his attention on forms of immorality: lying, murder, dishonesty and sloth; and on pain and disease and misfortunes that come from infra-human creatures, such, for example, as those which destroy crops. The use of a proper name for evil, Angra Mainyu, has led to much discussion as to whether Zoroastrianism is an ultimate dualism, of an all-wise Ahura Mazda and an evil Angra Mainyu, not created by God. Orthodox Zoroastrian scholars have rejected such a view. The term 'spirit' as applied to evil is in its usage to refer to a mental disposition.

In the period immediately following that of Zarathustra, the Avestan, from about the sixth century B.C. to the second A.D., aspects of pre-Gathic religion found renewed expression. Under the influence of Zarathustra and his teachings that religion had for a time been pushed into the background. Earlier mythology, ideas as to the Iranian deities, traditional rituals and ceremonies became regarded as a part of Zoroastrianism. But the essential teachings of Zarathustra still dominated among the leaders of thought and religion. The world was created by divine wisdom, and it would end through that wisdom. The radical distinction between good and evil was emphatically proclaimed. It was expressed as a difference of two worlds: 'the world of the righteous' and 'the world of the wicked'. These 'worlds' were two hostile groups and tendencies in human history which is largely constituted by the conflicts between them. There was in this Avestan period a change of attitude with more attention to the idea of the future life. Righteousness had its greatest importance with reference to the attainment of a blissful immortality. The chief significance of history was in its relation to a final goal. Nevertheless, it was still maintained that terrestrial history is also of worth in itself. Ahura Mazda was given the names of All Happiness, Full Happiness, the Lord of Happiness. He created 'joy-giving lands for mankind'. Being Himself abundant joy, He gives happiness to men. The householders prayed for all the boons of earthly life and that happiness should never leave their houses. Each individual was called on to take his part in the struggle against evil. Contrasted with the Gathic period there was some change of emphasis in an insistence that each generation profits by what the past achieved and on the duty of working for the good of future generations. The triumph of the good is of social import. The idea was maintained that in the final triumph there would be a renovation of the world. According to Plutarch the Persians believed that in this renovation there would be one human commonwealth and one language.

Despite the misfortunes of the Persians, including the

destruction of much Zoroastrian literature and the disorganization of the priesthood, there was a revival of Zoroastrianism after the establishment of the Sasanian dynasty, about 224 A.D. Though there was much concern with rituals and ceremonies and mythological ideas were widely current, the fundamental concepts and attitudes of Zarathustra were still accorded their importance and given their due attention. Mani preached a doctrine in which matter was treated as the principle of evil. This was regarded as heretical and he was executed in 274 A.D. Manichaeism spread widely in the Mediterranean area. The orthodox Zoroastrians insisted that the body as physical is not in itself evil, nor is it necessarily the source of evil. In contrast with Mani's advocacy of celibacy, they encouraged marriage and the production of children as virtuous. Fasting, they maintained, was conducive to a weakening of the body, thus lessening its effectiveness in the fight against evils and in the effort for the good: it was also a neglect of enjoyments that God had made possible. Spiritual being was more important than worldly goods, but the effort for riches was meritorious. The communistic teachings of Mazdak (d. 528 A.D.) were chiefly to do with political and social organization, but they were opposed by Zoroastrian thinkers on the ground that they were contrary to God's purposes in His differentiation of men in their creation.

In the latter part of the Pahlavi period, from the third to the ninth century A.D., there appeared a work entitled *Skikand Gumanik Vijar* defending a form of dualism different from that of spirit and matter propounded by Mani. If there is no independent opponent of God, who is Himself able to create beings free of misfortunes, why did He not create them? If He wished to do so and could not, then He is not almighty. If He could and did not, He is not completely merciful. The discussion was of the problem of evil in the form in which it concerns the theist. The author's final argument rests almost entirely on the nature of God as central in Zoroastrianism. God is perfect in goodness and thus only good could come from Him. If God wills good, some other being must will evil. It is absurd, the author contended, to think that God created evil that men might in contrast with it appreciate the good—poverty, pain and death so that they would value wealth, health and life. With His wisdom He would not create a being to be opposed to Himself; one whom with His foreknowledge He would know would turn against Himself. Evil must have originated from some other being existing independently of God. Evil cannot be described as originally due to man, for man is a divine creation. But man with his freedom may fall to the temptation of the evil one. With the belief that God is almighty, the author shared the Zoroastrian faith that eventually the evil will be entirely overcome. The orthodox have rejected this work along with all other theories of an ultimate dualism in existence.

Zarathustra had definitely taught that men have freedom to choose and strive for the good or to succumb to the temptations of evil. The significance of their histories depends in part on the use of their freedom. However, during the later Pahlavi period, mostly as a consequence of the political misfortunes the Persians had suffered and partly through the promulgation of astrology, a doctrine of fatalism was widely accepted. One Pahlavi work states: 'Fate holds sway over everyone and everything.' Striving for any end is of no avail to man if Fate has decided otherwise. An attempt was made to reconcile the idea of Fate with the Zoroastrian faith, with the theory that Fate controls only earthly affairs while men's spiritual welfare in the future life depends on their own attitudes and efforts. Such a theory was obviously not in conformity with Zoroastrianism which maintained man's freedom to fight against all that is evil and strive for all that is good, and this all includes earthly affairs.

Zoroastrian literature presents a well formulated system of thought, but it is analytic and expository rather than critically philosophical. It puts no emphasis on 'the way of knowledge' as the chief path to the ideal, as is done in Jain and some Hindu systems. With the recognition of the importance of knowledge, the dominant attitudes have always been, and still are, those of action and worship. With their central idea of God, their belief in a future life and the recognition that the values possible in this life are meant by God for man's enjoyment, it was doctrinally not difficult for Zoroastrians to adopt the faith of Islam. Apparently the majority of them in Persia did so. However Zoroastrianism has no dogma as to its scriptures such as is held by Muslims as to the *Quran*. In consequence the Parsis, especially in modern times, have had a freer development of thought and a wider appreciation of advances of civilization. Leading Parsis in India today have no difficulty in retaining the essentials of their ancient faith while discarding mythological ideas and some rituals that had become associated with it. Their full acceptance of the positive significance of history and of its dynamic progressive character is in accord with that faith.

An outstanding expression of a modern view of history from the standpoint of Zoroastrianism was given by M. N. Dhalla, formerly High Priest in Karachi, Pakistan, and a man of wide occidental and oriental scholarship. The title of his volume: *Our Perfecting World: Zarathustra's Way of Life* (1930) indicated both the dominant attitude to history and its basis for him in the teachings of Zarathustra. He contended that Zoroastrianism is not an obsolete mode of thought and way of life. Dr Dhalla incorporated much from the thought and the methods of the contemporary occident, but always bringing it into relation with Zoroastrian principles. In giving an account of his work, it is interesting to follow his own order of exposition. He placed the consideration of evil in the forefront, saying in his Introduction: 'Human evolution in its final analysis runs on the basis of resistance to evil.' He followed that statement almost immediately by an affirmation of the optimistic character of Zoroastrianism. The purpose of his volume was 'to show that our universe is unfolding towards an aim, that the life of man, imperfect in all its phases, has, throughout the period of human history, been slowly but steadily progressing towards perfection through the inexorable laws of co-operation with good and conflict with evil'. That was the implication of 'the message of hope' that Zarathustra brought to mankind.

The second section of the book was devoted to 'Religion in Evolution'. From an initial chapter on primitive religion, he proceeded through the historical stages of the religion of the prophets of all the leading faiths, to the periods of formalism and persecution, to the time of the clash between science and religion, to that of a falling away from religion, to the return to it, and ends the section with a chapter: 'From Religions to Religion'. Through these stages, with the movements backward and forward, Dr Dhalla saw a dominant advance of religion as a prime aspect of human history. Religion will 'continue mutually assimilating and absorbing the best that is embodied in every one of them'. A synthesis of all that is best in all religions will form man's future religion and mankind will not find it possible to think in terms of this or that religion but only of religion. Dr Dhalla's consideration first of religion is in accord with Zoroastrian theism. It is Ahura Mazda, the Wise Lord, the Divine, who is the source of all that makes history possible.

The Divine source is a Mind: thus the next section is concerned with 'Mind in Evolution'. Dr Dhalla traced that evolution with consideration of the intricate and rich development of thought and language and went on to the aims and achievements of modern education. Here, as in religion, he saw an advance to a universal outlook and universal co-operation. 'Knowledge knows no national frontiers, nor recognizes differences of caste or creed, and the cultured men and women of the world are becoming intellectual universalists. Universal education which is the objective of all civilized peoples of our times is the most powerful aid to promoting mutual understanding, trust and sympathy, leading to the goal of the universal brotherhood of mankind.'

Zoroastrianism has never represented the meaning of history as being specifically in society as such. It is the individual who has to cross Chinvat (the bridge) to submit to final judgment. Yet the importance of social relations has always been stressed: the good as such is unifying, the triumph of the good in the world is possible only with social co-operation. So in his next section Dr Dhalla treated of 'Social Life in Evolution'. The family as a social group has its own distinctive values. But Dr Dhalla was not optimistic as to the family in our time. Through economic and other conditions 'the family everywhere is disintegrating'. In Zoroastrianism a healthy family life has always been praised and God asked for His blessing of it. On the other hand, he recognized an advance in law, in the administration of justice, and in political government. Democracy 'the best form of government so far invented by human intelligence' is becoming more and more widely adopted. The phase of Nationalism is likely to be transcended. 'It is not altogether an idle dream to strive for the dawning of a day in some distant future when man may know neither nation nor race, but with the Stoic conception of world citizenship, only mankind, and when mankind may claim the world for its motherland.' Zoroastrianism fully acknowledges the necessity to fight against aggression; but there has been a growing opposition to war. But treaties, the preparation for war, the theory of the balance of power, diplomacy, imperialism, have all failed to end war. Writing in 1930 Dr Dhalla thought that there was an advance in international co-operation that would end war.

From his Zoroastrian standpoint of the deity being the creator of the world and of mankind, Dr Dhalla turned to the consideration of civilization. He traced the relations of the occident and the orient in past history, surveyed their present intercourse, and pointed to their respective future contributions to a world-wide civilization and culture. 'Human achievements during some seven thousand years of man's cultural ascendency are the creation neither of the East nor the West alone. Both have contributed their immortal heritage to humanity, each according to her peculiar aptitudes and distinctive genius . . . The progressive evolution of humanity depends on the combined services of the East and the West . . . Each by itself is incomplete and incapable of performing the stupendous task confronting mankind.' After a survey of economic evolution in history and the advances made relative to the physical well-being of men, the author turned in his final chapter to a consideration of 'Progressive Civilization'. The different civilizations in history did not appear to him to have been in radical opposition. Rather each has been an expression of parts of what is connoted by the concept of civilization taken in its completeness. History is in part an onward march to universal civilization. 'If, in a distant cultural millennium, humanity comes to embrace one universal civilization, it will not be a civilization of any one particular race, eastern or western, but a blend of the best in the civilizations of all races of mankind.' Dr Dhalla's account of the Zoroastrian view of history was one of universal progress inspired by the faith that with the dominance of God, the Wise Lord, the final goal, the complete triumph of the good, will eventually be attained.

II

The Jewish ideas as to the nature of history and their attitudes with relation to it are expressed in the Hebrew Scriptures. The historical character of most of those writings is evidence of the extent of the interest of the Jews in their history. We are not concerned here with questions of the dates of composition of the different books. The order in which they have been generally combined suggests a historical sequence from what was taken to be the beginning of mankind. The contents of the historical books and the manner of their presentation show that the Jews were interested in something more than any mere record of events. More important than that was the interpretation of events with reference to the attitudes of those concerned in them and the implied relations to God. The non-historical books have significance with regard to the fundamental ideas in that interpretation and in their descriptions of the right attitudes to God and their statements of the moral principles in accordance with which men should live.

The Jewish view of history is basically and comprehensively theistic. History is to be understood from the idea of the dominance of God. Though for a time there may have been a belief that different peoples had different gods, at an early date the conviction arose that there is only one God. Even though the early chapters of the first book, *Genesis*, may be regarded as mythological, they have the fundamental idea that the beginning of human history was due to God. He created the earth with all its characteristics that make history possible on it. He created human beings as psycho-physical, souls with bodies. He placed them in conditions of bliss, 'the garden of Eden'. But there is evil in history and the story of the 'fall' of Adam and Eve, the first human beings, is introduced to account for its origin. The story implicates two ideas that have persisted in the Jewish view of history. Man has a freedom of choice to obey or to disobey God. The alienation from God through disobedience is the root evil, and all other evil depends ultimately on it. But though God turned Adam and Eve out of the garden of Eden, He did not thereafter isolate Himself from mankind. The Jews have maintained that God has been continuously in relation with men in history. Though in *Genesis* it is represented as a curse that man should earn bread by the sweat of his brow, later in the Scriptures the need to work is treated as a blessing. God gave man 'wisdom of heart to work all manner of works'. The Scriptures give no suggestion of a conviction of a continuous advance in history. There is rather a succession of movements, forwards and backwards, times of prosperity and times of catastrophe. God intervened on particular occasions in history. Though evil was described as coming originally to man through his temptation by Satan, an evil spirit, the references to Satan in the Hebrew Scriptures are few.

The Jewish conception of God is of the utmost importance for their view of history. God is a spirit and there can be no visible representation of Him. Yet God made man 'in His own image'. Man is thus also a spirit. With this similarity of being, there is a use of terms for God analogous with those used for man. He has wisdom, will, and feelings such as love and righteous anger. The Jews have not confused or identified God with His creation: neither the physical world nor human beings are parts of God. The Jewish rabbis were in accordance with their traditional doctrine when they rejected the philosophy of Spinoza.

The Israelites came to believe that they were 'the chosen people' of God. The historical books recorded what God had done to and for them. The conviction was not just one of pride of race but of definitely religious import. God made a covenant with Abraham: 'I will make of thee a great nation and I will bless thee and make thy name great ... and in thee shall all the families of the earth be blessed.' God appeared at times in a manner to be perceived by particular individuals. He

INTERPRETATIONS OF HISTORY

came to Abraham on the plains of Mamre, and made His presence known to Moses in the burning bush on Mount Sinai. In a specific event in history He gave the law to Moses. That involved for the Jews a principle fundamental for their view of history. Morality was not invented by men, it was not simply a social product relative to changing conditions of life. Morality was conformity with God's will, its principles always and everywhere valid. It was God that revealed the moral to men: they did not discover it themselves. That was one main aspect of His guidance of men for their realization of His purpose in creating them and the intelligible world. God was a righteous judge and the Scriptures indicated some of His judgments in history as it went along.

The Jewish conception of history is not, and has never been, individualistic. It is of 'the people of Israel' primarily and then of mankind in general. The kings, as vice-regents of God on earth, were to promote the welfare of God's chosen people. The prophets preached righteousness and devotion to God. The Hebrew Scriptures did not advocate an 'escape from the world', in any forms of ascetic monastic life. A high estimate was placed on marriage and the command given 'to increase and multiply'. The goods of earthly life are gifts from God to be accepted with thankfulness and enjoyed. The attitude implied is 'this-worldly'. It is significant that little is said in the early Hebrew Scriptures of immortality in the sense of a continued personal life after death. The references to another world after death suggest a condition of desolation.

The Jewish attitudes to life have nowhere been more richly expressed than in the *Psalms*. They show them to have been not merely ethical but religious in a specific emotional experience. Central for the *Psalms* is the belief in God. Only 'the fool says in his heart: There is no God'. It is 'God who hath made us and not we ourselves'. 'The fear of the Lord is the beginning of wisdom.' Time is due to God: the night and the day are His. He is ever present in all times and places in history. 'Whither shall I go from Thy spirit? Or whither shall I flee from Thy presence?' God brings evil men to destruction, but He forgives the penitent, for He is merciful. The apparent prosperity of the wicked is only for a time, and inwardly they

THEISTIC CONCEPTIONS—I

are not truly happy. 'I have been young and now am old, yet I have not seen the righteous forsaken, nor his seed begging bread. . . . I have seen the wicked in great power and spreading himself like a green bay tree, yet he passed away and lo, he was not.' In the whole of religious literature it would be difficult to find an expression of the depth of true repentance to equal that of the fifty-first *Psalm*: 'I acknowledge my transgressions.' 'Cleanse me from my sin.' 'Create in me a clean heart, O God, and renew a right spirit within me.' 'Restore unto me the joy of Thy salvation.' Sin is not merely a breaking of social customs or laws, it is an alienation from God. For satisfaction in history man needs communion with God. 'As the hart panteth after the water-brooks, so panteth my soul after Thee, O God. My soul thirsteth for God.' More help is to be had from God than from men, and with trust in Him there should be no fear of men. 'God is our refuge and strength.' 'Except the Lord build the house, they labour in vain that build it; except the Lord keep the city, the watchman waketh but in vain.' Ultimately it is He who 'governs the nations' and enables them to attain the welfare they merit. The state of one in right relations to God, and therefore also to his fellowmen and the physical world, is one of joyfulness that leads to the praise of God. 'Praise the Lord O my soul.' The last sentence in the *Psalms* in their present order is: 'Let everything that hath breath praise the Lord.' But man's life on earth is brief. Man's days are as grass which withers so soon; like smoke they quickly fade away. Yet the *Psalms* do not stress any idea of a future life. It is once declared: 'God will redeem my soul from the power of the grave, for He shall receive me.'

It is maintained throughout the Hebrew Scriptures that suffering comes as a consequence of sin. But can all suffering be thus accounted for? That is the problem of the *Book of Job*, and it is of importance for the Jewish theistic view of history. Job was a man in good health, happy with wife and children, with much wealth, and of the highest virtue and devotion to God. His spiritual goodness and his worldly wellbeing seemed to go together. Then God allowed him to be deprived of his earthly happiness and afflicted with the pains of physical ailments. The few who came to talk to him insisted that as suffering and sin always go together, Job must be at heart sinful. Job could not accept that view as covering all the facts. He was not prepared to regard his sufferings as entirely punishment. Considering himself as mostly good, he was 'full of confusion' and in great despair. He accepted the idea that though he was virtuous God allowed him to suffer. He held fast to his righteousness and sought God: 'O, that I knew where I might find Him.' In conditions of despair he thought that 'man that is born of woman is of few days and full of trouble'; he is 'born into trouble'. The *Book of Job* presents the view that in history man has suffering not due to his own sin. Job's interlocutors maintained that idea to impugn the justice of God, and holding it was itself Job's sin. However, in that the Lord restored Job to happiness they were shown to be wrong. The *Book of Job* implies a definite rejection both of a merely humanistic and of a hedonistic conception of history. In history there is suffering that has for its purpose the strengthening of character and the turning of men to God. This Jewish view is in contrast with the Indian doctrine of the *law of karma*. The question is raised: 'If a man die, shall he live again?' Man cannot give a certain answer.

The *Book of Ecclesiastes*, or The Preacher, may express the ideas of an individual thinker, and they may be given different interpretations. They may not have been widely shared by his contemporaries or by many later Jews. The Preacher declared: 'All is vanity.' He gave this description to the details of worldly life. It may be taken as an expression of the transiency of the experiences in men's history. Like Marcus Aurelius, he considered history as always the same. 'The thing that hath been, it is that which shall be; and that which is done is that which shall be done; and there is no new thing under the sun.' History is to be experienced in all its variety as it goes along. 'To everything there is a season, and a time for every purpose under heaven.' Punishment comes to the wicked. Suffering and death come to the virtuous also. The Preacher touched a note of profound pessimism in saying that the day of death is better than the day of one's birth. All are dust and all turn to dust again. Nevertheless, only a superficial reader could understand the book as completely pessimistic with regard to this life. The

Preacher did not advocate a world-negating asceticism. Though vain in the sense of transient, the goods of life may and should be enjoyed. They are rewards for virtue and gifts from God. 'Go thy way; eat thy bread with joy, and drink thy wine with a merry heart.' 'Live joyfully with the wife whom thou lovest.' 'Every man also to whom God hath given riches and wealth and hath given him power to eat thereof and to take his portion and to rejoice in his labour: this is the gift of God.' Man must seek communion with God who is enduring. Devotion to God can give an abiding satisfaction. 'Let us hear the conclusion of the whole matter: Fear God and keep His commandments; for this is the whole duty of man. For God shall bring every work into judgment, with every secret thing, whether it be good, or whether it be evil.' Finally 'the dust shall return to earth as it was; the spirit shall return to God who gave it'.

Even the early history of the people of Israel was one of wars and misfortunes. The prophets interpreted these conditions as consequences of disloyalty to God, the failure to conform with His law and to make His worship central in life. The contention that their sufferings were due to sin was applied to them as a people and only to a less extent to particular individuals. Suffering was necessary to bring them to the realization that they were 'the chosen people' of God, and had a universal mission. Deutero-Isaiah called their attention to that: 'I will also give thee for a light to the Gentiles, that thou mayest be my salvation unto the end of the earth.' It may be questioned whether the Jews in general have consciously striven for this mission as a dominant purpose of their history. Many have believed in the coming of a personal Messiah. For them a goal of history has been the establishment of a Messiantic kingdom in which, if deceased previously to it, they would take their places by bodily resurrection. The principles of the Jewish faith formulated by Maimonides (1135-1204 A.D.) and widely accepted among orthodox Jews since his time, include these two statements: 'The Messiah, though he tarry, will surely come.' 'There will be a resurrection of the dead at the time when it shall please the Creator.'

The Messianic belief involved some change of attitude with

regard to history: the future was given more attention. The chief significance of history appeared to be, not in its present experiences, but in the future coming of the Messianic kingdom. It is an interesting question as to when and under what influences the Jews began to concern themselves definitely with the idea of a future life. Their continued misfortunes and perhaps the non-arrival of the Messianic kingdom may have led some to the thought that that kingdom was to be in another world. However, even when the belief in immortality began to be more frequently expressed, there was still an insistence on a full appreciation of the goods of this life. The writer of the apocryphal book *Ecclesiasticus* suggested how, with wisdom and goodness, earthly history might be enjoyed. Though he dealt little with the idea of a future life, he wrote: 'The knowledge of the commandments of the Lord is the doctrine of life; and they that do things that please Him shall receive the fruit of the tree of immortality.' The *Wisdom of Solomon* said: 'For God created man to be immortal, and made him to be an image of His eternity.' Similarly, the Second *Book of Esdras* declared: 'The present life is not the end. . . . But the day of doom shall be the end of this time and the beginning of the immortality to come. . . .' In 1799 David Friedlander in an assembly of cultured Jews in Berlin pronounced that only three doctrines are essential in Judaism: that of God, that of the immortality of the soul, and that of the mission to reach out to perfection. A conference of Jews in Pittsburgh in 1885 adopted a similar position, but with a re-affirmation of the universal Jewish mission in history. 'We maintain that Judaism preserved and defended, midst continual struggles and trials and under enforced isolation, this God-idea as the central religious truth for the human race.' In place of the belief in the coming of a personal Messiah they avowed the 'Messianic hope for the establishment of the kingdom of truth, justice, and peace among men'. Rejecting the doctrine of bodily resurrection, they professed faith in the immortality of the soul. Many Jews have thought that the greatest calamity in their history was when they finally lost their independence as a nation and became so dispersed from their native land. Some modern Jews have maintained that the dispersion of the Jews was not merely permitted by God but intended by Him for the carrying out of their religious mission as 'the chosen people'. The distinctive continuance of the Jews through nearly two thousand years without political power is a significant fact of history. Their wide and deep religious influence is obvious. Christianity arose within Judaism, and to judge by the contents of the *Quran*, Islām may owe more to Judaism than to any other factor in Muhammed's environment. With their acceptance of this world as God's creation, Jews have attained eminence on all sides of culture.

One of the most scholarly of Jews in recent times, Claude Montefiore, in his *Outlines of Liberal Judaism* (1912), gave indications of a modern, yet basically Jewish view of history. Accepting the orthodox conception of God as a personal spirit, he maintained that He 'controls and has a purpose for the history of man'. Terrestrial history has intrinsic worth and it is also a preparation for a future life. 'We believe that the race of men has progressed and is progressing—if slowly, yet surely—from a poorer righteousness to a richer righteousness, and from lower, cruder, more erroneous ideas about God to higher, purer and truer ideas about Him.' For His purposes in history God gives particular peoples and individuals different capacities and tasks. It is thus that the Jews are 'a chosen people', 'not chosen in order to acquire prosperity or power or numbers; not chosen for the sake of art or science or philosophy, but chosen to learn and to help in diffusing true doctrine and experience about God and righteousness, and the relations of man to God and God to man'. Montefiore believed that 'the preservation of the Jewish race' has not been due to chance: 'it has not been effected without the will and the intention of God'. The fundamentals of morality and religion as expressed in Judaism are universal. But the Jews are a race as well as adherents to a religion, and he regretted that some of them are more concerned with the former than the latter. With this they have not adequately appreciated the universalism of their religion. He confessed the opinion that the dissemination of the fundamentals of Judaism has been through Christianity and Islām more than through the Jews. However, 'Christianity seems to Jews only a stage in the preparation of the world for a purified, developed, and universalized Judaism.'

III

Islām arose in Arabia in the seventh century A.D. in communities with local religious cults. Orthodox Muslims believe it to have originated in a revelation made by God directly to Muhammed. Considering the accounts of Adam, Noah, Abraham, Jacob, Joseph, Moses, Aaron, and David in the *Quran*, as well as references to some Christian doctrines, occidental scholars are inclined to think that Muhammed had absorbed much of the traditional Jewish and Christian faiths in the travels he made. The historian may well believe that the *Quran* owes much to Jewish and Christian influences. Orthodox Muslims regard it as entirely revealed by God, the perfect and final revelation for men. The Islamic view of history is not considered by Muslims to have been reached by reflection on the facts of actual history. It is the way men are to regard history as implied in the *Quran* which gives much attention to what at the time of its promulgation was taken to be history. To confirm the attitude towards history that the *Quran* inculcates it gives many examples from actual history to show that it has conformed with the principles of that revelation. 'Travel in the earth and see how was the end of the guilty.'

For Islām, Allah, God, is central. The Islamic conception of history is theistic. God is a person, an individual spirit. The dictum: 'There is no God, but Allah', was not merely a declaration of opposition to any form of polytheism but also to the placing of anything or anyone else as supreme in one's life. Though in the occident writers on Islām have emphasized the all-dominant power of Allah, each chapter or *sura* of the *Quran* is headed: 'In the name of Allah, the Beneficent, the Merciful'. Of the many attributes ascribed to Him, three are most prominent: His mercy, His power, His wisdom. He is self-existent, eternal, omni-present, bounteous, and full of majesty and glory. The main purpose of the *Quran* is to draw men to an awareness of their relations with God. One can never get away from God in history. But He has not come into history as an incarnate being. The *Quran* definitely rejects the doctrine that Jesus was God incarnate, and frequently condemns it. God created Jesus 'from the dust'. 'The Messiah, the son of Mary, is but an apostle.' God had guided men through prophets and sacred books: Moses and Jesus were prophets and the Hebrew and Christian scriptures revelations at their own level. Muhammed was the last and the chief of the prophets. Henceforth mankind is to get its guidance in history from the *Quran* and personal communion with God in prayer. Thus the chief turning point in history was in the revelation of the *Quran*.

God created the physical world with its uniformities and other characteristics making human history possible and significant. It was not produced 'in sport' but for 'a serious end'. The world of Nature is not fixed once for all: God may continuously create: 'He adds to His creation what He wills.' In creating day and night and their succession, he has made life for mankind temporal. Time as men experience it is real for them and for God. He created men as souls and gave them bodies for this life. The *Quran* suggests that He has special consideration for men. The Lord 'chose' Adam, and 'turned towards him and guided him'. He made man His representative on earth. In their hearts men may come into spiritual relation with Him. There has been much discussion as to whether the *Quran* does or does not teach 'freedom of will'. But it must not be forgotten that the *Quran* is not a systematic philosophical treatise. It contains the recognition both of God's dominance and of human freedom, but has no reflective consideration of how these are held together in thought. It asserts that God dominates everything: He breathed into the soul 'its wickedness and its piety'. Yet throughout the *Quran* there is great emphasis on the use of freedom. God is not unjust to sinners: 'they are unjust to themselves'. 'Every soul shall receive as it shall have wrought.'

That Islām gives due consideration to the individual is clear. It also insists on the social group as such. God judges nations. Frequent references are made to cities that have advanced or been destroyed according to their conformity or otherwise with the moral principles expressed in the *Quran*. To apply a phrase from the German: 'World history is world judgment.' Each people gets eventually what it merits, for God rules men with righteousness. Muslims have often been accused of making war in order to propagate their religion. The extent to which that *may* be true must be decided by professional historians. Though educated modern Muslims contend that Islām stands for freedom in religion, the *Quran* enjoins opposition to those whose faith is in conflict with Islām. Followers were exhorted to fight 'in the way of Allah', that is, for that which conforms with the teachings of the *Quran*. Evil is to be fought. The *Quran* acknowledges some evil as due to men themselves and some to evil spirits other than men. The chief of the latter is *Iblis*, who, created by God, with his freedom turned away from Him. *Iblis* declared that he would make evil attractive to men and lead them from the right path. This temptation of men is at least to some extent used by God for the development of their characters. The *Quran* says: 'And for trial, We test you with evil and with good.' Without such temptation there can be no autonomous moral achievement. God also seized some 'with distress and afflictions in order that they might humble themselves'.

The Islamic attitude to history is meliorist. If individuals and peoples increasingly conform with God's will, things will get better, and Muslims maintain that they have done and will in the future, for eventually Islām will triumph. God enjoins justice, and history has already shown that eventually the unjust are not successful. Islām is universalist. 'The East and the West is God's; therefore whichever way ye turn there is the face of God.' The judgment as to whether there is progress is not to be made with reference to the externals of civilization but as to the condition of men's souls, their character and their disposition towards God. As a discipline to this end, the *Quran* requires fasting by Muslims. It is a form of self-control, strengthens character, and turns men from too great a concern with worldly goods. As the achievement of the Islamic goal is not to be easy, the *Quran* constantly advocates and praises patience. God is with the patient. Islamic meliorism being rooted in a theistic faith, it is insisted that for it divine help is needed. Past sins may not be a barrier to future progress, for God will grant forgiveness to the penitent and aid them in their striving for the good. However, the final goal is not terrestrial: a future life if open to man. In contrast with some oriental beliefs, the soul is not in itself eternal but has had a beginning; and it has had no lives previous to its one birth on earth. After death a man retains his being as a personal individual. Any other conceptions of the soul's post terrestrial condition, as found in the writings of some Sufis, are heretical. Believers are sure of the hereafter: it is promised in the *Quran*, God's revelation. God created the individual, and He can preserve his soul after death. Men were created with bodies and placed in the physical world, and life on earth may be good and should be enjoyed. But those who are content 'with this life' eventually go to perdition. The life hereafter 'is better' and 'more lasting'.

There has been a large amount of writing of history among Muslims. They have been interested in the lives of their leaders, both religious and secular, their wars and the establishment of their political power. Of Muslim historians, the most important for our purpose was Ibn Khaldun (1332-1406 A.D.). By some he has been called the founder of the science of history because he contended that history is a specific body of knowledge concerned with the whole range of the social phenomena of actual history with the discovery of the varied influences at work in it, the continuities of causes and effects, the physical and psychical constituents. For him history was not simply a record of events but a description of internal and external social relationships. In the Muslim world in the fourteenth century there was a decline of philosophy from the high level attained in the preceding centuries. There was a widespread distrust in rational reflection. Ibn Khaldun shared that distrust and looked for no help from traditional philosophy. He turned to what he considered the empirical facts of history. It has sometimes been supposed that he was Naturalistic, and that his references to the *Quran* were insincere, made to guard himself from persecution by ardent believers. That is probably incorrect. What he wrote was meant as an account of the historical, as actual, as it proceeds 'under God'.

Ibn Khaldun sometimes seemed to suggest that the course of history depends more on environmental conditions than on the free activities of individuals. But he did not present a rigid determinism. He acknowledged the rôles played by individuals and at times maintained that it was due to the nature of human responses that there has been a repeated pattern in the courses of empires. An empire has been established through the vigour of one generation; the next generation consolidated it and enjoyed its values with self-indulgence; the third generation sank to weakness and was overthrown. Ibn Khaldun traced the differences in the histories of different peoples according to their physical environments, climate, the character of the land, etc. It was in relation with their particular environments that they advanced little or much from a simple condition to civilization and developed their own types of racial or regional character. For their preservation and prosperity each people had to cultivate what they had there and then. He had great appreciation of the continuities within particular periods of time. Such prediction as he thought possible for the future was for historical conditions sufficiently similar to those of the past and the present as he knew them. Ibn Khaldun emphasized the social aspects of history and treated of individuals, their fortunes and misfortunes, as within the collective and common life of society. He could not leave unrecognized the facts of religion in society and he gave considerable attention to prophetism, the influences of persons of vivid religious experience. Yet his treatment of history was not explicitly from the standpoint of Islamic theism. He did not suggest that there is a divine purpose in history or concern himself with any idea of an ultimate goal.

The nature and meaning of history as conceived by a modern Muslim may be inferred from a work by Mohammed Iqbal, a native of India who studied in the occident and took into consideration its philosophies and ways of life: *The Reconstruction of Religious Thought in Islam* (1930). Though he did not call himself an Idealist, which with its various Western connotations might be misleading, he rejected the idea of matter as a distinctive substance and held that reality is completely spiritual. There are three sources of knowledge, and they all lead to God. There is the knowledge of the physical world through the senses; the knowledge of the empirical facts of history; and a knowledge of God by the inner being of man in what may be called 'religious' or 'mystical' experience. The last of these is natural to man and is the most significant for him. The chief aim and value in history is the religious communion with God. The purpose of the *Quran* was 'to awaken in man the higher consciousness of his manifold relations with God and the universe'. However, there is no radical opposition between the religious and the secular. 'In Islām the spiritual and the temporal are not two distinct domains, and the nature of an act however secular in its import, is determined by the attitude of mind with which the agent does it'. 'The ultimate Reality, according to the *Quran*, is spiritual and its life consists in its temporal activity. The spirit finds its opportunities in the natural, the material, the secular.... All this immensity of matter constitutes a scope for the self-realization of spirit. All is holy ground. As the Prophet so beautifully puts it, "The whole of this earth is a mosque".'

Despite the influence of Greek and Roman Classical thought on some Islamic philosophers, Iqbal insisted that Islamic thought is essentially 'anti-Classical'. Its mode of approach is empirical and is opposed to intellectual abstraction. Even more important is the rejection of the Greek philosophical attempts to impugn the reality of time. History involves time. Islām accepts time as real. Iqbal stressed the implication of the statement in the *Quran*: 'And it is He Who hath ordained the night and the day to succeed one another for those who desire to think on God or desire to be thankful.' He discussed what has been written in the West concerning time, and described different views maintained in the history of Islamic thought, but he finally agreed with the conclusion of a Muslin theologian who had examined all of the theories that had been expounded. Fakhr-ud-Din Razi wrote: 'Until now I have not been able to discover anything really true with regard to the nature of time.' 'The practical Arab mind could not regard time as something unreal like the Greeks did.'

History is an affair of individuals. 'To live is to possess a definite outline, a concrete individuality.' With his self-conscious being, man has to take the risk of conflicts with others. Iqbal insisted on individual spontaneity. The term 'creation' has meaning for us only because we ourselves have the capacity to initiate action. 'If history is regarded merely as a gradually revealed photo of a predetermined order of events, then there is no room in it for novelty and initiation.' The Islamic conception of history is of it as definitely dynamic. God is continuously creative. Any doctrine of His foreknowledge that limits His freedom is to be rejected. Nevertheless, in Muslim history there has been much acceptance of what Iqbal called a 'degrading Fatalism'. The adoption and promulgation of this doctrine of *qismat* was due, he wrote, 'partly to philosophical thought, partly to political expediency, and partly to the gradually diminishing force of the life-impulse which Islām originally imparted to its followers'.

Throughout his book Iqbal dealt very little with the evils of history and never gave any systematic consideration of the problem of evil. In discussing the Quranic account of the Fall of man, he maintained that it 'does not mean any moral depravity'. The story of Adam's disobedience was an account of the first act of free choice, and for that reason, according to the *Quran*, the transgression was forgiven. Further, the *Quran* does not treat the Fall as though one particular event of history; rather it represents a factor in the lives of men. The placing of Adam in 'a painful physical environment' was not a punishment: the earth is not 'a torture hall where an elementary wicked humanity is imprisoned for an original act of sin'. The earth is a divine creation manifesting the glory of God. It is adapted to the development of men's intellectual capacities and moral character. The Islamic idea of hell is of 'a corrective experience' which may make some sensitive to God. The implication is that some of the suffering in human history is caused by God for the moral and religious welfare of men.

Considering some modern political developments in Muslim countries and the discarding of the idea that there must be one Khalif for the Muslim world, Iqbal maintained that in contrast with the Arabic Imperialism of the early centuries there is the birth of an international ideal. Islām is universalistic. Its principle is loyalty to God and not, except in a secondary manner, to any human government. Men of every race and clime and of every social status may stand together, shoulder to shoulder, to participate in prayer in the mosque. Iqbal did not think of history in general as an advance towards a fixed predetermined goal. Any such idea he considered to be in opposition to the continuity of the free creativity of God and, indeed, of man also. 'To my mind nothing is more alien to the Quranic outlook than the idea that the universe is the temporal working out of a preconceived plan.' What is important is the belief that the Divine wisdom is continuous in His creative processes and that there may be a spiritual conformity of man with Divine goodness. The life history of the individual has some unity and its values are not merely relative to a final goal to be attained in a future life. The values are in what God has created and creates; in the experiences of the individual's own spiritual self-hood; and in mystical communion with God.

Metaphysics cannot prove that men will have spiritual continuance after death. Kant's ethical arguments for it lead only to a 'postulate' and are inconclusive. Against Nietzsche's theory of eternal recurrence, Iqbal contended: 'We can aspire only for what is absolutely new, and the absolutely new is unthinkable on Nietzsche's view which is nothing more than a Fatalism worse than the one summed up in the word *qismat*. Such a doctrine, far from keying up the human organism for the fight of life, tends to destroy its active tendencies and relaxes the tension of the ego.' Maintaining that the *Quran* teaches that every finite ego is 'irreplaceably' unique, he accepted belief in human immortality. 'Whatever be the final fate of man it does not mean the loss of individuality.' 'It is highly improbable that a being whose evolution has taken millions of years should be thrown away as a thing of no use.' The significance of history is in this world and the next. The *Quran* gives men guidance for it, a knowledge of all the fundamentals for the attainment of human good in its entirety. 'In view of the basic idea of Islām, there can be no further revelation binding on men.'

CHAPTER V

THEISTIC CONCEPTIONS OF HISTORY
II. CHRISTIAN

I

CHRISTIANITY is definitely concerned with history in two ways. It regards certain events, real or merely alleged, as fundamental, and it has implications with reference to the significance of history in general. The traditionally orthodox relate the latter specifically with the former. It is with consideration of the particular events that Christianity is maintained to be distinctive. Christianity presents a sort of drama of history. The first act was the Fall of Adam, with the subsequent continuance of sin, an alienation from God, among his descendants. The second act was the coming of God into history, incarnated as man in Jesus Christ. This act included (*a*) his foundation of the Christian church by gathering disciples through his personal influence, his way of life, and his teaching; (*b*) his redemption of mankind by his death on the Cross; (*c*) his resurrection and his ascension to heaven giving men an assurance of their immortality. The third act is the evangelization of the world with the extension of the Christian church. This act is still in progress. The fourth and final act is to be the second coming of Christ with a 'day of judgment' and the inauguration of the perfected Kingdom of God with complete blessedness. For the life of Christians and the expansion of Christianity in history, God is present as the Holy Spirit. With this idea God was conceived as a trinity in unity, Father, Son, and Holy Spirit. The Father was thought of pre-eminently as the creator of the world and men, making history possible; the Son as redeemer to bring history to its divinely intended goal; the Holy Spirit as the sanctifier of men in the process of history. Fundamental to this orthodox Christian view is the conviction that after their contamination by sin through Adam it was necessary for their salvation that God should come as man into history. This doctrine of an incarnation of God, once for all, constitutes the basic difference between Christianity and the theistic conceptions of history considered in our previous chapter.

By the methods of what may be called 'scientific' history it is not possible to prove that the events taken as basic for Christianity actually occurred. They cannot be established nor can they be refuted on philosophical grounds. They can be, and are, accepted by faith. Though modern theological scholars often adopt critical methods of study of the New Testament and of the history of Christian doctrine, almost without exception they continue to adhere to the articles of the faith as expressed in the creeds, Thus, notwithstanding the fact that there are some individuals at the present time, as in the past, who profess a form of Christianity with the rejection of some of the articles of faith of the creeds, it is the traditional orthodox view that must here be treated as giving the specific Christian interpretation of history.

That historical Christianity has been Christo-centric has not made it any the less theistic, because Jesus Christ was himself believed to be God. As expressions of divine revelation the attitudes and teachings of Jesus as to history are thus of the utmost significance. His divinity has been accepted with reference to his birth of the Virgin Mary, his miracles, and his resurrection after death. For a time considered to be the Messiah in the manner of some contemporary thought, he was confessed by Peter and eventually regarded by his followers as 'the Son of God'. He taught that the most important in life is the inner spiritual attitude, central for which is the love of God, conforming with His will, leading to the true love of self and of one's neighbours as one's self. He accepted the sufferings of the Cross as due to the will of the Father, and by that suffering 'took away the sins of the world'. He promised a future life of bliss 'in Paradise'. Though he lived a life of much self-denial—('the Son of Man hath nowhere to lay his head')—and called others for sacrifices to follow him, he recognized for some the joys of marriage and did not refrain from some participation in feasting. Thus, though his attitude was in a measure ascetic, it was not a thoroughgoing escape from the world, or a rejection of temporary history for the eternal. The ideal he preached was of individual character and of the harmony of men in the Kingdom of God. For both of these aspects of history repentance is necessary, turning from selfishness and the neglect of God to service for others and communion with God. Assured of divine forgiveness for themselves, men are to forgive their fellows. In his parables and otherwise, Jesus expounded how men should act in history: praying to God; making full use of their God-given talents; being 'good Samaritans' to those in need and suffering; welcoming back the prodigal; casting out the beam from one's own eye; doing good for righteousness sake and not for the praise of men; treating all men as brothers and not with invidious distinctions such as that between Jew and Gentile. In his youthful discussions with the rabbis, Jesus has been considered as concerned with knowledge as involved in 'his Father's business', and in his reference to the lilies of the field as having an appreciation of beauty.

It has been widely accepted among New Testament scholars that Jesus may, at least for a time, have shared the belief of many of his contemporaries that there would be an early termination of history as they knew it and the inauguration of an earthly messianic kingdom. His ideas may have changed in the course of his life. He certainly rejected any political aspects of the popular Messianism, and discouraged the questionings of his disciples as to when the kingdom would come. 'Of that day and hour knoweth no man, no, not the angels of heaven, but my Father only.' Some of his teachings may have been affected by this eschatological belief. Moral injunctions ascribed to him that now appear impractical may have been intended as an 'Interim ethic' in preparation for that imminent event. Even after his crucifixion his disciples believed in his early return to set up the kingdom. In the course of Christian history at different times small groups have declared that Jesus was about to return immediately. But though some belief in a second coming of 'the Christ' has continued among Christians, the goal of history has come to be predominantly considered to be in a future life. Associated with this have been the ideas of a general resurrection and 'a day of judgment' at the end of history.

All types of Christianity have included the belief that God is intimately concerned with history; and all have acknowledged spiritual continuance beyond earthly life. The early Christian conviction of a bodily resurrection was related with the conception of a millennium on earth, to participate in which the righteous persons of the past would rise again with their bodies. But the belief has been held by some as suggesting some manner by which individuals may recognize one another in a future life. To this the Pauline term 'spiritual body' has been applied. Three theories of the ultimate destiny of individuals have been maintained by Christians: (*a*) Universalism, that all without exception will finally attain perfection; (*b*) Conditionalism, that only those worthy of continuance will survive, all others being annihilated; and (*c*) Eternal Bliss or Perdition, that good souls achieve the bliss of heaven and the wicked suffer the perpetual evil of the hell of separation from God. Terrestrial history does not contain complete meaning in itself.

To the early Christian disciples Christ may have appeared as the culmination of the Hebrew faith, as the expected Messiah. Paul, in his missions to the Gentiles, pointed to Christ as the divine being Greek philosophers had sought. Some later thinkers represented all the past history of which they knew, of the Jews, the Greeks, and the Romans, as preparatory to the coming of Christ and the founding of the Christian church. All previous history had led up to Christ and all future history was to be considered as bringing the realization of that for which he had come. The Incarnation, Crucifixion, Resurrection and Ascension constituted the central facts of history with reference to which its significance is to be seen. That significance is the realization for mankind of all that is involved in right relations with God. The Christian conception of history is centrally religious, communion with God; and secondly ethical in personal integrity and the welfare of mankind as a social unity. It includes other particular values. Some of these are suggested by stories of Jesus's miracles (whether the miracles actually happened or not): provision of food for the hungry and the cure of disease. The range of particular values of history acknowledged by Christians has varied greatly with individuals. For the enlightened in the modern era it may be said to include all that comes within the concepts of the true, the good and the beautiful.

II

Considering St Augustine (354-450 A.D.) to have been the most important thinker in the whole history of Christianity, and his treatment of the nature of history as of special value, particular attention is given to him here. Augustine's attitudes varied at different times and there were diverse emphases in his thought. There are inconsistencies in his writings due to tensions which he did not completely harmonize. Of his many writings, consideration of his *The City of God* and his *Confessions* is sufficient for our purpose. Though a philosopher of eminence, Augustine took his stand not so much on philosophy as on his acceptance of the Christian faith. The philosophers, he declared, have laboured to find a way for 'laying hold of blessedness', but philosophy is 'uncertain' as contrasted with the 'certainty of the Christian faith'. With the Christian conception of God as basic, he opposed pantheism and any confusion of God with His creation. If God were conceived as the whole of reality, 'who cannot see what impious and irreligious consequences follow, such that whatever one may trample he must trample a part of God, and in slaying any living creature, a part of God must be slaughtered'. Further, if 'offenders are parts of Himself . . . why is He angry at those who do not worship Him?' He rejected the idea that God is 'the soul of the world'. The true God is not a soul, but 'the maker and author of the soul'. God is spirit. Spirit is something more fundamental than what man in his self-consciousness calls his soul. God is not bound by any necessity: as He created nature, He can also change it. He has prescience. 'To confess that God exists and at the same time to deny that He has foreknowledge of the future things is the most manifest folly.' Thus the future of history is under His control.

According to Augustine, history is concerned both with the temporal and the eternal. God is eternal and He creates time. The eternal is not to be understood or described from the standpoint of the temporal. God is pan-temporal as well as eternal. Though time cannot be comprehended with the concepts of the intellect, it is definitely experienced. 'For what is time?' he wrote, . . . 'Who can even in thought understand it so as to utter a word about it? By what in discourse do we mention more familiarly and knowingly than time? . . . What then is time? If no one asks me, I know; if I wish to explain it to one that asketh, I know not.' The relation of the temporal and the eternal, considered by Augustine to be real and significant for religion, is not intelligible to man. Within human history God is providence. The affairs of earthly history are 'ruled and governed by the one God as He pleases'. He 'can never be believed to have left the kingdoms of men . . . outside the laws of providence'. Human kingdoms are established by providence; they are not fortuitous or of necessity. There is to be a 'final judgment', and though we may not always be able to discern it, His judgment is present in the web of human affairs. Even when one views the apparent misfortunes of the good and the prosperity of the wicked, God cannot rightly be called unjust.

Much has been written as to Augustine's views of the nature of man, and especially as to the freedom of the human will and to the predestination of man by God. In this regard there were different tensions in his thought that he did not reconcile. His conviction of the all-dominance of God took precedence over the idea of the freedom and responsibility of man. But his less prominent recognition of human choice should be adequately appreciated. He did not arrive at a satisfactory expression of the relation of the two. The freedom and the moral responsibility of the individual are important for his conception of history. The basic question for him in this connection concerned the extent of man's capacity by his own will to attain spiritual values, the peace and bliss which is the supreme meaning in the history of the individual. The human will that may control the body is not capable of entire control of the mind. To overcome this deficiency there is need of the grace of God.

The spiritual life involves a two-fold relationship between man and God, and the part God has in it is greater than man's.

In the *Confessions*, Augustine indicated how the problem of evil troubled him before his conversion. He came to hold, philosophically, that all evil is privative, the absence of the good. 'No nature at all is evil, and this is the name for nothing but the want of the good.' 'Evil is of two sorts, one which a man doth, the other which he suffers. What he doth is sin; what he suffereth, punishment. The providence of God governing and controlling all things, man doth ill which he wills, so as to suffer ill which he wills not.' Sin in man is his lack of devotion to God and his failure to attend to the goods of earthly existence, to personal character and to social love which God intends for him. Augustine could even write that though sin is a 'sad blemish' in the individual, 'the universe is beautified even by sinners'. When he described hell as eternal he must have meant a condition of endless privation. God causes the temptations by the devil to benefit man. When God 'exposes us to adversities, it is either to prove our perfections or correct our imperfections, and in return for our patient endurance of the sufferings of time, He reserves for us an everlasting reward'. 'Everywhere the greater joy is ushered in by the greater pain.' Redemption from evil was one of Augustine's chief concerns. The significance of Christianity is in large measure in such redemption. The death that is the end of a good life is not to be judged evil.

Augustine rejected the theory of recurrent cycles in history, in part because he considered the Incarnation to be 'once for all'. On an analogy with the Biblical account of God's creation of the world in six days and resting on the Sabbath, he divided history into seven periods: 1, from Adam to the deluge; 2, from the deluge to Abraham; 3, from Abraham to David; 4, from David to the captivity; 5, from the captivity to the birth of Christ; 6, the present age; 7, in which God 'shall rest as on the seventh day and shall give us rest in Himself'. Augustine contrasted two ways of life in history. They express the attitudes of individuals and different social groups. 'There are no more than two kinds of human society which we may justly call two cities, according to the language of the Scriptures. The one consists of those who wish to live after the flesh; the other are those who wish to live after the spirit. . . .' But in that the phrase living 'after the flesh' may suggest to some that the 'flesh' is evil—which Augustine did not believe—it is better to take his other description of the earthly city as constituted of those who 'live merely according to man' and the heavenly city of those 'living according to God'. The ideas concerning the two cities served to indicate the basic contrast between men in history. The earthly city rests on love of self. In it 'the princes and the nations it subdues are ruled by love of ruling', pride of power. The earthly city 'has its good in this world and rejoices in it with such joy as such things can afford. But, as this is not a good which can discharge its devotees of all distresses, this city is often divided against itself by litigations, wars, quarrels, and such victories as are either life-destroying or short-lived'. The earthly city is not everlasting. The heavenly city rests on the love of God. In it 'the princes and subjects serve one another in love, the latter obeying while the former take thought for all'. According to it 'life eternal is the supreme good, death eternal the supreme evil'. While it sojourns on earth, the heavenly city 'calls citizens out of all nations and gathers together a society of pilgrims of all languages, not scrupling about diversities in the manners, laws and institutions whereby earthly peace is secured and maintained. . . .' This last passage suggests not an identity of the heavenly city on earth with the actual Christian church, but the invisible unity by which it is to be developed. The bliss of the heavenly city is not to be fully experienced in this life; the goal of history is beyond the terrestrial. 'The peace which we enjoy in this life, whether common to all or peculiar to ourselves, is rather the solace of our misery than the positive enjoyment of felicity.'

It would be a serious error to consider Augustine's distinction between the two cities as that of an evil earthly city in opposition to a good heavenly city. Though some aspects of asceticism towards the earthly may be acknowledged in both Augustine's life and in his teachings, his intention was not radically ascetic. His opposition to the dualism of Manichaeism was contrary to any merely other-worldly view of history.

His *Confessions* contain many expressions of his appreciation of worldly goods. But they are merely temporary, not to be accorded the supreme place in life or pursued without concern for spiritual values, which are eternal. If one's life is dominated by the spiritual one may also pursue and enjoy what God gives to men in His creation of the physical world. Insisting that beauty is 'indeed God's handiwork', he was aware that it is 'only a temporal . . . lower kind of good not fitly loved in preference to God, the eternal, spiritual and unchangeable good'. Earthly goods have their own place in human life, being part of God's purpose for man. He expressed this in a noteworthy passage of the *Confessions*. 'For whithersoever the soul of man turns itself, unless towards Thee, it is riveted upon sorrows, yea, though it is riveted on things beautiful. And yet they, out of Thee, and out of the soul, were not, unless they were from Thee. They rise and set, and by rising they begin as it were to be; they grow that they may be perfected; and perfected they wax old and wither; and all grow not old, but all wither. So then, when they rise and tend to be, the more quickly they grow that they may be, so much the more they haste not to be. This is the law of them. This much hast Thou allotted them, because they are portions of things which exist not all at once, but by passing and succeeding they together complete that universe of which they are portions. And even thus is our speech completed by signs giving forth a sound; but this again is not perfected unless one word pass away when it hath sounded its part, that another may succeed. Out of all these things let my soul praise Thee, O God, creator of all; yet let not my soul be riveted unto these things with the glue of love, through the senses of the body. For they go whither they were to go, that they might not be; and they rend her with pestilent longings, because she longs to be, yet loves to repose in what she loves. But in these things is no place of repose; they abide not, they flee; and who can follow them with the senses of the flesh? Yea, who can grasp them when they are hard by? For the sense of the flesh is slow, because it is the sense of the flesh; and thereby it is bounded. It sufficeth for that it was made for; but it sufficeth not to stay things running their course from their appointed starting place to the end appointed. For in

Thy word, by which they are created, they hear their decree, "hence and hitherto".' God made us 'for Himself' and 'our heart is restless until it repose in' Him. The love of God, the supreme value in human life, gives a satisfaction which nothing else can give. It should be the fundamental meaning in man's history on earth and beyond. The significance of the term 'eternal' for Augustine was not so much philosophical as religious. God is eternal essentially in that He is ever present for men to 'rest' in Him.

III

In the Middle Ages the belief in revelation as distinct from reason was emphasized. God revealed Himself in history in Jesus Christ. Through his suffering and death, he brought atonement to men and his resurrection assured them of a future life. History was conceived primarily as a time of trial and of preparation for a life after death. Specific expression was given to this idea in the many ascetic orders. Monks and nuns desired to escape as much as possible from participation in the ordinary affairs of history. 'The world,' said Peter Damiani (c. 1007-1072 A.D.), 'is so filthy with vices that any holy mind is befouled even by thinking of it.' *The Divine Comedy* of Dante (1265-1321 A.D.) gave expression to a Christian view of history as held in the Middle Ages. Human history is not limited to earth but goes beyond to future conditions of hell, purgatory and paradise. Even though men may be associated in groups for good or evil, spiritual attitudes and acts of conduct are of individuals, depending basically on their own wills. The principle of justice runs through the whole of the *Divine Comedy*. Described by Dante as being in hell are those adopting an unchanging opposition to God. Those in purgatory, though still sinful, have their wills turned to God, striving to overcome sin. But Dante's interpretation of human history was not entirely an other-worldly one. He had the idea of an earthly paradise which may eventually be achieved.

With the influence of Renaissance Humanism, the Catholic Church in Italy began to pay more attention to the goods of earthly life. The traditional Christian view of history was not profoundly affected. In 1681 A.D. that view came to a classical expression in Bossuet's *Discourse on Universal History*. Bossuet insisted that the affairs of history go on in a causal sequence, the events of one century depending on those that preceded. 'Let us talk no more of chance or fortune; or let us talk of them only as a description by which we cover up our ignorance. That which in our uncertain view is chance is a definite design in a higher view, that is, in the eternal view which embraces all causes and all effects in one order.' It is in accordance with this divine plan that empires rise and fall. In history men are dominated by a power above themselves, and under its influence, doing more or less than they themselves intend, promote the divine design. The central purpose for mankind is in religion, and it was from its standpoint that Bossuet mainly surveyed history. He rejected the claims of religions other than those of the Hebrews and Christians. 'The God whom the Hebrews and Christians have always served has nothing in common with the divinities, so imperfect and vicious, which the rest of the world has worshipped.' Eventually God appeared incarnate in Jesus Christ, showing men a 'new way' and giving the Christian direction to history. Jesus made clear the truth of the future life and revealed that the Cross is the 'way to heaven'. Jesus carried the Cross all his life and died on it. Thereafter, according to Bossuet, the Church becomes the central factor in history. Neither external opposition nor internal dissension has been able to destroy it. He maintained that the truth of this view was evidenced by the 'facts' that the Church has always been victorious and that the Jews who rejected Jesus have continually suffered. 'The Church has an ever-enduring body from which one cannot separate one's self without being lost. Those who are united with it and do works worthy of their faith are assured of eternal life.' J. B. Bury commented that Bossuet's theory is based on 'the hardly disguised axiom that mankind was created for the sake of the Church'. But with his upbringing and environment Bossuet could not conceive of true religion apart from the Church. Mankind was created not for the sake of the Church but for eternal life, for the attainment of which Bossuet believed that the Church had been established.

The Protestant Reformation of the sixteenth and seventeenth centuries brought no fundamental change with reference to the Christian attitude to history. The Reformers continued to hold the view that life on earth is a preparation for the life to come. Protestantism did not arise from influences of the Renaissance conception of values. That in later centuries most Protestants have come to acknowledge intrinsic meanings of culture was an accommodation to Humanistic developments and the advance of freedom of thought. At most the Reformers opposed the ascetic orders of monks and nuns and allowed priests more part in normal life by rejecting the necessity of their celibacy. Though Protestants have promoted attention to mundane affairs, they have not sought the meaning of history in the temporal flow of events. God is in history primarily for the spiritual welfare of individuals. Calvin encouraged diligence in one's calling, yet demanded simplicity of life and abstention from luxuries. Worldly success depends on God. Industry will not advance anyone 'unless God extends His hand and bounty'.

Both Calvin and Luther in one sense or another denied human free will. Luther admitted some freedom in secular affairs. Calvin did not mean to deny all freedom. In a passage written against some Free-thinkers, he declared: 'They attribute to man no free will, any more than if he were a stone; and they remove all distinction between good and evil so that nothing can be done wrongly in their opinion, since God is the author of it.' Calvin insisted on human responsibility. Ultimately what Calvin and Luther intended was to bring into the forefront that man's spiritual salvation depends far more on God than on man himself. That God in history does more for the well-being of man both physically and spiritually than men do is a fundamental of Christian theism.

It has often been maintained that there is a difference in the Protestant from the Roman Catholic attitude to history in that the former has acknowledged and insisted on the status of the individual person in a manner that the latter has never done. The concern of the Catholic Church with the individual is basically religious and moral. That Church requires the individual to make his personal auricular confession before the priest who may give his spiritual guidance. That is a definite recognition of the individual. The Reformation was in part a protest against some practices and teachings of the Catholic Church, but also against the dominance of the Catholic hierarchy. It championed freedom from some forms of authority. But the chief Protestant Churches had kinds of authority, as that of the Bible and various confessions of faith. However, the emphasis on individual freedom led to the development of science, philosophy and political government. The idea of a unified Church as central in history was challenged. The relations of churches and states became varied. The principle of individual freedom has become fundamental in modern history, leading to the developments of modern civilization.

No theologian has described Christianity as concerned with the history of the individual as impressively as John Bunyan (1625-1688 A.D.) did in two of his noteworthy writings: *The Pilgrim's Progress from this World to that which is to come* (pt. I, 1678; II, 1685 A.D.), and *The Holy War* (1682 A.D.). Bunyan did not refer to actual events as a historian, yet he regarded these works as expressing truths of history. This is seen in the note at the end of *The Holy War*: 'We have thus been enabled to trace the "History of the Soul" throughout its various stages, its alternations, its vicissitudes, its sunshine and its tears, its night of darkness and its noontide glory. All sorts of spiritual experiences are included here—the willing service of Satan's bond-slaves, the rebellion of the disobedient sons, the sorrows of the soul's captivity, the alarms of a troubled conscience, the betaking of the soul to God in penitence and prayer, the return of the prodigal to his Father, the submission of the rebel to his King, the pleasantness of religious ways, the backsliding of transgressors, the hardening of the heart, the carnal security of the soul, the awakening of the soul to a consciousness of its danger, its cry to the Mighty for help, the long and weary discipline, the seeking back to God, the finding of the lost and loved One, the renewal of the holy allegiance and sonship, and the loving and affectionate counsel of the great Immanuel.' Though *The Holy War* may have some social implications, 'the city of Mansoul' is meant rather to be the soul of the individual with its multiple feelings, thoughts and volitions, its inner conflicts and its strivings for peace. *The*

Pilgrim's Progress (pt. I) represented Christians in general as individuals, with Christian as the central figure; and part II, his wife and children. *The Life and Death of Mr Badman* (1680 A.D.) described the attitudes and conduct of the worldly person in history in contrast with those of Christians portrayed in the other two books. Bunyan's belief was the traditional orthodox one that men are redeemed from the evils of history and peace attained by them through the death of Jesus as the incarnate Son of God.

IV

In the first half of the nineteenth century there were many attempts to present a conception of Christianity in terms of Classical German Idealism. They were forms of philosophical pantheism rather than expositions of Christianity as a religion. Their emphasis was on God as the immanent eternal Christ. Friederich von Schlegel's (1772-1829 A.D.) *The Philosophy of History* (1828 A.D.) was a statement and defence of the traditional view in opposition to these. It had a wide circulation and some of its main ideas were accepted by orthodox Christians throughout the nineteenth century and they still are. Acknowledging that a philosophy of history must arise from reflection on actual history, von Schlegel insisted that there are fundamentals of Christian faith dependent on something other than the professional historian can obtain from his study of history. The course of history has conformed, and conforms, with the implications of these fundamentals. 'The Philosophy of History, as it is the spirit or idea of history, must be deduced from real historical events . . . the one connected whole of history.' It is an attempt to gain 'a clear insight into the general plan of the whole'. Von Schlegel distinguished two main opposing views of history. According to one, 'man is merely an animal, ennobled and gradually disciplined into reason and finally exalted into genius'. For it 'the history of human civilization is but the history of a gradual, progressive, endless improvement'. According to the other, man's 'true nature and destiny consist in his likeness to God'. For it 'man's history must be the restoration of the likeness to God or of the progress towards that restoration'. The former view is held with the conviction of the 'perfectibility' of man, which von Schlegel admitted had something in it 'very accordant with reason'. However, 'corruptibility of man is quite as great as his perfectibility'. Actual history reveals a course of events contrary to the first view.

Von Schlegel maintained that 'the first historical fact' was that man fell under 'the dominion of nature'. 'The blind power of nature' acts within him. Thus discord originated in him and has been transmitted to all ages and generations. It recurs in each individual. It is universal and 'may be regarded as a psychological ... phenomenon'. The consequences of this fall are found within history. There is no limit to man's possible degradation. Progress or retrogression depend in part on man, as spirit, having freedom of will. 'It is precisely the conflict between the good or divine principle on the one hand, and the evil or adverse principle on the other, which forms the purport of human life and human history from the beginning to the end of time.' The great task of mankind in general and of each individual is 'to restore harmony between the natural and the divine will'. The progress and the retrogressions in that constitute an essential part of history. Von Schlegel maintained that when God first created man, He gave him a revelation of Himself and of the way of life He meant for men. Despite the degeneracy of peoples, in their sacred traditions there are 'the clearest indications and scattered traces' of the primitive revelation, though often mixed with errors. Von Schlegel tried to give evidence of this in his detailed surveys of the histories of different peoples. Those histories, he remarked, had different periods. 'The first ... of artless childhood; the next ... of youth; later the vigour and activity of manhood; and at last the symptoms of approaching age, a state of general decay.' But the different peoples have their special parts in history. 'The whole historical existence and destiny of the Hebrews, for example, is confined within one of those great epochs of providential dispensation—it marks but one stage in the wonderful march of humanity towards its divine goal.' However, 'the mighty course of divine justice' is present throughout all ages of the world. With this idea von Schlegel considered the Dispersion of the Jews and their later sufferings as just retribution for their rejection of Jesus Christ.

In the course of history, dominated by divine providence, the Jewish covenant and the revelation to the Hebrews, Greek language and thought, and the Roman empire were bases, 'foundation stones' for the rise of Christianity. As to the actual origin of Christianity, he wrote: 'When we view the whole transaction with the eye of faith—when we consider all that has since grown up in the world out of beginnings apparently so small—... we are inclined to believe that the mystery and miracles of our Saviour's life and death, nay, the whole system of his doctrine which is intimately connected with those mysteries and miracles ... should be abandoned exclusively to religion.' They 'transcend' the ordinary sphere of history. Though they have significance for philosophy of history, they are not to be explained by it. Any description of Jesus Christ as a mere man is 'unhistorical', or rather 'anti-historical'. With that statement, von Schlegel confessed his conception of history as conforming with the traditional Christian faith. 'If we once remove this divine key-stone in the arch of universal history, the whole fabric of the world's history falls to ruin.' Without faith in the Christian dogmas 'the whole history of the world would be nought else than insoluble enigma—an inextricable labyrinth—a huge pile of the blocks and fragments of an unfinished edifice—and the great tragedy of humanity would remain devoid of all proper truth'. Similarly, 'the mystery of grace in the divine redemption of mankind' must be 'tacitly presupposed' in the Christian philosophy of history: 'it transcends the sphere of profane history'. The successive stages of human progress are marked by 'three historical data': the existence of a primitive revelation; the establishment of Christianity; and the pre-eminence of modern Europe in civilization. The true purport of modern history is the progress and further development of what is involved in Christianity. At the end of his exposition von Schlegel brought into relief a contrast between the temporal and the eternal. 'The spirit of time' is 'opposed to divine influence and to the Christian religion.' This is the spirit 'apparent in those who consider and estimate time and all things temporal, not by the law and feeling of eternity, but for temporal interests or from temporal motives change or undervalue and forget the thoughts and faith of eternity'.

The Idealism which dominated the thought of Germans, including the theologians, during the early decades of the nineteenth century was largely abandoned by the middle of the century. Metaphysics were abjured. Chiefly under the influence of Albrecht Ritschl (1822-1889 A.D.) theologians turned their attention more to the historical Jesus. Ritschl maintained that Jesus was to be taken as divine on the basis of value-judgments. With the serious social problems of that period, the Social Gospel movement arose, presenting Jesus as essentially concerned with social well-being. The Cambridge historian, J. R. Seeley (1834-1895 A.D.), considering the Christian documents as a historian, in his *Ecce Homo* (1866 A.D.) described a merely human Jesus whose aim was to arouse 'an enthusiasm for humanity'. He maintained that such a social motive was the essence of religion and not concern with a metaphysical deity or a future life. Matthew Arnold (1822-1888 A.D.) in his *Literature and Dogma* (1873 A.D.) insisted that the language of the Bible is poetic and symbolic. Theologians have caused confusion by taking it as scientific and historical truth. Thus, with reference to Messianic ideas he wrote: 'Jesus came calling himself the Messiah, the Son of God, and the question is: "What is the true meaning of these assertions of his, and of all his teaching?" . . . Is the language scientific or is it, as we say, literary?—the language of poetry and emotion.' Arnold had no doubt of the correct answer. 'Orthodox divinity' was an immense literary misapprehension.

Yet, in the same period, the eminent French historian, F. P. G. Guizot (1787-1874 A.D.), defended the traditional view.[1] Having lived for half a century following the French Revolution, the idea of liberty was dominant in his mind. He maintained that the Protestant Reformation had meant 'the emancipation of the human mind'. Its abolition of absolute authority in the spiritual order was the greatest step ever taken for the attainment of liberty, the exercise of God-given freedom of the will. The study of the history of civilization leads us to the problem whether all is over with the end of life on

[1] For other aspects of Guizot's thought, see pp. 235-7.

earth. For the understanding of history we must acknowledge the reality of freedom of will which is incapable of being explained in terms of anything but itself and cannot be explained away. History does not show morality to be the invention of man, merely socially produced relative to conditions of time and place. There is a 'divine law' to which individuals and societies must conform if they are to attain happiness. 'The only foundation of our hope for humanity' is in the recognition, in theory and in practice, that 'there exists a law above human law, which by whatever name it is called, whether reason, the law of God, or what not, is in all times and in all places the same law under different names'. In the occident it has been Christianity which has brought this truth into view and continued to insist on it.

Human freedom has significance in a purposive world. All 'must choose between fatality and Providence'. 'The belief in the Supernatural is a fact natural, primitive, universal, constant in the life and history of mankind.' The meaning of history is not found entirely in terrestrial life; it has important implications with reference to a future life. The world was not only created by God; it is still affected by His activity. God is in history as providence. Guizot challenged the idea prevalent in his time, that the world is a fixed mechanism, its 'laws' absolutely unalterable. 'Who dare to say that God cannot modify, that He never does modify, according to His plans with respect to the moral system and to man, the laws which He has made and which He maintains in the material order of nature?' In the exercise of His power, God may still use His liberty. History gives evidence that man needs God's help. Though man has freedom of will, he is often too weak to achieve his good choices. With these basic convictions, Guizot expounded his Christian view of the significance of history.

Maintaining that in all men there is some disobedience of God, Guizot accepted the dogma of Original Sin. In view of this, God, as providence, gives men His grace in history. He has done more. The Incarnation was a historical fact. Jesus was God-man who came into history for man's redemption. Without this divine incarnation Christianity 'would never have accomplished what it has'. What Jesus did may be contrasted with what was achieved by other great men, as the Buddha, Zoroaster, Confucius, Socrates. 'Whatever fame attaches to the names of these men, whatever influence they may have exerted, whatever trace of their passage may have remained they rather appeared to have power than really to possess it; they agitated the surface far more than they stirred the depths; they did not draw nations out of the beaten tracks in which they lived. They did not transform souls.'

V

In Germany, prior to the first world war, there was a large amount of free historical study of the life of Jesus. Albert Schweitzer (1875-) gave an account of the most important publications of this research in his *The Quest of the Historical Jesus* (Eng. trans. 1910). From that volume one may conclude that the scientific historical study of the New Testament leads to more doubts than certainties. Schweitzer went so far as to say: 'We must be prepared to find that historical knowledge of the personality and life of Jesus will not be a help, but perhaps even an offence to religion.' Leaving the traditional ideas as to the Incarnation, Crucifixion and Resurrection entirely out of his final discussion, he declared: 'The abiding and eternal in Jesus is absolutely independent of historical knowledge and can be understood only by contact with his spirit which is still at work in the world. In proportion as we have the spirit of Jesus we have the true knowledge of Jesus.'

Early in the twentieth century a discussion was published in England under the title: *Jesus or Christ? Is the historical Jesus or the Christ of dogmatic theology central for Christianity?* Most of the participants were ordained ministers and maintained that Christianity has to do with Jesus Christ and not simply with an alternative of Jesus *or* Christ. In the same period the leaders of Catholic Modernism distinguished between 'truths of fact' and 'truths of faith', contending that the latter did not depend on the former. Thus, while the Abbe Loisy in his New Testament studies arrived at conclusions definitely opposed to the traditional views, as, for example, taking the stories of the Resurrection as not a record of historical fact, he emphasized the value of the living religion of

Christians within the Church. At the same time the French exponents of Symbolo-Fidéisme, doubting or definitely rejecting the orthodox historical teachings, treated Christian dogmas as symbols for living religion. Scepticism as to the historical Jesus eventually reached its ultimate point with the suggestion that he never lived. Those who adopted that position were not antagonistic to religion. They surmised that Christianity had arisen in relation with a 'Christ-myth', as symbolic for God in His relations with men. For them, as for Schweitzer, the Catholic Modernists and the Symbolo-Fidéists, the Christian attitude to history did not depend on any historical events as alleged by traditional orthodoxy.

The German Idealism of the earlier decades of the nineteenth century had encouraged a form of optimism which persisted to the end of the century and beyond. Even the biological theory of evolution seemed to support the belief in human progress to higher levels. There were advances in industry and commerce and a great increase in wealth. But the first world war undermined the confidence of many in mankind. Among Christian leaders there was great emphasis on the wickedness of mankind, and an insistence that the only salvation was that of redemption by Christ. Few theologians continued efforts for a liberal interpretation of Christianity such as was being sought in the latter half of the nineteenth century. The creeds were regarded as expressing the true and full significance of the Christian faith. The second world war strengthened the sense of the 'crisis' in human history due to man's wickedness. No ideas of human civilization appeared adequate to deal with that evil. Thus from early after the first world war up to, and including, our own times, there has been a dominant presentation of Christian ideas as to history in terms of traditional orthodoxy with particular emphasis on the dogmas of Original Sin and of redemption through Christ alone.

One of the foremost leaders of Christianity today, Reinhold Niebuhr, has given an exposition of this Christian view of history in his *Faith and History* (1949). In that volume he described and criticized ancient and modern non-Christian views of history, with regard to which he made the general comment that they are too 'simple'. Classical thought reduced history 'too simply to natural recurrence'; and modern thought 'is betrayed into utopian illusions' about it. He gave only incidental attention to theistic conceptions of history other than those implied in his own Christianity. His whole consideration of history was dominated by the idea that man's ever present main concern has been and is redemption from evil. Despite his frequent acknowledgment of good in our present life, he declared that our contemporary situation is 'desperate' though not 'hopeless'.

Time is a mystery. It is fundamental for Niebuhr that history as temporal is not self-explanatory. It cannot itself bring the redemption that is sought in it. 'History does not solve the enigma of history.' In so far as man 'transcends the temporal process, he can discern many meanings in life and history by tracing various coherences, sequences, causalities and recurrences through which the events of history are ordered'. Yet he has to find its real significance by reference to something beyond time. 'In so far as man is himself in the temporal process which he seeks to comprehend, every sequence and realm of coherence points to a more final source of meaning than man is able to comprehend rationally.' Niebuhr said that though cultures are interrelated they are so disparate that it is not easy to correlate them empirically. The sense of universal history is possible only for faith. By faith he meant religion. 'History in its totality and unity is given a meaning by some kind of religious faith in the sense that the concept of meaning is derived from ultimate presuppositions about the character of time and eternity, which are not the fruit of the detailed analysis of historical events.' Thus 'the real centre of meaning for history must transcend the flux of time'.

Christianity is in part a continuance of Hebrew theism. In the Bible 'history is conceived as unity because all historical destinies are under the dominion of a single sovereignty'. But the significance of Christianity is specific in going beyond that theism. 'The Christian faith begins with and is founded upon the affirmation that the life, death and resurrection of Christ represent an event in history, in and through which a disclosure of the whole meaning of history occurs.' The revelation of Christ is both the 'centre' of and the 'clue' to the meaning of history. It challenges the adequacy of partial meanings. In maintaining that it leads to the fulfilment of the partial meanings, Niebuhr gives recognition to the values of human culture. The faith in Christ's revelation is, according to the New Testament, 'possible only by the Holy Spirit'. The truth of the Gospel may be known only by 'a gift of grace'. The study of history and philosophy cannot lead positively to it. Faith needs to be 'prompted by repentance', an acknowledgment of evil in one's self. There are few, if any, who would not agree with Niebuhr's contention that the proposed alternatives to Christianity do not do justice to all aspects of human existence. But many would seriously challenge his assertion that 'the basic presuppositions of the Christian faith, though transcending reason, make it possible to give an account of life and history in which all facts and antinomies are comprehended'.

Considering mankind in history as centrally concerned with redemption, Niebuhr focused attention on evil. He held that according to Biblical faith, evil is 'at the heart of human personality'; 'a corruption which has universal dominion over men'. The mystery of this doctrine of original sin 'has the merit of being true to the facts of human existence'. It is generally agreed—on the basis of experience—that all individuals are defective in their morality, in religion, and many other ways. But did Niebuhr mean that they are *centrally* ('at the heart') evil and by 'universal dominion' that evil *dominates* all men? If so, his statement that that has been and is 'true to the facts of human existence' may be challenged. Hegel said: 'To him who looks on the world rationally, the world in its turn presents a rational aspect.' Does Niebuhr look on men as radically evil and finds them so? He has been widely known for his concern with the idea of original sin and his declamations against the evils of the present 'human situation'. Yet it is strange that he should say: 'St Augustine's Christian realism errs in its too consistent emphasis upon the sinful corruptions of the world's peace.' In face of this evil of history Niebuhr declared the Christian view to be that the 'final clue' 'to the mystery of the divine power is found in the suffering love of a man on the Cross'. This clue does not follow 'logically from the observable facts of history'. Its acceptance is an act of faith. 'There are no observable facts of history which cannot be interpreted in its light.' Divine love and power shining through the enigmas and antinomies of history are 'finally and definitely revealed in a drama in which suffering love gains triumph over sin and death'. 'The Cross . . . ceases to be merely a story in history and becomes a revelatory of a very unique divine "glory", namely the glory and majesty of a suffering God whose love and forgiveness is the final triumph over the recalcitrance of human sin and the confusion of human history.'

It is quite clear that Niebuhr's idea of eternity is not as timeless. But his view of history depends essentially on what he refers to as 'beyond time' and by the term 'transcends'. He would probably admit that 'eternity' is as great a mystery as time. It is difficult to see how this mystery overcomes the particular enigmas of history. Further, his conception of Christianity is not other-worldly in any sense of an ascetic denial of the goods of temporal life. 'There are provisional meanings in history . . .' 'renewals of life individually and collectively'. Men must realize themselves in 'a responsible and loving relation' to their fellow-men. But the love of Christ, which is the clue to history, transcends all else.

A large volume would be required to survey the obscurities that have come into Christian thought during the centuries by the introduction of ideas of eternity as timeless or as a now comprehending all the past, the present and the future. Those ideas have led to confusion as to the Christian view of history. In this connection reference must be made, though it can only be brief, to the study by Oscar Cullmann, *Christ and Time* (Eng. trans. 1949). That work is a survey of the New Testament, especially of the Gospels. Cullmann shows clearly that these documents are consistently and unequivocally concerned with time. He maintains that the idea of timeless eternity is foreign not only to the New Testament, but also to the Old. 'Primitive Christianity knows nothing of a timeless God.' For it the eternal God is the everlasting pan-temporal God, who was in the beginning, is now and ever shall be. The main stream of history is God's redemption of man, and the mid-point of history is the unique time of the Incarnation, Crucifixion and Resurrection of Jesus Christ. All that went before and all that has (and will) come after has its central meaning with relation to this mid-point.

Niebuhr's interpretation of history is that of a Christian preacher. H. Butterfield, the author of *Christianity and History* (1949), is an eminent professional historian. Butterfield insisted that scientific methods in history cannot rightly be understood as attempts to treat man in naturalistic fashion as merely a part of physical nature. The historian 'does not treat man . . . as essentially a part of Nature, or consider him primarily in this aspect'. 'History is a human drama . . . taking place as it were on the stage of Nature', a drama 'of human life as the affair of individual personalities possessing self-consciousnesss, intellect and freedom'. Technical history does not acquaint men with the meaning of life. Mundane history is not self-explanatory. Nevertheless, actual history 'is the business of making personalities, even as it were, by putting them through the mill . . .' Butterfield stressed a fundamental idea in his insistence that technical history is in principle opposed to looking for meaning *solely* or even predominantly in a distant future. 'The technique of historical study itself demands that we look upon each generation as, so to speak, a world of people existing in their own right.' 'The purpose of life is not in the far future, nor, as we so often imagine, around the next corner, but the whole of it is here and now, as fully as it will ever be on this planet. It is always a "Now" that is in direct relation to eternity—not a far future; always immediate experience of life that matters in the last resort. . . .'

As history is essentially an affair of self-conscious individuals, and technical history cannot give authoritative judgments on its meaning, each individual 'as standing alone in the universe' has to make his own decision as to the significance of history. Technical history gives some help. It shows that, whether one believes in God as providence or not, there is a sort of providential order in history-making that goes beyond and is other than what men consciously intend and deliberately strive for. 'Millions of men in a given century, conscious of nothing save going about their own business, have together woven a fabric better in many respects than any of them knew.' Sometimes only later generations become aware of its pattern and 'over-arching theme'. Technical history gives evidence of the defective knowledge among men. 'It is a very serious distortion of the picture' to assume 'a world of normally wise and righteous men'. History uncovers 'man's universal sin'. This is a fact of history and not merely a Christian idea. Technical history supports the idea of judgment in history, though it cannot affirm that it is complete and exact. It seems to find much in accord with the conviction (expressed early in the Old Testament) that men suffer in history not merely for wrong-doing. Some suffering is known to develop personalities. Vicarious suffering is often inspired by love. 'Because there is tragedy in history, love itself is brought to burn with an intenser flame in human experience.'

'The whole interpretation of the universe and of history' depends on whether one believes in God or not. That belief does not rest on technical history, nor finally even on philosophy. 'I am unable to see how a man can find the hand of God in secular history, unless he has first found that he has an assurance of it is his personal experience.' Though God as providence in history must be 'capable of bringing good out of evil', He does not guarantee progress. We should 'conceive ourselves not as sovereign makers of history but as born to co-operate with providence', who 'has the last word about the results'. With this belief in God, we 'envisage our history in the proper light, therefore, if we say that each generation —indeed, each individual—exists for the glory of God; but one of the most dangerous things in life is to subordinate human personality to production, to the state, even to civilization itself, to anything but the glory of God'.

As we have presented them so far, Butterfield's views may be said to conform with Christian theism, but they could also be held by non-Christian philosophical theists, and mostly even by Jews, Muslims and Zoroastrians. We turn now to what he has otherwise to say of Christianity. Continuously with the religion of the Hebrews, Christianity acknowledges God as 'the God of history'. But, further, traditional

Christianity is a 'historical religion in a particularly technical sense', for it claims that the Incarnation, the Crucifixion and the Resurrection were events in time. It regards these 'as capturing into time a portion of eternity' (whatever that may mean). It is not clear whether Butterfield himself believes they do that, nor what he conceives to be their particular significance, other than this vague reference to eternity. Viewing the history of the occident as a technical historian he is prepared to say that Christ's years on earth must appear 'in any case the most central date'. Judgment, tragedy, vicarious suffering, providence, 'are brought into stronger focus at this point'. 'To anybody considering the moral aspect of the human drama, here is the climax and crisis of the story—the place where we can discern something fundamental about the very nature of history.' But the decision as to whether one should accept the traditional beliefs in the Incarnation, Crucifixion and Resurrection as historical 'passes out of the hands of the historian'. 'If any man were to say that history has scientifically established or disproved the Divinity of Christ, he would for the same reason be guilty of that intellectual arrogance which works in all the sciences as each of them transgresses its bounds to gain a usurped authority.' In this volume Butterfield wrote little Christological doctrine, and gave no emphasis on the belief in immortality as affecting terrestrial history. He contended that the assured Christian has 'in his religion the key to his conception of the whole human drama', but he did not make clear whether he regarded orthodox dogmas as an essential of the key. He ends his book with the exhortation: 'Hold to Christ, and for the rest be totally uncommitted.'

PART TWO

PARTICULAR THEORIES OF HISTORY
Occidental

CHAPTER VI

SOME INDEPENDENT REFLECTIONS ON HISTORY FROM THE RENAISSANCE TO THE NINETEENTH CENTURY

I

WITH the continuance of ecclesiastical authority the Christological philosophy of history has been maintained by orthodox Christian thinkers into our own time. But in the last four centuries in the Occident, other views of and attitudes towards history have been developed by independent thinkers. Whatever they may have thought of men's spiritual redemption from evil, their treatments of history were not focused on it. They widened the scope of the outlook on history. Influenced by them, the adherents to the non-Christological Christian theistic conception of history have gained a fuller appreciation of the terrestrial values in history. With this they have returned to some neglected aspects of Augustine's view. The beginnings of these independent reflections on history may be found in the Renaissance in Italy. Though the thinkers of the Renaissance had different theories with varied emphases, they all contributed to an emancipation from the thought and attitudes of 'other-worldliness' of the Middle Ages. With the conviction that the Middle Ages had been a period of degeneration, many of them wanted a return to some of the modes of life and ideals of ancient Greece and Rome. There was a concentration on the cultivation of the values of terrestrial life. It was against the exaggeration of the worth of the mundane that Savonarola (1452-1498) raised his protest.

One type of challenge to some Mediaeval ideas (still widespread in his time) was made in the works of Machiavelli (1469-1530), especially the *Discourses* (? 1512-17) and *The*

Prince (1513). In opposition to the contention of the leaders of the Church that temporal political rulers were subject to the higher authority of the spiritual hierarchy, Machiavelli insisted on their independence of it. In this he was expressing not merely an opinion of his own, but an idea becoming current amongst secular rulers of his age. Like Polybius (some of whose work he copied), he treated the political facts of history as natural phenomena. Like Polybius, he also held that there is always a rising and a declining in human affairs. But Machiavelli endeavoured to show how political power could at least be secured and prolonged. He believed that in all ages men are essentially the same in nature. It was thus that recorded history could have pragmatic value, and a true political theory be formulated. With the conviction that the course of history would be towards the establishment of larger political wholes, he dreamed of the unity of Italy. He charged the Church with causing and perpetuating divisions. Further, Christianity 'glorified meek and contemplative men rather than men of action'. He had a higher opinion of the conditions of the Pagan Roman Republic than those of his own day under Christian dominance. He was actually anti-Christian in placing political expediency above morality. A ruler 'should, if possible, practise goodness, but under the pressure of necessity should know how to pursue evil'. In his own time intrigues and murders were resorted to in the various States in Italy, and that, apparently, without evident perturbation of conscience or thought of retribution after death. Some have thought the recent Italian Fascism, German National Socialism, and contemporary Russian Communism to be types of Machiavellianism in history.

Concentrating his attention on the political State as of society organized independently of the Church, Machiavelli did not concern himself with the private lives of individuals as such. He had comparatively little to say of culture in general, art, letters and religion. Thus, taken alone, his works would suggest a false view of the dominant Humanist attitudes to history. The Humanists placed considerable stress on the importance of individuality, with the idea of the many-sided man. That idea was of continuous influence in Occidental education until the needs of recent times led to emphasis on specialization. Much of the art of the fifteenth century was concerned with religion and there was general conformity with Christian rites, even if with silent rejection of Christian dogmas. But there was a diversity of views as to the nature of history. There were many works on 'Fate'. 'They tell,' wrote Burckhardt, 'of the turning of the Wheel of Fortune and of the instability of earthly, especially political things. Providence is brought in only because the writers would still be ashamed of undisguised fatalism, of the avowal of ignorance or of useless complaints.' For some the idea of a future life was of 'a shadowy realm, as in Homer'. In 1513, Pope Leo X felt it necessary to promulgate a defence of the individuality and immortality of souls against those teaching that there is only one soul in all men. It is to be doubted whether the Humanists who outwardly accepted Christianity held a religious conception of sin or treated the belief in divine redemption seriously. However, in the Platonic Academy at Florence there was, in Burckhardt's words, 'an unreserved Theism' which 'treated the world as a great moral and physical cosmos. While the men of the Middle Ages looked on the world as a vale of tears in which Pope and Emperor were set to guard against the coming of the Anti-Christ, while the fatalists of the Renaissance oscillated between the seasons of over-flowing energy and seasons of superstition or of stupid resignation, here in this circle of chosen spirits, the doctrine was upheld that the visible world was created by God in love, that it is the copy of a pattern pre-existing in Him, and that He will ever remain its eternal mover and restorer. The soul of man by recognizing God can draw Him into its narrow boundaries, but also by love of Him itself expand into the Infinite, and this is blessedness on earth.' The loftiest Renaissance conception of humanity, according to Burckhardt, was uttered by Pico della Mirandola (1463-1494), in a speech on the dignity of man: 'I have set thee, says the Creator to Adam, in the midst of the world that thou mayest the more easily behold and see all that there is therein. I created thee a being neither heavenly nor earthly, neither mortal nor immortal only, that thou mightest be free to shape and to overcome thyself. Thou mayest sink into a beast, and (yet) be born again to the divine likeness . . . To thee alone is given a growth and a development depending on thine own free will. Thou bearest in thee the germs of universal life.' The thinkers of the Renaissance did not enquire directly into the intrinsic significance of history, yet their attitudes implied that it is mainly in it as it goes along. Their concern with the past was for the sake of the present. They did not develop any progressive theories as to the future. Occupied with their own activities and the glories of ancient Greece and Rome, they gave comparatively little thought to the possible future course of events. However, from the time of Italian Humanism, the idea of history on earth as merely a preparation for a future life beyond it became subordinate in the Occident. Italian Humanism was of fundamental importance as a transition to modern life, a breaking away from the narrowness of vision of so many of the thinkers of the Middle Ages, but further steps had to be taken before our modern points of view were reached.

II

Italian Humanism had been a reaction against the narrow Christian conception of history as having significance simply in the spiritual redemption of mankind. But though in its creation and enjoyment of art it had been a specific enrichment of present life, in its thought it had been largely backward-turning. Francis Bacon's (1561-1626) works, though he did not consciously intend it, militated against the Christian view. However, he took the chief steps needed beyond Italian Humanism in pointing to the future, and that in specific ways. Bacon acknowledged that there was a place for 'divinity', but insisted that it should not be confused with other knowledge. It is folly to build 'a natural philosophy on the first chapter of the book of Genesis, the book of Job and other parts of Scripture'. He affirmed his belief in God. 'While the mind of man looketh upon second causes scattered, it may sometime rest in them and go no further, but when it beholdeth the chain of them confederate and linked together, it must needs fly to Providence and Deity.' However, in his Essay

SOME INDEPENDENT REFLECTIONS

On Death, he made no mention of immortality as a basis for any consolation. Otherwise with regard to Christianity he simply pointed to faith: 'It is most wise to render to faith the things that are faith's.' He did not discuss Christological doctrines or relate the meaning of history to them. He also endeavoured to avoid the metaphysical ordinarily understood as abstractly rational.

Bacon wrote a *History of Henry VII* (1622) and left fragments of a projected general history of Britain. But though accorded no great importance as a historian, his work has had wide and continuous effects on actual history. Felt only later, and rarely recognized, he had indirectly an influence on the 'science' of history in his insistence on the examination of facts and enquiry into causal relationships. He made a clarion call to men to turn from their dominant concern with the ideas of the past to the investigation of realities, physical things, minds, and their processes. Much of his *Advancement of Learning* (1605) was devoted to describing the hindrances to the growth of knowledge. In his *Novum Organum* (1620), he proposed methods of scientific study. In detail those methods were not so valuable as Bacon himself supposed. His importance was not specifically in them but in his arousing men to occupation with Nature and in the comprehensiveness of his range of vision as to aspects to be investigated. Men were thus led to a wider actual history and to conceptions of it different from the Christian ones of the Middle Ages. His imaginative *New Atlantis* (1627) indicated the very varied realms of life in which he expected benefits from knowledge in the future. The purpose of 'Salomon's House' (a fictitious organization in *New Atlantis*, supposed to have suggested the foundation of The Royal Society) was 'the knowledge of causes and secret motions of things, and the enlarging of the bounds of human empire, to the effecting of all things possible'. Bacon expected progress in history but not as inevitable: he gave grounds for reasonable 'hope' of it. His outlook on history was essentially of it as including an ever-widening knowledge of Nature with an ever-increasing amelioration and enrichment of human life. The advances of the last three centuries in the attainment and appreciation of secular values may be considered as due in no small measure to the attitudes aroused by Bacon.

Another form of transition to modern thought was initiated by Descartes (1596-1650), the pioneer character of whose work led to his being called the 'father' of modern philosophy. In opposition to the credulous acceptance of ideas from the past he taught the necessity of a primary method of doubt. Applying that method, he came to the first conclusion that as the act of doubting could not itself be doubted, 'I think, therefore I am.' By steps that need not be described here, he accepted the ideas of matter and of minds. Matter is extended: minds are not. Minds have the functions of thought, feeling, and will: matter has not. It has been from the standpoint of such a Dualism that history has been viewed by common sense and that most historians have written of it. But Descartes occupied himself predominantly with the mathematical and physical and made no significant contribution with regard to history. He defended the belief in God. He gave no overt expression of applying the method of doubt to Christological doctrines, and up to the present there has been little, if any, adoption of the method by official Christian teachers.

The works of Thomas Hobbes (1588-1679) also had implications as to history. Hobbes was interested in history and one of his earliest works was a translation of Thucydides. He is best known for his *Leviathan* (1651). Hobbes maintained that men are by nature entirely egotistic, seeking their own preservation and power. 'In the first place I put for a general inclination of all mankind a perpetual and restless desire of power after power, that ceaseth only in death. And the cause of this is not always that a man hopes for a more intensive delight than he has already attained to, or that he cannot be content with a moderate power; but because he cannot assure the power and means to live well, without the acquisition of more.' In the condition of Nature, with 'every man enemy to every man', 'there is no place for industry, because the fruit thereof is uncertain, and consequently no culture of the earth, no navigation nor use of commodities that may be imported by sea, no commodious building, no instruments of moving and removing such things as require much force, no knowledge of the face of the earth, no account of time, no arts, no letters, no society, and, which is worst of all, continual fear and danger of violent death, and the life of man solitary, poor, nasty, brutish, and short'. To theologians this account of the inherent nature of man may have seemed to accord to some extent with their idea of man's radical corruption. But Hobbes did not point to a redemption by an incarnation of God in history. He maintained that men had achieved what they had of the goods mentioned by the acceptance of governmental control. It is not to be supposed that Hobbes thought there were times in history when men deliberately and formally made a 'social contract' for political government. They came to accept such government and to continue it 'as if' there were a contract. The values men have had in history have been made possible because of the promulgation of rules for their social conduct by a sovereign power with the motive of the well-being of all. Actual history in the past and in his own time had fallen short of this ideal, but it may be regarded as intended by Hobbes that it was the goal for the future. It has sometimes been said that Hobbes considered morality as merely relative to time and place, even as dependent on the arbitrary will of the sovereign power. But Hobbes works contain many inconsistencies, and in the *Leviathan* time after time he introduces moral ideas as of 'reason' and employed the term 'natural law' with the same implication it had for the Middle Ages and for the Stoics. Nevertheless, though he talked occasionally of the 'immortal God', he made no reference to a supreme reason dominating history. Hobbes's position ought not to be misunderstood. He did not intend by his theory that the individual was to be entirely subordinated to the State. Rather, political government was to accord him the greatest liberty possible in the conditions of social life. He considered the essential function of government to be the protection of its subjects—from interference one with another, and from external attack. That view of government played a part in later history, until it was widely rejected for the conception of political power as concerned with constructive efforts for social progress and the general advance of civilization. Hobbes was violently opposed to the Roman Catholic Church. 'The Papacy is no other than the ghost of the deceased Roman empire sitting crowned on the grave thereof.' The Church in any country should be subordinate to the civil sovereign.

Machiavelli and Hobbes had presented theories of the rôle of the political state in history. The philosopher, Leibnitz (1646-1716), formulated a metaphysics with quite different emphases. Though his influence on conceptions of the nature of history may have been felt first in the late eighteenth century, and then indirectly rather than directly, he propounded some ideas fundamental for later views. A complete account of his philosophy, even as bearing on history, would require far more space than can be given here: only a few of his ideas of special importance can be mentioned. His contention that ultimate realities are spiritual entities or 'monads' indicates the basis for the consideration of history from the standpoint of individual persons as spiritual beings. Philosophically speaking, each exists 'in and for himself', whatever his relations to others, and each is unique with his own position in the whole of existence. The monads have an inherent activity, a spontaneity or freedom. His belief that they strive for perfection may have been one root of the later theories of the perfectibility of the human race. In this connection his dictum: 'This is the best of all possible worlds' has its significance. The future and not merely the past and the present are to be taken into consideration. Through the past and the present perfection is to be attained in the future. His dictum could not be proved by reason or experience but rested on faith in God. The co-ordination of the parts of Nature and of men with Nature is due to God, being referred to by Leibnitz as a 'Pre-established Harmony'. In the *Theodicee* (1710) Leibnitz treated of evil in history. Part of it is in the immoral use of freedom: the suffering associated with sin is to cure men from sin. Suffering not due to men is instrumental for their development to perfection. The spiritual beings or monads, not being extended, do not arise by composition. They are created by God. Each has a history of his own. It may extend into a future life. It could end only by his annihilation by God. However, the goal intended by God is the perfection of the individual along with that of all others. There are many serious difficulties in the philosophy of Leibnitz, but there can be little doubt concerning the main characteristics of his view of history.

III

Before Leibnitz there had been beginnings of a scientific, even philosophical, consideration of history in the works of Jean Bodin (1530-1596). Though some have been inclined to describe him as the founder of the Philosophy of History, he was not concerned so much with the significance of history as with the methods of its study. He published a volume on methods in 1576. With an attitude of independence towards traditional religion and the Church, he shared something of the theological scepticism of the post-Renaissance period. The study of history is of intellectual interest and of pragmatic value for morals and politics. The divine must be regarded as immutable and the physical world also appears to be a stable system. Yet, at first glance, human history seems to be a realm of continuous change. Nevertheless, studied carefully it manifests some orderly principles. Man, as body and mind (or spirit) has some of the persisting orderly characteristics of the physical world and of the divine. History involves both Nature and God. One aspect of order in history is to be seen in the development of civil law. Underlying the particular laws of different people there is 'universal law'— (the natural law of the Stoics)—and this may be ascertained by studying the facts of history. Bodin was thus opposed to the notion that morality in history is merely relative to conditions of time and place. He maintained, further, that empirical investigation gives no ground for belief in a Golden Age in the past or that men have continuously degenerated. Though there have been periods of decline, in the main there has been progress. Considering man's dual nature, an adequate treatment of history involves both the sciences of the physical world and a comparative study of religions. Human history is not fully determined by physical conditions and social customs, but depends in part on the individual's freedom of choice. To a considerable extent men may resist external forces and even turn them to their cultural ends. History began from divine creation and terrestrially it will come to an end.

A new approach to the study of history was made by Giambattista Vico (1668-1744) in a work entitled *The New Science* (1725). Too enthusiastically, Jules Michelet called Vico the father of the Philosophy of History. A pioneer in introducing certain methods for the study and in suggesting some general principles, he may rather be considered one of the founders of the science of history. He did for it something the same that Bacon had done for the investigation of the physical world. He broke away from the pragmatic attitude to history common in the period of the Italian Renaissance. Any practical significance of the study of history must be considered secondary. In his *Autobiography* (? 1743) he admitted his debts to Plato, Tacitus, Bacon and Grotius. From Plato he derived a conception which lies behind his whole treatment; from Tacitus he gained an appreciation of historical facts; from Bacon he learned methods of the investigation and organization of the empirical data; and from Grotius some main aspects of universal law in the historical. On the other hand he contrasted his position with that of Descartes. While not denying the validity of abstract mathematics, he questioned their value for any demonstration concerning concrete facts. The historian has to pay attention to the empirical data of history, with regard to which he may reach probabilities and not logical demonstration. Nevertheless, men may have more significant knowledge of human activities than of the realm of Nature. He maintained this on the ground of the general principle that only the creator of a thing can properly know it. At least in part, man creates his own history. 'When it happens that he who creates things also describes them, then the history is certain in the highest degree.' With this principle Vico insisted on the reliability of knowledge of the changing ideas, persons and events of history as against those who considered mathematics and the sciences of the physical world as alone worthy of acceptance. Whatever be said of his principle and the details of his theory of knowledge he was a pioneer in contending, even at the beginning of the eighteenth century, that there are valid scientific investigations other than the quantitative. He emphasized the importance of philology for the historian. Only with it can he avoid reading later ideas into earlier times.

Vico adopted the distinction of 'sacred' and 'profane' history, taking the former as the history 'of the Jews and the Christians'; the latter as that 'of the gentiles'. The greater part of his work, dealing with 'profane' history, has been regarded as positivistic, seeking the causes of the processes solely in the empirical data. With his insistence on mankind as social and that history is made by men, his interpretation has been declared to be purely humanistic. Both in his statements as to the general character of his work and in its details are definite grounds for rejecting such a view. He made a significant contrast between his position and that of traditional Natural Theology. Of Natural Theology, Vico had a poor opinion, as it was based chiefly on consideration of the physical world. In contrast with it, he pointed to 'a rational civic theology'. The New Science, he said, in one of its principal aspects is 'a rational civil theology', 'a demonstration, so to speak, of the historical fact of Providence, for it must be a history of the forms of order which, without human discernment or intent, and often against the designs of men, Providence has given to this great city of the human race'.

Vico used the term 'Providence' in two ways, similar to what have been referred to in theology as 'General' and 'Special' Providence. General Providence operates in history, immanent in all natural processes and dominating all peoples. History is not created simply by men. Providence sometimes leads to other ends than those men have themselves intended. His most definite statement of this is in the 'Conclusion of the Work', in which what is obviously Providence is described as 'a mind'. 'It is true that men have themselves made this world of nations . . . but this world, without doubt, has issued from a mind, often diverse, at times quite contrary and always superior to the particular ends that men had proposed to themselves, which narrow ends, made means to serve wider ends, it has always employed to preserve the human race on earth.'

Providence dominates men with their particular aims, and does so in a manner 'superior' to them. This is seen in the facts of history which refute both the Epicurean belief in chance and the Stoic (and Spinozist) belief in fate. Though history is in part due to the genuine freedom of choice of men, that freedom is exercised only within the limits permitted by Providence. 'The divine Plato,' wrote Vico, 'affirms that Providence rules the affairs of men.'

If history is something more—different from and superior to the particular ends of men—what is this something more? In the answer to that question one might hope to reach the main idea of Vico's interpretation of history. But the only suggestion of an answer in his work is a phrase evidently Platonic in character, repeated on a number of occasions, yet never explained: 'an ideal eternal history' . . . 'whose course is run in time by the histories of all nations'. This phrase gives a little justification for Croce's contention that 'Vico was of the stuff of Plato and not of Bacon'. Yet all that Vico suggests of the 'ideal eternal history' are the fundamental characteristics of the universal history of nations as discovered empirically in their 'course run in time'. Despite the Platonic phrase, his work is actually in accord with the attitude of Bacon. He never discussed the relation between his Platonic 'idea' and the historical as temporal processes.

Vico adopted the conception ('which the Egyptians handed down to us') of three ages of the world: (i) 'The age of the gods, in which the gentiles believed they lived under divine governments and everything was commanded them by auspices and oracles, which are the oldest thing in profane history; (ii) The age of the heroes, in which they reigned everywhere in aristocratic commonwealths, on account of a certain superiority of nature which they held themselves to have over the plebs; and (iii) The age of man, in which all men recognized themselves as equal in human nature, and therefore there were established first the popular commonwealths and then the monarchies, both of which are forms of human government.' All peoples have gone, or go, through these stages; then they have lapsed, or will lapse, into a condition of barbarism. The whole process is then repeated. This flux and reflux, this cyclic character of history, is due to the inherent nature of mankind. Though Vico acknowledged some similarities among peoples as due to transmission, he considered them in the main as independently produced from common human nature. The high point of this natural historical process is at the level at which, with the establishment of political equality among men, order is maintained through the functioning of a good monarch. Applied to details, Vico's law of flux and reflux is, as Croce remarked, 'riddled with exceptions'. With reference to early history there is a recognition in *The New Science* of the significance of mythology, folk-lore and such like. Books II and III are devoted to the ages of the gods and the heroes, and are of no special importance for our present purpose. It is, however, interesting to note that even in the age of the gods men 'made out this great truth: that divine Providence watches over the welfare of mankind'. Within these early conditions there were developments of social organization (as of marriage) and of law. In all this Vico saw the influence of Providence. 'Human passions are to be made into virtues.' 'Our treatment of natural law begins with the idea of Providence.' 'The first laws everywhere were the divine laws of Jove.'

There is very little in *The New Science* concerning 'sacred' history. Whatever Vico himself really thought, his statements in this connection are confusing. It is in sacred history that one may talk of Special Providence. Yet Vico gave no specific attention to the relation between General and Special Providence. Both are expressions of intelligence, the former in the laws of nature and the orderly natural processes of history and the latter in what leads men to the highest type of life. While he declared that even the 'most savage, wild and monstrous men' have some notion of God, and that 'religions alone have the power to cause the peoples to do virtuous works', he said: 'Our Christian religion is true . . . all the others are false.' Sacred history is due to 'divine grace', an aspect of or identical with Special Providence. Was Vico a sincere Christian or did he say what he did of 'sacred' history to avoid persecution and the suppression of his work? Croce affirms the former. Though he is probably correct, it is significant that Vico ignored the specific (alleged or actual) historical events considered basic to traditional Christianity. 'The Hebrew religion was founded by the true God on the prohibition of the divination on which all the gentile nations arose.' The Hebrews were 'illuminated by the true God—believing in Him as all mind, who searches the hearts of men, and the gentiles believed in gods composed of bodies and mind who could not do so'. There is a 'divine reason' of which men may know only what has been revealed to them. 'To the Hebrews first and then to the Christians this has been by internal speech to their minds as the proper expression of a God all mind; but (also) by external speech through the prophets and through Jesus Christ to the Apostles by whom it was declared to the Church.' Of his own time, and the centuries immediately preceding it, Vico wrote little. In the Dark Ages, mankind had lapsed to barbarism. But God 'permitted a new order of humanity to emerge' that the true religion might be firmly established. Yet, not withstanding this reference to a new order of humanity, he went on to deal in detail with the 'recurrence of human things' in the same way as he had described gentile history. Then, at the close of his account, he asserted that 'Christian Europe is everywhere radiant with such humanity that it abounds in all good things that make for the happiness of human life, ministering to the comforts of the body as well as the pleasures of mind and spirit.' Though he did not discuss the relation of General and Special Providence, in acknowledging them both Vico implied definite opposition to any view restricting the activity of God in history to the orderly processes of Nature. Providence is concerned not merely with the constitution of the physical world making history possible, but also with the character of history itself as involving an ideal of life for men.

Some interpreters of Vico's work have treated his references to 'Providence' as camouflage, maintaining that his real position is that the historical processes have definite uniformities that are to be discovered by scientific investigation of the empirical data of history. They discard any Theistic expressions and anything of the character of Special Providence, and describe his position as positivistic and merely humanistic. Vico may have some contributions of value for that type of view of history, but that it was his own view cannot be established. To us it does not seem to have been. Croce wrote, surely on good grounds: 'We find here and there a theological Vico, an agnostic Vico, or even a fanciful Vico composing cosmological and physical romances, but look where we will among his works, we shall never find a materialistic Vico.'

By one writer, Montesquieu (1689-1755) has been called the founder of Philosophy of History and by some others the inaugurator of scientific historical method. Though neither of these descriptions is justified, he was a pioneer in the study of the facts of history as contrasted, e.g. with Bossuet's view of history from the standpoint of previously accepted religious conceptions. *The Spirit of Laws* (1748) was only indirectly concerned with history in general. He treated of causes and effects in history and not of its significance. He sought, first and mainly, to account for history by physical causes, as climate and other geographical conditions. But he failed to distinguish adequately between the direct and inevitable effects of them and the different kinds of reaction that peoples have adopted towards them. The ways men have responded to their environments, whether they have submitted to or actively fought against and changed them, have been of far greater importance in history than Montesquieu acknowledged. Though he professed to believe in the free agency of man, he gave his attention almost solely to external forces on him. Even in his consideration of civilization there was little recognition of the creative contributions of individuals and the effects of particular events. He viewed history rather as of broad general movements changing their character only slowly. Men may change them by the formulation of new laws. Montesquieu was a forerunner of the 'scientific' history which has concerned itself predominantly with social currents. Yet, though his treatment of history was factual as to the physical, the economic, the political and religious, ignoring chronology he failed to view historical development as a set of temporal processes. Emphasizing tradition, he minimized the part played by reason and Voltaire ridiculed him. With the attitude to the past that dominated at the time of the French Revolution, Montesquieu's work was thrust on one side.

INTERPRETATIONS OF HISTORY

The historian, J. B. Bury, credited Voltaire (1694-1778) with the first use of the term 'Philosophy of History'. He employed it in a dissertation in 1756, later affixed as an introduction to his *Essai sur les Moeurs et l'Esprit des Nations* (1753-1758). He gave no systematic discussion of the meaning of the term. For him, it meant the consideration of history with the attitude of eighteenth century rationalism. Bury said that Voltaire 'flung down the gage of battle to that conception of history that had been brilliantly represented by Bossuet'. Voltaire believed in God but rejected any idea that history included His activity in the manner implied by the term 'Special Providence'. He certainly did not view history from the standpoint of Christological doctrines. He was an outspoken opponent of the Roman Catholic Church. The historical religions are superstitious formulations of natural religion, theistic belief and piety. God has given men a 'principle of universal reason', and they are to put their faith in it. He had no appreciation of emotions associated with religious worship. Though recognizing pity and justice as fundamental aspects of history, he himself had a contempt rather than a love for the mass of mankind, whom he considered to be mostly weak and sensuous. They have been dominated by a selfish and more or less unscrupulous minority.

Of Voltaire's historical works, it is the *Essai* that is significant for us. A Berlin edition described it as 'Outlines of a Universal History'. One of the basic motives of Voltaire's writings was an opposition to the Christian ecclesiastical view of history. In contrast with the mainly European outlook of its defenders, he presented a survey that has been called 'the first real world-history'. With the knowledge available in his time, he included accounts of the Arabs, the Chinese, and some peoples of India, paying attention, though unevenly, to their thought and art, their economic and political conditions. Lanson wrote that Voltaire was the first to realize 'the modern conception of history, of history which is the picture and explanation of civilization'. The meaning of history was for Voltaire in science, art, literature, the refinements of social life, and natural piety. Often cynical as to the events of history, with its vagaries of chance, crimes, stupidities and miseries, he nevertheless looked for an advance in civilization with the increasing triumph of reason. His faith in reason may have implied an acceptance of the idea of the perfectibility of man, but he developed no clear conception of a goal, or goals, in history. In *Candide* (1758), depicting vices and misfortunes such as occur in history, he satirized Leibnitz's dictum that this is the best of all possible worlds. Had he been alive, Leibnitz might have retorted: 'Judge not the play till the play is done'. Voltaire had himself previously written, in *Zadig* (1747): 'Men are wrong in judging the whole by the very small part which alone they are able to perceive.'

Voltaire's younger contemporary, Robert Jacques Turgot (1727-1771) left a sketch of a proposed, but apparently never written, *Discourse on Universal History*, partly in opposition to Bossuet. Acknowledging the influences of the physical (climate, etc., as emphasized by Montesquieu) he considered internal psychical factors to be more important. Admitting belief in God, but not interventions by Him, he viewed history as an organic whole working out a plan of advance in civilization—science, art, morality, government, and religion. Even periods of degeneration involve something beneficial to the general progress: errors and calamities have had some stimulating effects, and passions have provided driving power. In distinction from Voltaire, he did not rest progress so largely on reason. Both he and Voltaire represented a change in attitude from that common in earlier times, in abandoning any reliance on Providence and promoting a definitely humanistic interpretation of history.

In the work of Jean Jacques Rousseau (1712-1779) there was a double challenge: to traditional teachings of the Church and to the prevailing secular organization of society. In opposition to the doctrine of the corruption of human nature, as taught in the dominant Christian view of history, he contended that man is born naturally good. In opposition to the organization of society as he found it, he maintained that man is born free but that the social organization had put him in chains. Man's capacity of free choice and his ability to perfect himself are what specifically distinguish him from infrahuman animals. If he is to retain his true status as man he must preserve this liberty. Rousseau admitted that there is a 'natural inequality' of men, but that in itself it is not very great nor of such influence as is too often claimed. Much passes as natural inequality which has actually been engendered in society. The past evolution of society has given rise to civil inequalities, contrary to Natural Law, and these have led to the greatest human evils. In contrast, society should be organized in accordance with an implied social contract to ensure civil equality. Along with the civil inequalities have gone the inequalities from claims to property. Rousseau definitely recognized the significance of personal individuality. He complained that in traditional society a man always lives in the opinion of others as though he derives the feeling of his own existence only from their judgment. His contention that the capacity to perfect himself is a distinctive feature of man was echoed by many later writers and became an underlying principle of theories of progress in history.

In the turmoil of the French Revolution, while in danger of execution, the Marquis de Condorcet (1743-1794) wrote an optimistic account of history as a progressive advance of mankind towards truth and happiness. He maintained that there had been such development in the past and that it would go on, as by a law of nature, indefinitely in the future towards human perfection. 'Perfectibility . . . can be regarded as one of the general laws of nature.' To judge by the past 'Nature has put no limits to our hopes.' Nature binds together truth, virtue, and happiness by an indissoluble chain. Development is to be seen in art, and what is more important, there is progress towards 'the brotherhood of nations'. 'Our hopes concerning the future condition of the human species can be reduced to these three important points: the destruction of the inequality between nations; the progress of equality within a people; and finally the perfecting of man.'

IV

The Rationalism that came to dominate so much of eighteenth century thought was not adopted by Bernard Mandeville (1690-1733). Mandeville's personal position is open to doubt. Thus, as Dr Kaye, the editor of the latest edition

SOME INDEPENDENT REFLECTIONS

of his work, points out, William Law and George Bluet 'combatted Mandeville's asceticism because they felt that he did not really believe it', while Adam Smith and John Brown 'objected because they thought that he did'. The title of Mandeville's work is immediately arresting: *The Fable of the Bees, or Private Vices, Publick Benefits*. It went through a number of varied editions from 1714 and aroused much discussion and opposition, in part because of some misunderstanding of the implications of the latter part of the title. The question involved rests on the meaning of the term 'vices'. That depended for Mandeville on what he took to be an accepted view of virtue, as conformity with immutable, eternal, rational principles. Mandeville suggested that such virtue involved extreme asceticism, the suppression of impulses. He complained, at the outset of his book, that 'most writers are always teaching men what they should be and hardly ever trouble their heads with telling them what they really are'. As contrasted with the rationalistic character of virtue (as above described) he believed man, other than his obvious physical organism, 'to be a compound of various passions, that all of them, as they are provoked and come uppermost, govern him by turns, whether he will or no'. Whether Mandeville himself ultimately accepted the concept of transcendent principles of morality, he clearly maintained that men cannot realize them in terrestrial history. He left undiscussed whether they could attain to them in a future life after death. Human history appeared to him to be an affair more of impulses and desires. Reason is the servant of desires. All are rooted in self-love. Even the 'sociableness' of man arises from the 'multiplicity of his desires' and 'the continual opposition he meets with in his endeavours to gratify them'. 'Hunger, thirst, and nakedness are the first tyrants that force us to stir: afterwards, our pride, sloth, sensuality, and fickleness are the great patrons that promote all arts and sciences, trades, handicrafts and callings; while the great taskmasters, necessity, avarice, envy and ambition, each in the class that belongs to him, keep the members of society to their labour and make them all submit, most of them cheerfully, to the drudgery of their station, kings and princes not excepted.'

With a wealth of illustration, Mandeville showed that the general welfare was benefited by some conduct contrary to the supposed absolute principles of virtue. The women who live by the vice of prostitution are a prevention of others being dishonoured. Without prostitutes 'the chastity of women of honour' would 'be daily exposed to public violence'. He challenged the 'received notion' that luxury is destructive of social and individual welfare. By luxury he meant anything beyond what is necessary for self-preservation. He asked where luxury could be supposed to begin, if the line were not so drawn. He rebutted the charge that luxury leads to corruption and to the enervation of peoples, maintaining that these are due to 'mal-administration' and 'bad politics'. Mandeville evidently thought of history in terms of an ever-increasing richness of life in contrast with asceticism. Avarice involves industry and contributes eventually to that increase. Every vice leads indirectly to something for the public good. But vice must be kept within limits: beyond them it becomes 'crime' detrimental to society. In other words, Mandeville gave dominance to social virtues. What are to be called 'vices' and 'virtues' depends on the conditions of time and place. The chief effects of Mandeville's work, as regards history, were in its emphasis on desires as contrasted with reason and in its concentration on the possible richness of terrestrial history contrasted with the asceticism of a rigorist morality. Dr Kaye said that 'future events followed the trend foreshadowed' by Mandeville's book.

David Hume (1711-1776) wrote a history of England, but in the present sense of the term is not regarded as a scientific historian. As a philosopher he joined with those who rejected Hobbes's view of human nature as inherently egoistic, maintaining that men in general have 'sympathy' with others. On the basis of natural sentiment they get satisfaction in social co-operation in history. The scepticism he expounded may have been essentially an indication of the position that one *should* reach accepting the previous views of Locke and Berkeley. As an eighteenth century thinker he was important as challenging the dominant belief in the efficacy of reason to give solutions to the problems of human life. Much of his writings suggests his acceptance of the attitudes of 'commonsense'. Though he showed that the arguments of Rational Theology provided no proof of the existence of God, his writings suggest that he held vaguely to Theism. His interests became less philosophically speculative and more historical. Thus, in his *Natural History of Religion* (1759) he traced (with the information then available) the place of religion in history. Nevertheless his attitude to history was empirical. Even his view of religion implied nothing of a significant relation of men to a transcendent reality. He acknowledged something 'secret and silent' in religion, seldom coming 'under the cognizance of history' but otherwise described its 'proper office' 'to reform men's lives, to purify their hearts, to enforce all moral duties, and to secure obedience to the laws and civil magistrate. In a brief essay, *Of the Study of History*, he insisted first on it as an 'agreeable entertainment' more interesting than fiction. In this he revealed his attitude to history as actual: 'human activity, in its infancy making its first faint essays towards the arts and sciences; ... the policy of government and the civility of conversation refining by degrees, and everything that is ornamental to human life advancing towards its perfection'. In history, one observes 'the rise, progress, declensions and final extinction of the most flourishing empires; the virtues which contributed to their greatness and the vices which drew on their ruin'. The study of history, as it were, 'extends' a man's life, in itself so brief: 'A man acquainted with history may, in some respect, be said to have lived from the beginning of the world . . .' History has to do with the actual, and Hume was convinced that the ethical dominates in it. Historians, he wrote, 'almost without exception' have been 'the true friends of virtue'. With their speculations some philosophers 'deny the reality of all moral distinctions'. Even Machiavelli, who, when talking was a politician 'considering poisoning, assassination and perjury as lawful arts of power', as a historian showed a 'keen indignation against vice'. History 'places objects in their true point of view'. Hume was convinced that in it the differences of vice and virtue are fundamental.

Adam Smith (1723-1790) made much use of history as

empirical evidence of the validity of the views he expounded in *The Wealth of Nations* (1776). He was not concerned with the whole meaning of history, but with the economic. The importance of the economic in history needs no discussion. Though Smith's views do not dominate economics today they are still basically held by some politicians and represent one side of a conflict in contemporary history. For a period they held sway in England and the United States. In his earlier volume, *The Theory of Moral Sentiments* (1759), Smith insisted on the social factor in morality. Yet, though man can 'subsist only in society', he even then asserted that 'every man is by nature first and principally recommended to his own ends'. In *The Wealth of Nations* he placed 'self-interest' definitely in the forefront. A man cannot expect help from others 'from their benevolence only'. 'He will be more likely to prevail if he can interest their self-love in his favour . . .' 'Every individual is continually exerting himself to find out the most advantageous employment for whatever capital he can command. It is his own advantage indeed, and not that of society which he has in view.' But, he goes on, 'the study of his own advantage naturally, or rather necessarily, leads him to prefer that employment which is most advantageous to society'. He believed that there is a natural identity of public and private interests and that social welfare would be best served by each pursuing his own interests. He did not verify his belief, resting it rather on faith in 'the invisible hand' (? God) ruling history. The course of industrial history has surely given grounds to doubt the truth of this belief. He contended that there is very little difference in the natural talents of men. The differences are mainly due to environment. 'The difference between the most dissimilar characters, between a philosopher and a common street porter, for example, seems to arise not so much from nature as from habit, custom and education.' Smith treated the wealth of nations as dependent on labour, especially with the divisions of labour, rather than on natural resources, to which he gave inadequate attention. Though he acknowledged some exceptions, labour must be without governmental or other restrictions. It is to be pursued with 'natural liberty'. 'The natural effort of every individual to better his own conditions, when suffered to exert itself with freedom and security, is so powerful a principle, that it is alone and without any assistance, not only capable of carrying on the society to wealth and prosperity, but of surmounting a hundred impertinent obstructions with which the folly of human laws too often encumbers its operations.' Most references to the 'individualism' of the eighteenth century are to this 'economic man' of self-interest.

V

In contrast with the predominantly humanistic French conceptions of history, a religious view was again formulated by the German, Lessing (1729-1781) in *Education of the Human Race* (1780). History is a process of education of the human race towards the knowledge of God. In conformity with eighteenth century rationalism, Lessing agreed that revelation gives nothing that could not be acquired by the exercise of reason. However, by revelation the knowledge of God has come and comes earlier and more easily. The teacher is God, who has revealed His nature to mankind at different levels according to men's capacities to comprehend it. As the chief purpose of human life is essentially personal and religious rather than social civilization, the most important aspects of history are in the series of divine revelations in the sequence of religions. As this education of the individual is not completed in one life on earth, the full significance of his history cannot be found in such. It extends beyond, either in a succession of lives on earth, or in some other world or worlds. In the final sentence of his treatise, Lessing asked: 'Is not the whole of eternity mine?'

Herder (1744-1803) modestly called his work: *Ideas towards a Philosophy of the History of Man* (1784-1791), but it came to be regarded as a pioneer study. He remarked that because they can perceive no plan in history, some 'peremptorily deny the existence of one'. Considering that everything in history is transient, some have recurring doubts concerning mankind, as though 'chained to an Ixion's wheel, to the stone of Sisyphus, and condemned to the prospect of a Tantalus'. In opposition to these, he attempted to describe history as an onward march, a sequence to those processes of the physical world of Nature which in stages have led up to man. Man, the culmination of the physical development, is also the beginning of another, of a mental order. Though man is, as it were, a 'link between two worlds', the life of mankind is to be considered part of the universal order which includes Nature. That is what he meant in saying: 'The whole history of mankind is a pure natural history of human powers, actions and propensities, modified by time and place.' 'Every phenomenon in history is a natural production.' Recognizing the influence of climate and the physical environment, though not as all-controlling, he developed the conception of 'national character'. The physical diversities of the earth have helped in the development of different 'national characters'. Each nation 'bears in itself the standard of its perfection, totally independent of all comparison with that of others'. The national character influences all the history of a nation, it is 'unequivocably displayed in all their operations on earth'. Nations have sometimes exaggerated different sides of human civilization, but in the course of history may tend to supplement one another 'till at length a certain symmetry takes place in the whole'.

Herder's use of the idea of 'national character' has sometimes led to a misrepresentation, as though he stood for a solely sociological interpretation of history. Asserting that men are 'born for society', he nevertheless insisted that 'the whole species live solely' in 'the chain of individuals'. 'The whole consists of individual members.' 'No individual can suppose himself to exist for the sake of another or posterity.'[1] Happiness is an 'individual good'. Apart from the biological group of the family, all other forms of social organization are dependent on the conduct of men. History is the set of processes in which mankind, with its freedom of choice, strives to realize its own capacities and powers. In this there is a development of and a progressive triumph of reason, together with an ever closer approximation to ideal justice. In the course of time the destructive tendencies decrease and give

---

[1] His position, as understood from the whole work, suggests that 'only' should be understood before 'for the sake of'.

place to the preservation and constructive. Education and tradition are essential factors, but there must be some breaking away from tradition which may become 'the narcotic of the mind, as well to nations and sects as to individuals'. Though his aim was to describe the nature of human life on earth, Herder did not hold that alone to give complete understanding of history. Rejecting as unjust that an earlier generation should suffer simply for the welfare of a later one, he insisted on belief in immortality. 'The history of the human species, with what it has attempted, and what has befallen it, the exertions it has made and revolutions it has undergone', sufficiently prove 'that the earth' is but 'a place of exercise and trial for the powers of our hearts and minds'. He frequently referred to God as the designer and ultimate cause of Nature with mankind as its final purpose. His exposition, otherwise leaving God out of the picture, was allied by some with the humanistic accounts of history.

Some pertinent criticism of Herder was made by Edgar Quinet (1803-1875) who translated his work into French. He charged him with being too Naturalistic, exaggerating the power of Nature over man. There is something distinctive in history, in which men sometimes use Nature and sometimes fight against it. This is seen especially in the lives of individuals. The wills of individuals are always operative in history and no account of history is satisfactory which does not give them full recognition. They are central in all human history. Individuals strive for freedom and the ideals of human personality. In this, though there have been backward eddies they have advanced in history. Nations and civilizations endeavour to express dominant ideas; they decline more frequently through faith in false ideas than from external aggression.

Though from the times of Italian Humanism and of Francis Bacon there was increasing concern with the secular values of history, most of the writers previously considered in this chapter gave at least a formal recognition of religion. But the Deists of the seventeenth and eighteenth centuries placed emphasis on religion in history. They contended that throughout history men had had a 'natural' religion. Discarding

Christological doctrines they were pioneers of the wider view of history described at the end of our previous chapter. The impression has often been given that the Deists believed that God created the world but thereafter remained so aloof from it that He was unconcerned with human history. That view was certainly not held by the more eminent exponents of Deism. This may be illustrated from the *De Veritate* (1624) of Lord Herbert of Cherbury (1581-1648), who has been called the father of Deism. He maintained that among all men, in all times and places, there were 'Common Notions' underlying a universal 'natural' religion, involving relations between God and men. The five fundamental Common Notions of this religion, as a persistent constituent of history, imply the following beliefs: There is a Supreme God, 'blessed', 'the end to which all things move', 'the cause of all things in so far as they are good'. Universal Providence is manifested in Nature, but also 'we are bound to assume a Special Providence' . . . 'from the universal testimony of the sense of divine assistance in times of distress'. God is eternal, wise and good. 'Experience and history bear evidence at every point that the world is ruled under His Providence with absolute justice.' Religion cannot be based on historical records which can give only probability. But history may give examples of the truths known through reason. Thus, in it, we shall find evidence of 'the laws of Divine Providence, particular and general'. The second Common Notion is that God is to be worshipped. The third that the most important part of religion is 'Virtue with Piety', from which 'springs true hope', from that 'true Faith', from that 'true Love' and from that 'true Joy, Blessedness'. The fourth that 'vices and crimes' must 'be expiated by repentance'; and the fifth that there is 'reward or punishment after this life'. He maintained that that is the religion of the only truly 'catholic' or universal church. It comprehends all places and all men, and not just 'a single period of history'. The goal of history is 'eternal blessedness'. 'Some advance is granted in this life, and this encourages us with the promise of a better life whose nature we mystically strive to penetrate.' Eternal blessedness is 'possible'. But as thought of the future only gives us 'possibilities', our confidence with reference to it is 'genuine faith in God'. Herbert ardently defended belief in immortality. As the child in the mother's body is eventually born and becomes conscious of this world, so man may pass from this to another world. 'What embryo has ever succeeded in examining itself, what mature man will ever do so?'

The Deists did not all deny revelation. However, in so far as what was represented as revelation was something from the past it was maintained (as by Lord Herbert) that one could talk at most of probability. But the test of revelation must ultimately be its conformity with the Common Notions of natural religion. So judged, the alleged revelations were either a sort of republication of these universally recognized truths—and thus in a way superfluous—or in conflict with them—and so to be rejected. That was the contention of Matthew Tindal's *Christianity as Old as the Creation, or the Gospel a Republication of the Religion of Nature* (1730). God has given all men the possibility of knowledge of true religion. 'If God's ways are equal,' wrote Tindal, 'and He has at one time as well as another, the same goodness for the sons of men in relation to their eternal happiness, how can we suppose He left all mankind for so many ages and the greatest part, in a most miserable state of doubt and uncertainty about the pardon of sin and consequently about the possibility of any man's being saved?' With this attitude the Deists could not accept the idea that the historical events alleged by the theologians of traditional Christianity—the Incarnation, Redemption by Jesus's death on the Cross, and his Resurrection—had any fundamental relation to the significance of history. They rarely, if ever, directly discussed them, but that they considered them of no importance is clear in their ignoring them. Tindal criticized the Biblical story of the 'Fall' of Adam and the idea of 'original sin' based on it, with which the specific traditional Christian view of redemption by particular events is related. He questioned whether those events had produced the results they were supposed to have done. He asked: 'What impartial man . . . though ever so well versed in Church history, can, from the conduct of Christians, find that they are arrived at any higher state of perfection than the rest of mankind, who are supposed to continue in their degeneracy and corruption?' History does not confirm the claim made for the special revelation affirmed in ecclesiastical Christianity. With their belief in the goodness of God, the Deists insisted that what was necessary for human happiness could be known by all men in all times and places. That knowledge could not be regarded as having been withheld from man until the time of the (alleged) Christian revelation. God has been in relation with men throughout all history adequately for their good life. It has been through their own fault (with their freedom of will, as urged particularly by Herbert) if they have disregarded the moral and religious aspects of their nature which God had given them.

It was on account of its treatment of Christianity, in chapters xv and xvi of Volume I, that *The Decline and Fall of the Roman Empire* (1776-1788) by Edward Gibbon (1737-1794) aroused most discussion. There have been very divergent judgments on Gibbon as a historian. Some have considered him to be the greatest of English historians. His work is truly impressive in the vastness of its canvas and the continuity of its survey for so long a period. He studied history without preconceptions of superhuman influences in it. Probably with a wish to avoid controversy with Christian dogmatists, he described his account of Christianity—specifically its expansion in the Roman empire—as dealing with 'secondary causes'. He did not deny that there were supernatural causes as primary. Yet it is hardly open to question that he himself had no faith that there were any, though he wrote: 'the theologian may indulge the pleasing task of describing Religion as she descended from Heaven arrayed in her native purity'. He endeavoured to survey the facts of the expansion of Christianity as ordinary historical phenomena. He maintained that it was with the aid of 'exclusive zeal, the immediate expectation of another world, the claim of miracles, the practice of rigid virtue, and the constitution of the primitive church that Christianity spread itself with so much success in the Roman empire'. At the end of the xvith chapter, in which he reviewed the early persecutions of Christians, he wrote that 'a melancholy truth . . . obtrudes itself on the reluctant mind, that even admitting . . . all that history has recorded, or devotion has feigned, on the subject of martyrdom, it must be acknowledged that the Christians in the course of their intestine dissensions have inflicted far greater severities on each other than they experienced from the zeal of the infidels'. In his opinion life had been better in one part of Roman history than at any time in the Christian era. 'If a man were called to fix the period in the history of the world during which the conditions of the human race were most happy and prosperous, he would, without hesitation, name that which elapsed from the death of Domitian to the accession of Commodus. The vast extent of the Roman empire was governed by absolute power under the guidance of virtue and wisdom.' Though he pointed to the rise of the modern world on the ruins of the ancient, his view of history was more pessimistic than otherwise. History 'is little more than the crimes, follies and misfortunes of mankind'. Every page of history 'has been stained with civil blood' 'from the ardour of contention, the pride of victory, the despair of success, the memory of past injustice and the fear of future dangers' which 'all contribute to inflame the mind and to silence the voice of pity'.

Gibbon's German contemporary, the philosopher Immanuel Kant (1724-1804), had no faith in Christological doctrines. Jesus was simply a man who may be honoured as the highest representative of the ideal of the good. It is not his historical person but the ideal of the good that is significant for religion. But Kant was apparently devoid of mystical love of God, though his awe was aroused by 'the starry heavens above' and 'the voice of conscience within'. His philosophical works were almost entirely formal and abstract and did not do justice to the empirical in any sphere of life. He failed to appreciate adequately the details of the religious, moral and aesthetic aspects of history and paid little attention to its events and great men. He devoted no major work to philosophy of history, but some of his fundamental concepts influenced later thought concerning it. His ethical doctrines were of especial importance in their opposition to any type of view that morality is merely relative, a product of changing social conditions in history. In his emphasis on the autonomy of the moral, that it is to be willed by the individual for its own sake, he maintained the reality of spiritual freedom. The central meaning of the individual's history is to be sought in moral character. Each person is to treat himself and others as of intrinsic worth. All together are to form a 'realm of ends'. The moral is universal, rational, unconditional, and social. In his defence of the postulate of immortality, he implied that no adequate understanding of human life can be attained with reference solely to earthly existence. The significance of the history of the individual extends beyond this life. But in his comparatively little known essay entitled *The Idea of a Universal History on a Cosmo-political Plan*, he objected to looking for a purpose 'only in another world'. Though rejecting the ecclesiastical doctrine of 'original sin', Kant nevertheless believed that there is something radically evil in human nature. Perhaps it was in accordance with that belief that he described the actions of history as so often arousing 'a certain degree of disgust'. For 'with all the occasional indications of wisdom scattered here and there, we cannot but perceive the whole sum of these actions to be a web of folly, childish vanity, or even of childish wickedness and spirit of destruction'. In contrast with these actions, he maintained that though metaphysically the freedom of the human will may be admitted, giving rise to particular contingencies, 'individuals and even whole peoples are little aware that men, concerned with their own purpose according to their own views, often in opposition to one another, are unconsciously following the guidance of and working to promote a natural purpose unrecognized by themselves, which, even if they recognized, would be little regarded by them'. In general he ascribed this dominant purpose or plan to 'Nature', but in one place he wrote: 'or rather of Providence'. It is the task of a philosophy of history to try to find a clue to this plan. Apart from what is given mechanically in Nature, or is due to instinct, all that man attains in history, all that otherwise makes for his 'happiness or perfection' is 'what he has created for himself'. Progress in history depends on the fact of instabilities and tensions. While feeling their gregariousness, individuals are not in complete harmony. Man 'wishes for concord', but 'Nature knows better what is good for man as a species and she ordains discord' as that through which he will be led to higher levels. Man 'would live at ease and passive content, but Nature wills that he shall abandon his indolence and inactive complacency for labours and hardships, in order that he may devise remedies to raise himself intelligently above them'. The values of civilization are due to individuals, but they can be fully attained and harmony reached only in world-wide social conditions. So, the significance of terrestrial history, 'the final purpose of Nature with regard to man', viz. 'the development of all his tendencies' requires the establishment of 'a universal civil society founded on the empire of political justice'. To achieve this is the central task of historical activity. In the short treatise *To Perpetual Peace*, Kant outlined some requirements for 'a federal league of nations', which he suggested in the earlier essay referred to above. At the basis of his thought in this connection is the fundamental that ethical right is not conditional nor a matter of expediency but an imperative of universal reason.

There are many obscurities and some radical inconsistencies in Kant's works. In the nineteenth century, forms of thought as different as those he had tried to co-ordinate were claimed to be derived from his philosophy. Kant refused to accept Idealists such as Fichte, Schelling and Hegel as his philosophical off-spring. Schopenhauer, Herbart, and Fries, despite their great differences, professed to follow Kant. With the breakdown of Classical German Idealism, in the middle of the century, there was a movement 'Back to Kant'. In the Heidelberg School of this Neo-Kantianism there were important studies relative to history.[1] The name 'Critical' given to Kant's philosophy indicated the character of his thought. But it suggested nothing of the nature of reality, as do the terms 'materialistic' and 'idealistic' used by others. Kant's philosophy involved an unavowed Dualism. If he had explicitly acknowledged a Dualism of matter and mind, he might have contributed to our knowledge of their differentiation and of their relations and helped to reconcile forms of thought that through one-sided exaggeration led to conflicts as to the nature

[1] See below, Chapter IX, especially on Heinrich Rickert.

of history. He failed to do that, and the oppositions known in the eighteenth century between empiricism and rationalism have continued through the nineteenth century and into the twentieth in the forms discussed in our chapters VII and VIII.

VI

But in the last half of the eighteenth century and the early years of the nineteenth there were events affecting man's views of history far more than the philosophy of Kant could ever do: the American and the French revolutions. Attitudes involved in these were expressed in writings by Thomas Paine (1737-1809) who with residence in America and in France was associated with both. Paine made no appeal to technical philosophy or to erudition but relied on ordinary reason and common sense. His influence must have been considerable, for he reported that the demand for his first publication, *Common Sense* (1776), ran to not less than one hundred thousand copies. That work was concerned solely with maintaining that separation of the American colonies from Britain was historically inevitable and their independence a demand of common sense. It was said that Washington was opposed to independence until he read Paine.

There were probably many in the eighteenth century who disbelieved the doctrines on which the Christian conception of history rests, but comparatively few who explicitly rejected them in published writings. Paine has some significance in having done that in *The Age of Reason*, published in two parts in 1794 and 1796 respectively. He wrote that work with the conviction that traditional Christianity, especially with the relation of the churches to the political governments, had been a means of exploitation of the masses. His main attack was against what he took to be the foundation of the whole system of Christianity: the authority of the Old and the New Testaments as the Word of God, a divine revelation. On the basis of internal evidence he challenged the historical accuracy of the traditional views of the authorship of many of the books. His essential contention was that there is no historical authority for the claims made for the Bible. He emphasized 'the obscene stories', 'the cruel and tortuous executions' and 'the unrelenting vindictiveness' recorded in the Old Testament, and with amazingly inadequate attention to its other contents, declared its conception of God unacceptable. More important for our purpose was Paine's unequivocal opposition to the doctrines basic for the traditional Christian account of history: of original sin, of divine incarnation and redemption. The doctrines of 'the fall of man', 'of Jesus Christ being the Son of God and of his dying to appease the wrath of God, and of salvation by that strange means, are all fabulous inventions'. There are no adequate historical bases for the Christological teachings of the Church: they are a form of mythology with unworthy ideas of God. Paine was not antagonistic to religion: every religion is good which teaches men to be good. But in contrast with the 'fabulous theology' of Christianity, he pointed to the 'true theology' obtained by knowledge of God's creation. 'The Word of God is the creation we behold and it is in *this word*, which no human invention can counterfeit or alter, that God speaketh universally to man.' Do we want to contemplate His power, His wisdom, His munificence, His mercy? We see them 'in the immensity of creation', 'in the unchangeable order by which the incomprehensible whole is governed', 'in the abundance with which He fills the earth', an abundance not withheld 'even from the unthankful'. 'The first act of man, when he looked around and saw himself a creature which he did not make and a world furnished for his reception, must have been devotion.' Emancipated from traditional dogmas, Paine described Jesus as 'a virtuous and amiable man. The morality that he preached and practised was of the most benevolent kind; and though similar systems had been preached by Confucius and some of the Greek philosophers many years before, and by many good men in all ages, it has not been exceeded by any'.

Paine had reached those convictions as a young man and they were a background for his activities. Though he did not explicitly say it, there is an implication that moral principles are an accordance with the divine as revealed in creation. He insisted that political government should conform with moral principles as applied by common sense. He presented that view in *The Rights of Man*, published in two parts in 1791 and 1792 respectively. We need not concern ourselves with its criticisms of Edmund Burke's *Reflections on the French Revolution* (1790) and of government shared by a hereditary monarch and peerage. Paine's main purpose was to state and defend the rights of man in terms of common sense. He did not depend on the authority of any political philosopher. He considered these rights as providing the fundamental motive of the American and French revolutions—whatever immediately and superficially may have appeared to be their motives. He contended that those revolutions had been a main turning point in history because they were revolutions of *peoples* in contrast with earlier ones that had solely affected ruling minorities. 'The revolutions which formerly took place in the world had nothing in them that interested the bulk of mankind.' The first form of government was by priestcraft, the second by conquerors, and the third is, or is to be, by reason.

Paine accepted the idea—shared by most American and French revolutionists—that man's rights are inherent in him as divinely created. 'Every child born into the world must be considered as deriving its existence from God.' These natural rights are universal and permanent. Civil rights, which a man has as a member of a political group, are ultimately for the protection of natural rights and may be changed according to circumstances. The American Declaration of Independence and the Declaration of the Rights of Man by the national assembly in France contain affirmations of these rights. The statements differ. In the conclusion of part I, Paine used the French form. He claimed that the revolutions were justified by 'principles as universal as truth and the existence of man, combining moral with political happiness and prosperity. (i) Men are born equal, and always continue free and equal in respect to their rights. Civil distinctions, therefore, can be founded only on public utility. (ii) The end of all political associations is the preservation of the natural and imprescriptable rights of man, and these rights are liberty, security, and resistance of oppression.' As is well known, the American Declaration gives them as life, liberty, and the pursuit of happiness. Paine was convinced of the possibility, even the probability, of progress. 'Man always has it in his power to improve circumstances'; but he did not over estimate the part played by political government. 'Formal government makes but a small part of civilized life.' Safety and prosperity depend more on the particular activities of individuals and their cooperation in established usages. Thus he declared that, apart from what flows immediately from moral principles, 'the greatest approach to universal civilization' is through commerce.

The fundamental ideas of the American and French revolutions have continued to affect conceptions of history up to the present. They have been ever more widely applied in different countries, changing the nature of their histories. But they have not been universally adhered to: the National Socialist government of Germany and the Fascist government of Italy were in contradiction with them, as is the present Communist government in Russia. The thought of the eighteenth century had given due consideration to the individual as such. Paine's contentions were basically with reference to the individual. For National Socialism, Fascism, and Communism as so far actualized, individuals are regarded as mostly pawns in the drama of history.

From the time of the Renaissance to the end of the eighteenth century there were two fundamental changes with regard to history. There was a great increase in the meaningful contents of actual history, and a vast broadening of the scope of history as scientific record. For most thinkers not subject to ecclesiastical commitments there was an emancipation from the Christological view of history.

CHAPTER VII

IDEALIST TREATMENTS OF HISTORY IN THE NINETEENTH CENTURY AND AFTER

I

IN the eighteenth century there was an increasing tendency towards empirical interpretations of history, with God as traditionally conceived as Providence relegated to the background, entirely ignored, or explicitly denied. In the nineteenth century that type of interpretation was challenged by Idealist philosophies which substituted for the traditional idea of God the conception of a spiritual Absolute. Apart from the continued Christian views of history, there have been in the nineteenth century and since two opposing interpretations of history. Taking the terms in a broad sense these may be described as Idealist and Naturalist. Writing in 1817, Frederick Ancillon (1766-1837) in a short but noteworthy essay on 'The Philosophy of History' gave definite recognition of the distinction between these two ways of looking at history. He called the former 'the metaphysical point of view' and the latter 'the political' chiefly the empirical and social. The 'metaphysical' is 'sterile, born in the field of abstractions'. It starts with the being of God or the Absolute as the eternal self-existent. Its concept of Nature is of a realm of necessity with inevitable uniform processes. As mind man has liberty, 'the power to act in conformity with reason'—the faculty by which he grasps eternal, universal, divine ideas which he takes as directive. Man is regarded as 'perfectible'. An essential condition for human development towards perfection is the constant conflict between 'necessity' and 'liberty', external and internal, of Nature and man, of man with his fellows, of man with himself, 'The history of the human race, and of its great divisions, peoples, is occupied principally with the struggle against Nature and human passions, of which the physical world is the stage.' 'The inner struggle that occurs in the heart of each individual is the secret of the man and of God. It is not properly within the province of history, which cannot know the details and can speak of it only so far as it is necessary for the explanation of the former' (i.e. the external struggle). But 'perfectibility' points onward to another place and time than those of earth. Urging that the idea of progressive perfectibility and of unlimited development is contradicted by the actual history of peoples, Ancillon passed to a description of the 'political point of view'. This keeps to the facts, explains effects by causes, and does not lose itself in ideas of eternity. It 'considers peoples as organized beings subject in life and in death to invariable laws, and approaches civil history from natural history'. It does not find 'progress to perfection in its entirety, in all its bearings'. 'One sees that the body politic has its infancy, its youth, its maturity, and its old age, and that the frame always presents a picture of the same scope and the same nature.' Sooner or later it will die. 'There is a necessity in things over which liberty never triumphs; there is a liberty in man which can triumph over an apparent necessity, which only appears such to common monds. One should exaggerate neither the one nor the other.' While it is clear that Ancillon held this 'political' point of view to be 'preferable' and to have 'practical' advantages, he wrote in his Preface that 'there is no question of proscription of the metaphysical'. Even while Ancillon was writing, in Germany itself, the most elaborate metaphysical Idealist philosophy in modern history was being formulated with the fundamental idea that human life (and thus history) is to be understood only within Reality as a whole, involving something more than the transitory experiences of the mundane. The most impressive and influential exponents of this philosophy were K. C. F. Krause (1781-1832); J. G. Fichte (1762-1814), F. W. J. Schelling (1775-1854) and G. W. F. Hegel (1770-1831).

Krause's lectures, entitled *The pure, that is, general Doc-*

trine of Life and Philosophy of History (published posthumously in 1848) might well be judged the first systematic philosophy of history. Though a contemporary of the others in the Classical German Idealist group, he meant to keep closer to traditional Theism both in his ideas and in his terminology. He used the term 'God' instead of 'The Absolute', yet in accord with the concept of the Absolute described God as the Whole and as such Perfect. Calling his view 'Panentheism', he maintained that all is *in* God. The world is not God, but is in God, who is more than it. The world, with all that is in it, is finite: God is infinite. As the finite is within the infinite, the meaning of human history involves the relation of man to the infinite. Man is to be understood primarily not by consideration of his finite being but from the concept of the infinite deity. In his history on earth and beyond man strives to become 'godlike', realizing in his life goodness, wisdom, beauty, and holiness. In the detailed development of his views, Krause insisted on important implications. All time being within God, every portion of it has some intrinsic significance. The time of childhood is not merely for preparation for youth, nor youth for maturity. To hold, as many have done, that man's existence on earth is simply preparatory to a life beyond is 'to mistake the worth of this life'. Expressed otherwise, the meaning of history is at least partly within it as it goes along. So again, Nature being within God, man's body as a part of it is to be perfected and enjoyed. 'Each finite being can perfect its life only in and through the whole of life.' Though Nature has its own intrinsic meaning and is not merely instrumental for human minds, the spiritual life of man is developed in part in relation with it. Krause struggled hard with the problem of evil. Conceptually in agreement with most Idealists of his time he described it as essentially privative, the lack of something. As such it is characteristic of the finite beings in God but not of God as infinite. However, he felt the need of acknowledging evil positively in history as due to the wrong exercise of human will. God helps in the good: He permits but does not help in the evil. Admittedly on faith in God's perfect goodness, Krause maintained that He turns evil towards the

IDEALIST TREATMENTS

realization of greater good by what is called forth to overcome evil. Actual history includes constant spiritual rebirth and renewal. The history of the individual, as of mankind, may be considered in three stages: 1. of initial simple unity; 2. of variety in the multifold strivings for values; and 3. of harmony in which, with comprehensive worth, unity is again achieved. Mankind is at present in the second stage. In the latter half of the nineteenth century, with the reaction against the more definite forms of Absolute Idealism, some thinkers returned to positions similar to Krause's.[1]

An analogous contemporary treatment of history was given by the Belgian, J. J. Altmeyer's (1804-1877) *Course on the Philosophy of History*, which appeared in 1840, before Krause's volume. Philosophy of history is based on history 'as a science of facts' spatial and temporal, and on 'pure ideas', eternally immutable. God is in direct union with every individual and intervenes in his life. Altmeyer asserted that facts prove divine intervention in the great turning points of history. 'When humanity, breathless and exhausted, arrives at the end of one of its evolutions, God gives it new wings and projects it along new ways.' Man is in the image of God, and in conformity with this nature, desires and strives for perfection. Thanks to this nature, there is nothing which man cannot 'comprehend with his intellect'; nothing which he cannot 'embrace with his love'; nothing upon which he cannot exercise 'the sovereignty of his will'. Like Krause, Altmeyer gave divergent views concerning evil. Though he described it as negative, he still insisted that among men in history it is largely due to wrong use of free will. The aim and hope of humanity lies in the admission of 'one God and one Fatherland for all', with the love of mankind the only law.

Absolute Idealism in the writings of F. W. Schelling was mainly a discussion of concepts. It is sometimes suggested that a distinction must be made between his earlier and his later thought, but in neither did he reach a significant interpretation of history covering all its details. Except (and that very rarely) in the work of an occasional pantheistically inclined

---

[1] As e.g. Herman Lotze. Krause taught at Göttingen where Lotze developed his own philosophy.

German theologian, his influence has ceased. He gave at least the appearance of regarding the evils of history as within the Absolute in a manner which Krause tried to avoid. Nature and history are the 'evolution', the self-manifestation, of the organic Whole, the Absolute Spirit. The finite in all its forms is the symbol of the infinite, the temporal of the eternal.

J. G. Fichte, keeping closer to the ethical side of Kant's thought, conceived the Absolute essential as moral order. By his fundamental concept of the 'Ego', he meant (as he constantly insisted) not the individual 'I' but the Absolute. Individual finite spirits are the modes in which the infinite life expresses itself. Though according to this each has his unique position in history, in his Berlin lectures on *The Way towards the Blessed Life*, Fichte declared: 'He who still has a self—in him assuredly there is nothing good.' In a lecture on *The Idea of Universal History*, he said that 'this earthly life with all its subordinate divisions may be deduced from the fundamental idea of the eternal life already accessible to us here and now'. Discussing *The Absolute Vocation of Man*, he described 'perfection' as the highest 'unattainable end of man' and 'eternal perfecting his vocation'. 'I know assuredly in every moment of my life what I ought to do and this is my whole vocation so far as it depends on me.' But 'my entire complete vocation I cannot comprehend: what I shall be hereafter transcends all my thoughts'. However, 'the Eternal Will will dispose all for the best'. 'At last all must arrive at the sure haven of eternal peace and blessedness.' Fichte admitted that his mode of thought could never be the result of the mere observation of the world. Indeed, he argued that our first maxim is to be: 'Not to accept apparent existence in time as itself true and real, but to assume a higher existence beyond it.' From Fichte's standpoint, the irrational phenomena of actual history remain an insoluble riddle. In his *Addresses to the German Nation*, Fichte endeavoured to arouse Germans to their part in history, saying that to them 'the germs of human perfection are especially committed'. Urging that 'a nation becomes a nation through war and through a common struggle', he yet proclaimed: 'Yours is the greater destiny—to found an empire on mind and reason—to destroy the

IDEALIST TREATMENTS

dominion of rude physical power as the ruler of the world.'

Even though many of its conceptions be rejected, the philosophy of G. F. W. Hegel has important implications for philosophy of history and it has been of greater influence in the nineteenth century and since than any other Idealist philosophy. Hegel's treatment of history in his posthumously published *Lectures on the Philosophy of History* (1837; 1840) was an application of the ideas and principles of his general philosophy arrived at by logical reflection rather than from empirical consideration of Nature or history. Though he said that 'It is only an inference from the history of the world that its development had been a rational process', his actual procedure accords with his other statement: 'The only thought which philosophy brings with it to the contemplation of history is the simple conception of reason . . .' So far, perhaps, that must be agreed by all engaged in philosophy or science. But Hegel went further: '. . . that reason is the sovereign of the world, that the history of the world therefore presents us with a rational process'. His surveys of the Orient and the Occident were so composed to illustrate this conception which he brought to the study of their history. He paid attention to what he wanted to find, for 'to him who looks upon the world rationally, the world in its turn, presents a rational aspect'. Nature, the stage of universal history, is an embodiment of Reason, though its influences (geographic, climatic, etc.) do not dominate history. But Hegel's notion of 'development', important for his treatment of history, was ambiguous. For Spirit, as the Absolute, is eternal: 'with it there is no past, no future, but an essential now'. Yet, in order to treat of history, he had to maintain that 'the life of the ever-present Spirit is a circle of progressive embodiments'. His ultimate position may be best stated in his own words: 'What Spirit really strives for is the realization of its Ideal being; but in doing so, it hides that goal from its own vision, and is proud and well-satisfied in this alienation from it.' With that it is easy to understand that the most serious criticisms of Hegelianism as regards human history have been directed against the implications of this Absolutism. If the historical is only the *appearance* of the development of the Absolute

Spirit, all temporal processes are in some sense unreal. If the real is the rational, the oppositions and conflicts in history might well be called 'a bloodless strife of categories'.

The constructive influence of Hegelianism on theories of history have been chiefly through its important implication that rationality is characterized in systems and not merely in abstract universals. Not repetitions of similar particulars but co-ordinated wholes, or processes towards the systemization of diverse particulars, are to be sought in history. Actual history manifests oppositions and conflicts. Hegelians have endeavoured to show that these are progressively resolved into something more comprehensive, synthesizing the factors from both sides in a historical dialectic. Much in the actual processes of history fits in with such a conception, but there are many contingencies which cannot be accommodated in Hegel's logical scheme.

Hegel thought that his survey of history justified him in describing it with reference to rational freedom. 'The history of the world is none other than the progress of the consciousness of freedom.' It is in the exercise of freedom, in choice, that man is aware of his spiritual being. The destiny of man in history lies in that he knows what is good and what is evil and has ability to will either good or bad. However, freedom at a low level is caprice: its 'positive reality and completion' are in 'Law, Morality, and Government'. 'Only that will which obeys law is free.' The conditions for the realization of freedom are in society and the state. Hegel gave comparatively little attention to particular persons in history. 'In the history of the world, the individuals we have to do with are peoples, totalities that are states.' Individual persons are to realize their freedom in the state, which involves their subjectively free participation in aims transcending those of purely selfish interests. Complete spiritual freedom for any constitutent of the Whole can be only with harmony in the Whole. Objection has been rightly made to Hegel's view that the self-development of the Absolute reached its goal politically in the Prussian State of his day. But that absurdity, and others, such as the statement that 'Europe is absolutely the end of history', do not entirely negate or seriously detract

IDEALIST TREATMENTS

from his principle that through oppositions and their overcoming there is an advance to wider and wider spiritual life. Hegel recognized that religion in history is concerned not merely, or chiefly, with moral attainment in time, but is in essence an immediate relation of the finite with the infinite, the eternal. This conception of religion was in contrast both with that of the traditional ideas of Providence and with naturalistic accounts of history. Religion has the highest position in spiritual activity. 'In it, Spirit, rising above the limitations of the temporal and secular existence, becomes conscious of the Absolute Spirit, and in this consciousness of the self-existent Being renounces its individual interest.' 'It was for a while the fashion to profess admiration for the wisdom of God, as displayed in animals and plants and isolated occurrences. But if it is allowed that Providence manifests itself in such objects and forms of existence, why not also in Universal History?' He ended his whole discussion with the declaration: 'The history of the world, with all the changing scenes which its annals present, is the process of development and the realization of the Spirit—that is the true theodicy—the justification of God in history.'

Though Hegel's conception of Christianity was certainly not that of traditional theology, he said that it included a 'new principle' which was 'the axis on which the History of the World turns', and represented both the starting point and the goal of history. The Fall was man becoming conscious of himself as an individual. It is persistence in separation from God that is evil. Suffering entered history 'as an instrument for producing the unity of man with God'. The essence of Christianity is not to be found in any thought of 'Christ only as an historical bygone personality'. 'Christ—man as man—in whom the unity of God and man has appeared, has in his death and in history generally, himself presented the eternal history of Spirit—a history which every man has to accomplish in himself, in order to exist as Spirit, or to become a child of God, a citizen of his kingdom. The followers of Christ, who combine on this principle and live in the spiritual life as their aim, form the Church, which is the Kingdom of God.' The supreme significance of Christianity in history is that through it 'the Absolute Idea of God, in its true conception, attained consciousness'. In it, man understood 'his true nature, given in the specific conception of the "Son". Man, *finite*, when regarded *for himself*, is yet at the same time the Image of God and a fountain of *infinite in himself.*' Life in the State, and all that is secular, is to be with moral rectitude involved in the fundamental principle of religion.

There was a general impression throughout the nineteenth century that the Classical Idealism of Germany and the Idealisms of other countries which were derived from it were essentially optimistic. The idea of a dialectical process by which oppositions were overcome in wider syntheses conformed with the belief in human progress. But from another point of view, it could be maintained that if the present *appearance* of evils (appearances experienced at least by man) constitute something of the eternal perfection of the Absolute, they might always persist as such. The position of Absolute Idealism was thus ambiguous. By the middle of the nineteenth century, with widespread social discontents, the doctrine that history is fundamentally rational was seriously doubted and often denied. Arthur Schopenhauer (1788-1860) had lived during the early period of the dominance of Fichte, Schelling and Hegel, but it was not till the middle of the century that much attention was paid to his *The World as Will and Idea* (1818) and his many Essays. Metaphysically, Schopenhauer's position was Idealist, however, the essence of spiritual reality for him was not conscious reason but unconscious will. He had an important influence on later views in turning attention to human will in history and from the Hegelian effort to find reason overwhelmingly dominant in it, if not completely controlling it. In contrast with the theories of development and progress, he maintained: 'The true philosophy of history consists in the insight that in all these endless changes and their confusion we have always before us the same ever unchanging nature, which today acts in the same way as yesterday and always.' 'History shows on every side only the same under different forms . . . The chapters of the history of nations are at bottom only distinguished by the names and the dates, the really essential content is everywhere the same.'

Having described something of life in times of war and of peace, he asked: 'But the ultimate aim of it all: What is it?' He answered: 'To sustain ephemeral and tormented individuals through a short span of time, in the most fortunate case with endurable want and comparative freedom from pain, which however is at once attended with ennui; then the reproduction of this race and its striving.' This is the truth of individuals and their conduct: 'the excellence, the virtue, even the holiness of a few; the perversity, meanness and knavery of most; the dissolute profligacy of some'. Applying an essentially hedonistic criterion and in opposition to some Idealist views that evil is merely negative, Schopenhauer described evil as positive and good negative. Even if there is an appearance of social and intellectual progress, it is accompanied by increase in suffering. 'What history narrates is in fact only the long heavy and confused dream of humanity.' The contemplation of beauty may give some redemption though most often brief. It is futile to try to find meaning in history. Our attention should be turned from it. That, he contended, is the fundamental attitude of the greatest religions of history. The true spirit, the kernel of Christianity, as of Brahminism and Buddhism, 'is the knowledge of the vanity of earthly happiness, the complete contempt of it'. That attitude appealed to comparatively few: Schopenhauer himself conformed with it very little in practice. Whether from biological urges or spiritual aspirations, or both, most men, including the leaders of thought in the nineteenth century, continued to regard history from the standpoint of the idea of progress. The view of Schopenhauer was most often ignored. In the United States the thought of Emerson had a wide appeal for its people with their pioneer spirit. In England the virile teachings of Carlyle aroused a response quite contrary to Schopenhauer's pessimism.

II

Ralph Waldo Emerson (1803-1882) presented his Idealist conception of history not as systematic philosophy but as indicating an attitude to life. He expounded it in his *Essays*, particularly in those on History, Nature, the Over-Soul and

Self-Reliance, and in the Introduction to *Representative Men* (1850). He wrote: 'I am ashamed to see what a shallow village tale our so-called history is.' In contrast, he described history with reference to ultimate reality as one eternal universal Spirit, an 'over-soul'. Within that Spirit 'every man's particular being is contained and made one with all others'. Before Its revelations, 'Time, Space, and Nature shrink away'. 'The Soul of the Whole', 'the eternal One' is within man. He emphasized this as his dominant point of view for considering history in opening the essay *History*, with the affirmation: 'There is one mind common to all individual men. Every man is an inlet to the same and all of the same.' History is constituted of the works of this universal Mind. The Whole is represented in every part, in an atom, in a moment of time. History cannot be accounted for simply by the physical world and conscious human activity. 'I am constrained every moment to acknowledge a higher origin for events than the will I call my own.' 'The web of events' is the 'flowing robe' in which the universal soul is 'clothed'. It is present in all persons in every period of history. So-called physical Nature is not a distinctive 'substance' but a part or aspect of the spiritual whole. With an 'aboriginal push' Nature has gone on from stage to stage and forces every creature onward. 'The lover seeks in marriage his private felicity and perfection with no prospective end; and Nature hides in his happiness her own end . . . the perpetuity of the race.' But Nature seems to mock us in that it never leads to our complete satisfaction. He asked: 'Are we tickled trout and fools of Nature?' And answered: 'One look at the face of heaven and earth lays all petulance at rest and soothes us to wiser convictions . . . We are escorted on every hand through life by spiritual agents and a beneficent purpose lies in wait for us.' The enjoyment of the infinite variety of Nature is part of the significance of history. The human mind comes to love Nature as its 'home'. History is thus to be written and read in the light of these two facts: 'that the mind is One, and that Nature is its correlative'.

With insistence on the one universal Spirit, Emerson nevertheless emphasized human individuality. That emphasis was fundamental in his view of history. He had little sympathy for forms of thought giving a solely or predominantly sociological view, as the later conception of social progress in Comtean Positivism. 'Society never advances. It recedes as fast on one side as it gains on the other . . . (It) acquires new arts and loses old instincts . . . No greater men are now than ever were . . . Not in time is the race progressive.' The true test of civilization is the kind of men in general who are produced. Each individual is one more incarnation of the universal Mind. Each is unique. 'It seems as if the Deity dressed each soul which he sends into Nature in certain virtues and powers not communicable to other men, and sending it to perform one more turn through the circle of beings, wrote "Not transferable" and "Good for this trip only" on these garments of the soul.' Each of us expresses a divine idea. Though there are no 'common men', there have been outstanding, great, or representative men who have led mankind to the 'great moments' of history. 'The search after the great man is the dream of youth and the most serious occupation of mankind.' 'Mankind have in all ages attached themselves to a few persons who either by the quality of the ideas they embodied or by the largeness of their reception were entitled to the position of leaders and law-givers.' Though 'all history resolves itself very easily into the biography of a few stout and earnest persons', all individuals have their part in it.

The significance of history is not to be sought primarily in advance in time as though to a final goal. It is rather in the experience of the eternal now. Emphasis on a future life of the individual, as such, is wrong. True immortality is the experience of an infinite present. 'All that respects the individual is temporary and prospective, like the individual himself, who is ascending out of his limits into a catholic existence.' The ultimate fact is 'the resolution of all into the ever-blessed One'. Religion is the mingling of the individual soul with the universal soul. Emerson treated 'limitation' as the essence of evil. He said: 'The only sin is limitation.' Yet, though from his theoretical standpoint he treated evil as the absence of truth and virtue, he referred to many things that appear as positive evils. With such a general conception of evil, Emerson discouraged the attitude of strenuous struggle.

'There is no need of struggles . . . of the wringing of hands and the gnashing of teeth.' 'A little consideration of what takes place around us every day would show us that a higher law than that of our will regulates events; that our painful labours are unnecessary and fruitless; that only in our easy, simple, spontaneous action are we strong.'

With the organization of the masses in modern times in industry and national armies and with world-wide financial and economic relations, it is not surprising that the social aspects of history have been emphasized. But when the advances in culture have formed the central subject of attention, the importance of individuals has had to be acknowledged by historians. Though there are other ways of looking at history in his works, Thomas Carlyle (1795-1881) gave us the most forceful expression of the meaning of history as found pre-eminently in the achievements of great men. 'For, as I take it,' he said in his first lecture *On Heroes. Hero-worship and the Heroic in History* (1841), 'Universal History, the history of what man has accomplished in this world, is at the bottom the History of the Great Men who have worked here. They were the leaders of men, these great ones; the models, patterns, and in a wide sense, creators of whatever the general mass of men contrived to do or attain; all things that we see standing accomplished in the world are properly the material result, the practical realization and embodiment, of Thoughts that dwelt in the Great Men sent into the world. The soul of the whole world's history, it may justly be considered were the history of these.' 'The History of the World' is 'the Biography of Great Men'.[1]

Taking religion to be men's beliefs concerning and attitudes towards 'this mysterious Universe', their duty and destiny in it, Carlyle also maintained that in them 'the soul

---

[1] In an earlier Essay *On History* (1830) Carlyle wrote that 'History is the essence of innumerable biographies,' but in contrast with his later concentration on outstanding personalities, he drew attention to the importance of the forgotten, regarded generally as lesser ones. 'Which was the greater innovator, which the more important personage in man's history: he who first led armies over the Alps and gained the victories of Cannae and Thrasymene; or the nameless boor who first hammered out for himself an iron spade?'

IDEALIST TREATMENTS

of the history of man or nation' is to be found. 'It was the unseen and spiritual in them that determined the outward and the actual.' In history there has been an intimate relation between religion and great men. 'No nobler feeling than this of admiration for one higher than himself dwells in the breast of man. It is to this hour, and at all hours, the vivifying influence in man's life. Religions I find stand upon it . . .' The essence of religion in history, as he described it in *Sartor Resartus* (1833-1834), is the adoption in belief and practice of the Everlasting Yea, in opposition to the Everlasting No. It is the vital conviction that 'On the roaring billows of Time, thou art not engulfed, but borne aloft into the azure of Eternity. Love not Pleasure: love God. This is the Everlasting Yea wherein all contradiction is solved, wherein whoso walks and looks it is well with him.' The Everlasting No takes the universe as 'one huge immeasurable Steam-engine', and regards it as 'rolling on, in its deadly indifference to grind me limb from limb'. In short, Carlyle fought against the 'mechanical' and 'profit and loss' philosophies of uniform processes and against economic determinism, for an interpretation of history in terms of spiritual values with regard to which, not uniformities but the distinctive contributions of great men are of predominant significance. The essential in history is the striving for ideals under forms which are changing symbols of eternal goodness, beauty and wisdom.

Carlyle produced many books with titles of historical import; among them *The French Revolution*; *The Letters and Speeches of Oliver Cromwell*; *The History of Friedrich of Prussia, called Frederick the Great*. There are good grounds for the question raised by professional historians whether they are 'scientific history' in their understanding of it. *The French Revolution* is a prose epic, not concerned primarily with the record of facts, but an expression of his own way of regarding history. The whole is a dramatic portrayal of the leading individuals—in accord with his conviction that history is before all of great and forceful men. But through all he brought out the inevitable results of the abuse of power and the failure to perform duties and to accept responsibilities. In his work on Cromwell, Carlyle found scope for an expression of his own moral nature and the conviction of the importance of personal strength. Of his Frederick the Great, it might perhaps be said that Frederick could not be made actually to fit the romantic figure that Carlyle set out to describe him, with the coincidence of might and right. Carlyle wrote his historical works in the main to give forceful illustrations to his convictions of essential attitudes to life that he wished to be acknowledged in his own day as contrasted with materialistic economics and ideas of democratic political government based on the counting of heads of the 'mob'. An ethical motive was present in all his historical writing. One may assent to J. G. Robertson's judgment that Carlyle was 'the greatest moral force in the England of his day'. 'He laughed to scorn the pretensions of scientific materialism to undermine man's faith in the unseen; he heaped obloquy on the much vaunted science of political economy; he championed the spiritual against the material, demanded respect for justice and for the moral law, and insisted on the supreme need for reverence . . . not merely for what is above us, but also for what is on the earth, beside and beneath us.'

III

As Carlyle stressed the importance of individuals in history, so many professional philosophers criticized Classical German Idealism as defective in its conception of human personality. In Germany itself, Herman Lotze (1817-1881) accepted the reality of particular selves as fundamental in his philosophy. He influenced many German, British, and American thinkers. Well acquainted with the sciences of the physical world, he insisted that for the understanding of human life there must be definite recognition of individual personal consciousnesses for whom the concepts of ideals, of what 'ought to be' should be the bases for the consideration of 'what is'. In his *Microcosmos* (1856-1864) he discussed different views of history current in his time. The theory that history is the education of the human race is associated with the metaphorical idea of humanity as though one person living on and learning from one generation to another. This idea is metaphysically unsound and the continuity in history is not actually comparable to that of the life of one man. The Hegelian conception of history as the rational development of the Absolute Idea gives no place for historical contingencies, nor any intelligible relation between the evolving ideas and the beings working for them. 'He who sees in history the development of an Idea is bound to say whom this development of an Idea benefits and what benefit is realized by it.' He could not suppose that the Absolute needs the development of history. The other contemporary views, that history is a 'divine poem', and that it is a 'painful meaningless dream' contradict one another. Both are contrary to the facts of history which includes goods and evils.

Lotze was well aware of the limitations of what we may learn about history from the course of history. It will not reveal to us the origin or the destiny of mankind. 'History still seems to us, as it has seemed to all ages, to be a path which leads from an unknown beginning to an unknown end, and the general views as to its direction, which we believe we must adopt, cannot serve to indicate the course and the cause of its windings in detail.' Empirically known history cannot be the basis for a logically valid inference to necessary universal laws. What the philosopher may try to do is to formulate what is involved in history as we know it and that was a task Lotze undertook. History is the experiences of individuals in relation with the physical world, one another, and God. The significance of history lies within these experiences and not in any Absolute beyond them. It cannot be considered merely individualistically or humanistically. That people of one generation have been and are prepared to sacrifice themselves for the wellbeing of future generations and in general with an entire lack of envy towards them, Lotze regarded as a remarkable feature of history. He considered it as helping to confirm the belief in 'some unity of history transcending that of which we are conscious'. The interrelations of individuals includes both co-operation and opposition. Only because individuals have some freedom of choice and action is there real history. The conditions in which they operate are set for them. Within these conditions they may act rightly or wrongly, realize goods or evils. History manifests both. The dominant factor, to whom the conditions are mainly due, is God. The historical process is to be described in part as one of divine government. The meaning of history is not to be found entirely in its 'forward' movement, but also involves an 'upward' gazing and striving to God. 'In proportion as we estimate more highly the immediate relation of each individual soul to the supernatural world, the value for mankind of the coherence of history will decrease; history, however it may move forward or fluctuate hither and thither, could not by any of its own movements attain a goal lying out of its own plane, and we may spare ourselves the trouble of seeking to find in mere onward movement upon this plane a progress which history is destined to make not there but in an upward movement at each individual point of its course forwards.' He arrived finally at 'The idea of a history for the world in which we come to participate with God in some common experience. While this is something which is determined in accordance with His most general plan, it is still in its details by no means the mere result of original predestination. It is therefore not merely "development" according to the law of reason and consequent but actual history.'

In France, the fundamental dependence of history on individual personalities was maintained by Charles Renouvier (1815-1903), in *Introduction a la Philosophie Analytique de l'Histoire* (1864), *Uchronie* (1876), and *Le Personalisme* (1903). Renouvier emphasized the spontaneity, the basic liberty of individual persons in history. Civilization in its successive phases depends on the decisions of men. 'The life of the race, as that of the individual, is not a vain representation, a kind of performance given by marionettes, of which an external power pulls the strings and directs the movements; there is something serious, tragic in it—it is the drama of consciousness and of liberty, of which none may foresee the outcome, which is not predetermined.' 'The facts of history do not enter into a single system the inner logic of which sustains and predetermines them. Without doubt their consequences follow according to laws of phenomenal determinism, but they arise originally from the free will of man. The moments follow one another, they are not bound together, at each of these moments new tendencies are possible which depend upon individual initiative.' It rests on itself and it is evidenced by the uncertainties, the forward and backward tendencies of mankind.

Renouvier challenged the prevalent belief in an inevitable progress of civilization. It is impossible to show in human facts the law of progress said to be present. We neither know the starting point; nor can we define scientifically the end to which humanity proceeds. The theory of inevitable progress implies that institutions are more powerful than individuals, that instead of being an active and ever present agent the individual is a mere product. The evidences of progress are far too limited geographically and temporarily to justify the theory of continued universal progress. Further, there are also regressions and decay. The theory of inevitable progress is as dangerous as it is false. It approves not what is distinguished as good but what is in accordance with the tendency of the time. It seeks guidance for the future in a justification of the past—a method, as Renouvier says, more calculated to teach us how to restore or to continue the past. There is no definite law of progress; the true law consists in the equal possibility of progress or regression for societies as for individuals. 'Progress has to be willed and realized, and this by each individual.' 'We have duties as members of humanity and of a country; the moral law requires us to work for progress. Progress must be possible, at least we must believe progress possible.' History is the product of human freedom. As evil depends on man's will, so by his will he may overcome it. Evil is most often due to the acceptance of the momentary desire rather than its rejection for the sake of a greater good of the future. Renouvier placed the greatest possible emphasis on the conception of justice. Progress is essentially dependent on liberty and the realization of justice.

Renouvier was much opposed on the one hand to forms of Hegelian Idealism and on the other to some central doctrines of traditional dogmatic Christianity. 'It is not an ostentatious and hollow theory of the infinite which contains the truth for the usage of future generations; it is the doctrine of harmony or of perfect relations achieved in a finite order. And it is not grace from on high, the gift of a single being, nor the merit of a single being which brings salvation on earth, it is the golden chain of men of right reason and of great heart who from age to age have been the leaders in spirit, the true redeemers of their brothers.' He called his philosophy Personalism, and a comment made on his death bed indicates its fundamental attitude to human life and history. 'The last word of philosophy is not "to become" but "to do" and in doing to make oneself. It depends in part on our reason, on the reasonable use of our freedom, that we should be makers of ourselves. And that is Personalism.'

Though Rudolf Eucken (1848-1926) was a pupil of Lotze, he turned from the latter's emphasis on personality and reverted in large measure to the positions of Fichte and Hegel, but with the use of a different terminology. In most of Eucken's writings there are implications as to history. He gave a concise statement of his views concerning it in an essay, 'Die Philosophie de Geschichte' in *Kultur der Gegenwart* (2nd ed. 1924). Two volumes, published in English under the titles: *Christianity and the New Idealism* (1908) and *Life's Basis and Life's Ideal* (1911) show his treatment in more detail. His very widely circulated *Grosse Denker* (7th ed. 1907, English translation: *The Problem of Human Life*, 1910) is a history of the development of the problems of human life from Plato to his own time, and illustrates his main conception of historical processes as expressions of spiritual life. Instead of talking of one Absolute Being, Eucken described reality dynamically as a 'universal Spiritual Life'. The meaning of human history is to be sought in the experiences of time as involving time-transcendent values. 'We must establish history within an eternal Order, and understand it as a revelation of this Order on the plane of our human life.' 'History is only valuable— indeed, in its distinctively human sense only possible—as being the medium through which the Eternal reveals itself, as being that whose whole existence is but a struggle for the Eternal.' His activistic emphasis had special significance with reference to history. The periods of history do not arise with the 'quiet inevitableness of organic growth'. What is offered from the past becomes a real possession for any present only

IDEALIST TREATMENTS

by active appropriation in that present. In history there is unceasing re-creation and new creation. The present must 'shape its own life'—whatever in so doing it may use from its heritage from the past. Reminiscent of the Hegelian dialectic, Eucken viewed history as giving the possibility of ever-widening syntheses, taking in and yet transcending partial theories and modes of life. What is positive in Naturalism can and should be recognized within the wider whole of the Spiritual Life. The course of history is a transcendence of Nature, not a negation of it. Modern Socialism and Aesthetic Individualism are partial theories and attitudes, the essentials of which have validity in history. He asked: 'What is the whole to which the course of the movement of history trends?' and replied: 'The more we reflect over the question the more strongly we feel that it is a direction rather than a conclusion that is offered to us in this matter.' However, the chief significance of history is not to be found in its forward movement in time. History involves a conflict with the temporal. The more the individual strives for spiritual ends, the more he feels himself taken up in a universal supra-temporal spiritual life in and through which he finds peace and satisfaction. Men are raised above the flow of time to a participation of 'the Eternal in the midst of time'.

IV

The most distinguished exponent of an Idealistic conception of history in the twentieth century has been Benedetto Croce (1866-1952). He treated of history specifically in one section of a volume on *Logic*; in *History: its Theory and Practice* (1941); *Historical Materialism and the Economics of Karl Marx* (1914); and incidentally in *The Conduct of Life* (n.d.). His Idealism is explicitly formulated in his reference to 'thought' 'in so far as it is itself life (that is to say, the life which is thought, and therefore life of life) and in so far as it is reality (that is to say, the reality which is thought and therefore the reality of reality)'. He early rejected 'Philosophy of History' as ordinarily expounded. He said that it was a search for *transcendental* explanation, for 'designs' and ultimate purposes in history. 'The mythological character of philosophies of history is self-evident. They all want to discover and reveal the World-plan, the design of the world from its birth to its death, or from its entry into time to its entry into eternity.' Philosophy of history so conceived is 'dead' 'with all the other conceptions and forms of the transcendental'. He rejected just as definitely explanations of history in terms of 'causal chains of determinism'. Both historical determinism and philosophy of history 'leave the *reality of history* behind them'. The theistic conception of history was one form of transcendentalism which he opposed. 'The transcendental God is a stranger to human history, which would not exist if that God did exist; for history is its own mystic Dionysus, its own suffering Christ, redeemer of sins.' He objected that forms of 'Universal History' resorted to theological or naturalistic fictions as to origins; to revelations and prophecies or naturalistic socialist goals as to ends. He rejected all treatments of history endeavouring to trace it from its beginning to its end.

Croce's own philosophy has been described as 'the Philosophy of the Spirit', and as 'Historicism'. Reality is the life of the Spirit, and that is history as actual. Attempts to explain history in terms of Matter, God, Idea, or Will, are futile for they want to get 'outside' history, and that is impossible. But Croce used the term 'Spirit' as vaguely as those terms have ever been used. It is most often found in the singular and suggests, as Ruggiero contended, that for Croce history is 'the invisible God manifested in the visible world'. The same is implied in his treatment of the concepts of time, space and nature. These are 'abstract', useful for practical activity but not accurate of reality as 'the Spirit'. He talked of 'beyond time' and of 'the eternal'. Nature is not a physical reality standing over against minds. Sometimes he described it as the 'negative moment' (whatever that might mean), the 'non-being' which synthesized with the 'being' of Spirit, constitutes the 'becoming' of spiritual activity. At other times he gave the impression that Nature is a positive constituent of the Spirit, expressions of its will. The concepts of the Natural Sciences are distortions for practical purposes. Thus, the idea of the uniformity of Nature is not strictly valid. It is wrong

IDEALIST TREATMENTS

to talk of external 'brute facts' (as of Nature) for what are thus falsely so-called are 'acts of the Spirit, conscious in the Spirit that thinks them'. He criticized the concepts of efficient and final causes, yet he said that 'the Spirit' 'posits' the brute facts 'in that way because it is of use to it so to posit them'. The Spirit seems as invisible and as transcendent as the Hegelian Absolute or the theist's God. The terms 'posits' 'acts' suggest efficient causality, as 'of use to it' implies purpose, 'final cause'.

Croce defined his Historicism as 'the affirmation that life and reality are history and history alone'. As the life of the Spirit history has its 'goals' within itself; it has no transcendental aim or end to which its movement is directed. Though he gave definite recognition to the distinction of history as actual and history as record, he may be charged with often confusing them, in part because of his logic and his vague view of time and his ultimate idea of the Spirit as beyond time. This may be illustrated by his statement that when 'history has been raised to the knowledge of the eternal present it reveals itself as one with philosophy, which for its part is never anything but the thought of the eternal present'. With this identity of history and philosophy there can be no 'philosophy of history' as something other than history. Croce said that Hegel aimed at resolving history into philosophy, he himself equated philosophy with history. History is cognitive and practical activity; knowing, intuitive (as the true and the beautiful) and conceptual, and willing (as in the economic and the ethical). Reality, as history is dynamic, with ever new creations. The meaning of history is 'attained at every instant, and at the same time not attained, because every attainment is the formation of a new prospect, whence we have at every moment the satisfaction of possession and, arising from this, the dissatisfaction which drives us to seek a new possession'. Despite his many criticisms of Hegel, Croce's philosophy is much closer to Hegelianism than he has admitted. As Hegel described history as the advance to Rational Freedom, so Croce said: 'Liberty is the eternal creator of history and itself the subject of every history. As such it is on the one hand the explanatory principle of the course of history and on the other the moral idea of humanity.'

But liberty in history is not a passive condition of attainment: only in its active assertion of itself is the Spirit free. 'If anyone needs persuading that liberty cannot exist differently from the way it has lived and always will live in history, a perilous and fighting life, let him for a moment consider a world of liberty without obstacles, without menaces and without oppressions of any kind; immediately he will look away from this picture with horror as being something worse than death, an infinite boredom.'

Stimulated to no small extent by the work of Labriola, Croce wrote a number of essays on Marxism. He maintained that it should not be considered 'a philosophy of history' and that its description as 'Materialism' is unfortunate. Any supposed metaphysics in it may be discarded. It is rather a 'method', purporting to yield an interpretation of history. But even in its method, *Das Kapital* is abstract. 'Nowhere in the world will Marx's categories be met with as living and real existencies.' 'Marx's researches are not historical, but hypothetical and abstract.' Actually Marxism is not a method of historical *thought* but a 'cannon of historical interpretation' recommending that attention be directed to the economic basis of society. It is not an ethical doctrine. Croce challenged the notions that value is estimated in terms of labour and that history is fundamentally a realm of class war. With his justifiable endeavour to find the distinctiveness of Marxism as an expression of the economic history, he was wrong not to acknowledge its materialist attitude and the ethical demands it makes.

Like so many Idealists, Croce treated evil fundamentally as negative. The so-called 'irrational' in history is 'merely the shadow projected by the rational, the negative aspects of its reality'. It is always 'found to be a necessity in a certain particular order'. But his attempt to justify this by discussion of a particular example in his *History, the Story of Liberty*, is confused. Worse, he described suffering and even natural catastrophes as negative. 'History is about the positive and not about the negative, about what man does and not what he suffers. The negative is certainly correlated to the other, but just because of this it does not enter the picture otherwise

IDEALIST TREATMENTS

than through this correlation and in virtue of this office . . .' 'Both the natural disasters which fall upon human communities, like earthquakes, volcanic eruptions, floods and epidemics, and the disasters men inflict upon men like invasions, massacres, thefts and plunderings, and the wickedness, treachery and cruelty that offend the soul of man, all these may fill the human memory with grief, horror, and indignation, but they do not merit the interest of the historian . . . except as they provide the incentives and the material for generous human activity in which alone he is interested.' 'Evil and error are not forms of reality.' They are 'nothing more nor less than the transition from one form of reality to another, from one form of the Spirit to another of its forms'. 'We are denying the reality of evil by making it implicit in the good—an aspect, therefore, a constituent of the good as eternal as the good itself.' Progress is to be understood not as a passage from evil to good, but as from the good to the better, 'in which the evil is the good itself seen in the light of the better'. He complained that Hegel, after maintaining that the real is the rational and the rational is the real 'began all over again by redistinguishing the truly rational and necessary from the real which is bad and accidental'. In his *Autobiography*, Croce confessed: 'I am in the habit of recognizing whatever happens as rational.' From this point of view he contended that 'In an absolute sense and in history there is no such thing as decadence which is not at the same time the formation and the preparation of a new life, therefore, progress.' 'In no way is perpetual progress arrested.'

With close consideration the ambiguities of Croce's exposition are evident. 'Our history,' he wrote, 'is the history of our Soul and the history of the human Soul is the history of the World.' Are we concerned with an Absolute One or with many spirits? If the history of the human Soul is the history of the *World*, it would seem that the term 'human Soul' is just another name for 'the Spirit' conceived as the Whole, as including or identical with 'the World'. He frequently wrote as if history is concerned with a plurality of persons and as though rejecting an all-dominant, all-inclusive One as no more than an idea of transcendental character. Yet, on the other hand, he described history as 'the perpetual growth of' the spirituality of 'the Spirit'. Apparently, as such, history is spiral in character: the Spirit 'moves (sic?) in a circle'. 'This circle is the true unity and identity of the Spirit with itself, of a Spirit which feeds on itself, and grows beyond itself.' So, religion that 'blossoms' on philosophy is 'the consciousness a man comes to have of his oneness with the All, with true and complete reality'. The ambiguities of his exposition as to immortality are obvious in the passage: 'Every act of ours, the moment it is realized is disjoined from us and lives an immortal life of its own, and since we are nothing in reality than the series of our acts, we too are immortal, for to have lived once is to have lived for ever.' The 'our' and 'us' here suggest 'beings' who act and the term 'Spirit' similarly. Yet it is said that we are 'nothing' but 'a series of acts'. Is it meant that immortality is 'the Spirit' living for ever? It is clear that for Croce the significance of history lies within itself. While the nature of that significance is only vaguely indicated and is never considered in detail, he sometimes made statements coming under the charge of being abstract (a charge he made against those of so many others). Thus, if significance is concerned with value, the following is surely abstract in character. 'Activity is value. For us nothing is valuable except what is an effort of imagination, of thought, of will, of our activity in any of its forms.' 'It may be said that there is nothing in the universe that is valuable except the value of human activity.'

Later historians may find the chief importance of Croce in his political activities and his literary criticism. Of his work relative to history, his discussions of the inadequacies and onesidedness of various common forms of historiography are far more valuable than his own treatment of history. His significance for philosophy may be primarily in showing what an Idealism of the kind he espoused leads to: a contribution to the discrediting of Idealism! In a brief essay he wrote that 'common sense is a historical growth, a distillation of the thinking of the ages'. Croce's philosophy could not be so described. In consideration of its discursiveness and lack of thorough-going critical analysis, I would say, in his own words: 'I detest the incompetent philosopher.'

CHAPTER VIII

NATURALIST TREATMENTS OF HISTORY IN THE NINETEENTH CENTURY AND AFTER

I

The Idealist movements considered in the previous chapter had a common basis in their acceptance of the spiritual nature of reality. In contrast with them, in the nineteenth century and since, have been treatments of history by thinkers who implicitly or explicitly denied that conception or ignored it with the attitude of metaphysical agnosticism. In addition to their negative agreement in that regard, they were mostly inclined to give emphasis to the facts of Nature, and to adopt empirical methods similar to those of the Natural Sciences. For convenience these thinkers may be described as 'Naturalistic', understanding that term widely and indefinitely. They were led to their positions in part through their dissatisfaction with Idealism, to which some had adhered in their earlier years. But they depended more on aspects of contemporary life, the problems of which they approached in realistic fashion. This is evident for Marxism, which, with the actual organization of Communist societies, has been in its practical manifestation the most impressive Naturalistic treatment of history. The Naturalistic Positivism of Auguste Comte, while it has not led to any specific political organization, has had effects on the attitudes of some professional historians and in one way and another on many of the general public. But there have been many whose outlook was essentially Naturalistic who were neither Marxians nor Comtists. Presenting a variety of different conceptions of history, they have all had the conviction that they were keeping to the facts of history with no distortion of their thought by preconceived Idealistic notions. The question may be raised as to whether they gave attention to *all* the facts, whether deliberately or otherwise they ignored those commonly called 'spiritual'. Of the many thinkers of this kind only a few can be considered here as illustrative and of special significance: Marx, Bakunin, Kropotkin, Buckle, Nietzsche, Nordau, Reade, Metchnikoff, Spengler and Wells.

In definite opposition to Hegel's concept of reality as Absolute Spirit, Karl Marx (1818-1866) and Frederick Engels (1820-1895) based their ideology on the actualities of the world of men and things. Though they acknowledged human minds and repudiated the common notion of Materialism, they nevertheless described their theory as the 'materialistic conception of history'. The essence of the theory is, in Marx's words, that 'the modes of production of the needs of the material life condition the social, political and the spiritual course of life generally'. 'The first premise of all human history,' wrote Engels, 'is the existence of living human individuals,' but their nature 'depends on the material conditions determining their production'—both what they produce and how they produce. The forms of intercourse of individuals are determined by production. 'A fundamental condition of all history is the production to satisfy physical needs and it is a first necessity of any theory of history to observe all the significance and implications of this fact.' Underlying all psychological motives are material conditions. 'Men make their own history whatever its outcome may be, in that each person follows his own consciously desired end, and it is precisely the resultant of these many wills operating in different directions and of their manifold effects upon the outer world that constitutes history.' Whether man's conscious desires are achieved or not, history 'is always governed by inner hidden laws'. These laws are ultimately economic, involving a historical determinism. 'The key to the understanding of the whole history of society lies in the historical development of labour.' The processes of history are inevitable. Their development is in form similar to that described by Hegel: a dialectical movement through opposition to synthesis. Engels said that Marx had divested 'the dialectical method' of its Idealist trappings. In history the basic opposition has been and is in economic and political class struggles. 'The history of all hitherto existing society is the history of class struggles.' The final synthesis—of 'Labour' and 'Capital'—is to be achieved in a classless society in which there will be no need of the 'State' as an organized authority. When this is attained, 'pre-history ends and history begins'. Leaders, prominent personalities, good and bad, are fully recognized by Marxism, but their appearance is explained as determined by general causes in the prevailing social conditions. The Marxian theory, however its Dialectical Materialism is metaphysically understood, acknowledged no God, either as creator or as Providence in history. Religion with faith in these is superstition. In history it has been a means adopted by the minority to exploit the majority: turning the attention of the majority to their 'reward' and 'bliss' in a future life. The minority have assumed earthly control and have enjoyed worldly luxuries produced by the labour of the majority. But though the significance of history is solely terrestrial, the adherents of Marxism are inspired by thoughts of a future goal and even to make sacrifices for its attainment. It is 'humanity' for which men must work in history, enjoying for themselves in the onward march whatever part they may have of the values connoted by the ideal. To a large extent individuals of earlier generations are instruments for the attainment of something they will not fully share. It may be agreed with Marxism that efforts for the satisfaction of material needs, the preservation of physical life, are main factors in human history, but that all other aspects are merely by-products, determined ultimately by these needs and the modes of their satisfaction, can be and has been challenged on the basis of the facts of history itself.

For some time allied with Marx in efforts to arouse a social revolution of the masses, the Russian, Mikhail Bakunin (1814-1876) in *God and the State* (English 1895), later came to feel that his attitude was different from that of Marx. Central for his thought and life was the sentiment and ideal of liberty, but Marx, he wrote, lacked 'the instinct of liberty' and was 'from head to feet an authoritarian'. Bakunin eventually opposed the Marxian theory that men in history are inevitably determined by economic forces. Early in life he had been attracted by the Idealism of Fichte and Hegel, even translating one of the former's works into Russian. In violent reaction, he came to regard theism and the Idealist philosophies of his time as bases for authority external to the individual. God being the master, man is the slave. One who wishes to worship God ought to renounce liberty and his dignity as man. Religion has meant the dominance of an authority in history militating against the inner freedom of man. Admitting that the great merit of Christianity had been to proclaim the equality of all men before God, he contended that the significance of this for history had been eliminated by being taught as for 'the life to come, not for the present real life, not on earth'. For advance in human liberty, belief in God must be rejected. The authority of the State as found in history and as emphasized by Hegel, and the compulsion of the economic as involved in the teaching of Marx, are also to be challenged. Bakunin saw little if any help in a government through science, as implicated in Comte's view of the development of Positivism in history. 'Science is as incapable of grasping the individuality of a man as that of a rabbit. Not that it is ignorant of the principle of individuality: it conceives it perfectly as a principle but not as a fact.' With individual freedom as a fundamental aim of men in history, there is a striving for unity, but it is not to be realized by any dominant power over individuals. 'Unity is the end towards which humanity irresistably tends. But it becomes fatal, destructive of intelligence, of the dignity, of the prosperity of individuals, of peoples, wherever it is constituted apart from liberty, whether by violence, whether under the authority of any theological, metaphysical, political or even economic idea.' With due regard to the difference in the attitudes towards religion, there was a fundamental similarity between this anarchism of Bakunin and that of Leo Tolstoy.

Another Russian, Peter Kropotkin (1842-1921), also challenged all that restricted human liberty, in *Paroles d'un Révolt* (2nd ed. 1888) and *Conquest of Bread* (1906). 'From the cradle to the grave' the State 'strangles us in its arms.' The economic organization developed in the past and dominant today makes true liberty impossible. 'The history of our day is the history of the struggle of privileged rulers against the equalitarian aspirations of the people.' A revolution is necessary to base social organization on new principles. In the past absolute monarchy went with serfdom. Parliamentarianism and the wage system have gone with the exploitation of the masses. Having regained possession of the common inheritance, the 'people' must seek new organization in free groups and federations of groups. With material needs satisfied men will strive for a great variety of other values. Thus 'the more society is civilized, the more will individuality be developed'.

II

While conflicts were raging around Absolute Idealism in Germany, Auguste Comte (1795-1857) in France was developing a 'scientific', purely humanistic view of history. He claimed to have discovered 'the general law of evolution' suitable to constitute 'a true philosophy of history'. With an echo of Condorcet, Comte championed the idea of progress in human history, not as inevitable but nevertheless real as evidenced by the growth of man's mind. Social evolution is a continuance of general biological evolution. The 'Law of evolution' is manifested in history through three stages of thought and life: the theological or fictitious; the metaphysical or abstract; and the scientific or positive. Each stage itself includes development, the first, for example, from feticism through polytheism to monotheism. The main significance of the metaphysical stage has been by criticism to undermine and eventually eliminate belief in the earlier theological fictions. With the dominance of the empirical scientific attitude, history is concerned not with theological fictions or metaphysical abstractions but with realities, men in their physical environment. In *The Catechism of the Positive Religion* (1852) Comte wrote: 'Humanity definitely substitutes herself for God, without ever forgetting his provisional services.' Discarding God as fictitious, he also rejected the idea of an actual conscious future life for individuals. Immortality consists solely in 'an unconscious but permanent life in the hearts and minds of others'. He described history as advancing from conditions of war to those of peaceful industry. The spread of collective scientific thinking and of industry in modern history is carrying mankind forward to universal peace. The central aim, 'the principal object' of human striving is 'moral improvement', and by morality is to be understood 'living for others'. Comte's whole exposition appears to be amazingly superficial, a presentation of what in history may seem to fit in with his own view of the nature of science. Admitting that all the three types of attitude are still found among mankind, he believed that this is because the Positive standpoint has not yet been completely attained by all. He represented the progressive discarding of the theological and the metaphysical as the actual course of history. But the theological, the metaphysical and the scientific are not necessarily exclusive of one another. Indeed, history shows them as going along together as all permanently important aspects of thought and life. In giving his attention to the discovery and statement of 'the veritable laws of sociability' he treated of only one aspect of history. In discarding 'exceptional events and minor details' he neglected much that constitutes the essential character of history.

Though Comte's younger contemporary A. Cournot (1801-1877) avoided the metaphysical and in other ways accorded with the Positivist attitude, in his *Treatise on the Concatenation of fundamental Ideas in the Sciences and in History* (1861) he provided important correctives to Comte's position. In contrast with Comte's treatment of social laws, he insisted on the importance of the individual and the particular for the philosophical consideration of history. 'Individuality, the particular fact with that which it has about it peculiarly characteristic, is that which fixed our attention. For we are no longer in the ordinary condition of science which in general makes and ought to make abstraction from individuals, we find ourselves in genuine history, in face of all the singularities of destiny.' Philosophy of history 'enquires into the reason of events rather than of their causes'. Though he admitted that we have only the barest knowledge of the history of small portions of humanity, he wrote that 'it is necessary to observe the development of history as a whole, to consider not only its starting point but the final phase and the incidents on the way there'. He favoured the attitude of those historians who consider their task 'to bring into relief the progress of civilization through the differentiations of races and the revolutions of empires'. This progress of civilization, in language and literature, politics and morality, science and industry, art and religion, he opposed to the view that 'there is nothing new under the sun', 'that human experiences revolve in the same circle'. 'The phenomena of history which are repeated are only repeated with variations which witness by the constant significance of the variations that there is over and above the causes of reproduction and repetition a cause of continuous progress'. Although there is an alternating movement of progress and decline, the succeeding higher levels of civilization acquire the capacity for longer duration, with aspects of indefinite persistence. Cournot summed up his conception of history thus: 'History, as it is ordinarily understood, has for its starting point primordial facts, the description of which and the explanation, if it is possible, belongs to ethnology. It leads humanity progressively towards a final condition in which the elements of civilization properly so-called, have assumed a preponderating influence in all concerning the organization of societies over all the other elements of human nature. Thanks to the continual intervention of experience and of the general reason, all the primitive distinctions tend to become eradicated, even the influence of historical precedents tends to become weaker. Society tends to organize itself like a hive of bees, according to conditions *quasi* geometrical, the essential conditions of which experience gives evidence and theory demonstrates.' 'The philosophy of history has essentially for its object to discern in the totality of historical events dominant general facts, which as it were form the framework and skeleton; to show how to these general facts of first order others are subordinated and thus on to the facts of detail which can still offer a dramatic interest vividly arresting our curiosity, but not our curiosity as philosophers.'

In the period of its first exposition and early development,

Marxism did not arouse very much interest in Britain. There was no widespread adoption of its ideas and no great amount of criticism of them. Comtist Positivism aroused more attention because it was akin to the common empirical attitude of the majority of British thinkers. But the English cultural tradition with its acceptance of greater importance of individuals than Comte acknowledged prevented Positivism from becoming widely adopted. English treatments of history, even when predominantly empirical, were not in a Positivist framework. The independence of English works may be illustrated by Henry Thomas Buckle's *History of Civilization in England* (1857; 1867) in which he presented some fundamental ideas on the nature of history. He contrasted his own effort with what in the past and largely in his own day was given by the writers on history. 'I am deeply convinced that the time is fast approaching when the history of man will be placed on its proper footing; when its study will be recognized as the noblest and most arduous of all pursuits; and when it will be clearly seen that to cultivate it with success, there is wanted a wide and comprehensive mind, richly furnished with the highest branches of human knowledge. When this is fully admitted, history will be written only by those whose habits fit them for the task and it will be rescued from the hands of biographers, genealogists and collectors of anecdotes, chroniclers of courts, of princes and nobles—those babblers of vain things, who lie in wait at every corner and infest this public highway of our national literature.' Though his title makes reference specifically to the history of civilization in England, it is in the wider study in his General Introduction that his attitudes to history are systematically stated. The remainder of the work was conceived by him as indicating the bases of his views and an exemplification of them.

Living in the latter half of the nineteenth century with its rapid advances in the sciences of Nature, Buckle wrote that he wanted to accomplish for the history on man something equivalent or at all events analogous to what has been effected in the different branches of the natural sciences. He asked: 'Are the actions of men, and therefore of societies, governed by fixed laws, or are they the result of chance or of supernatural interference?' He was himself convinced that there are regularities and uniformities in the phenomena of human history analogous with the 'laws' formulated in the natural sciences. The regularity of events is 'at once the key and the basis of history'. Actions are due to motives, and these to antecedents, and 'if we were acquainted with the whole of the antecedents and with all the laws of their movements, we could with erring certainty predict the whole of their immediate results'. History is the human mind 'developing according to the conditions of its organization', 'obeying its own laws', modifying Nature, and Nature modifying man. 'Out of this reciprocal modification all events must necessarily spring.' The idea of 'chance' applied to the physical corresponds to that of 'free will' ascribed to minds. Buckle rejected both. The 'necessary connection' revealed in science is analogous with that of 'predestination', included in some theologies. Buckle accepted it not as a theological dogma but as a scientific truth, without any implication of the will of a Supreme Being. As far as events are of concern to man it makes no essential difference whether they come through a divine 'predestination' or are 'determined solely' by their antecedents. With a brief discussion he rejected the method of metaphysics, whether of the rationalistic, idealist type or that of sense empiricism. Metaphysics, 'so zealously prosecuted, so long continued' has yet been 'so barren of results'. Any reliance on introspection by the individual, he regarded with contempt: history is to be studied 'in the actions of mankind at large'. He gave no indication from his standpoint how those variations occur on which the progressive course of history (in which he ardently believed) depends. Insisting on the distinction of the human mind from the physical world, and recognizing the mind as fundamental in history, he did not enquire into its character. Had he done so, he might have definitely considered—as he did not—the goals or purposes striven for and included in progress.

The events of history are entirely due to the interactions of Nature and human minds. Buckle raised the interesting and important question as to which of these is the dominant factor. In the early stages of the histories of all people it is Nature, but it has not so remained with all peoples. The most important physical factors in history are food, clothing and soil, but there are also other general factors influencing ideas and emotions. Buckle contended that there has been, and is, a fundamental difference between what we should call 'Occidental' (but he called 'European') civilization and others, as e.g. the Oriental. 'The great division between European and non-European civilization is the basis of the philosophy of history, since it suggests the important consideration, that if we would understand, for instance, the history of India, we must make the external world our first study, because it has influenced man more than man has influenced it. If, on the other hand, we would understand the history of a country like France or England we must make man our principal study, because nature being comparatively weak, every step in the great progress has increased the dominion of the human mind over the agencies of the external world.' Considering Occidental civilization, he made the general statement: 'the only progress which is really effective depends, not on the bounty of nature, but upon the energy of man,' whose powers he declared to be 'unlimited'.

In the course of history as due to human minds Buckle distinguished between the influence of the moral and the intellectual. Does progress in history depend more on advance in morality or in intellectual knowledge? He contended that the influence of moral motives in the progress of civilization has been 'extremely small'. 'For there is, unquestionably, nothing to be found in the world which has undergone so little change as those great dogmas of which moral systems are composed. To do good to others; to sacrifice for their benefit your own wishes; to love your neighbour as yourself; to forgive your enemies; to restrain your passions; to honour your parents; to respect those who are set over you; these and a few others are the sole essentials of morals; but they have been known for thousands of years, and not one jot or tittle has been added to them by all the sermons, homilies, and text-books which moralists and theologians have been able to produce.' In contrast with that, 'the progressive aspect of intellectual truths' is 'indeed startling'. 'We have found reason to believe that the growth of European civilization is solely due to the progress of knowledge and that the progress of knowledge depends on the number of truths which the human intellect discovers and the extent to which they are diffused.' The results of intellectual advance are more enduring. Morality is essentially of personal character and is not transferable. The effects of philanthropy are comparatively short-lived. The advance of mankind has not been through a development of inherent moral and intellectual *capacities*. An infant born in a barbarous country may be equal in these with one born in the most civilized country of Europe. 'Here,' he wrote, 'lies the whole gist of the matter': 'the entire mental atmosphere in which the two children are respectively nurtured'—the circumstances after birth. That seems to imply that all progress is due to the environment, specifically the social. But there must obviously be some source of the progressive changes, and Buckle had eventually to acknowledge it. 'An immense majority of men must always remain in the middle state, neither very foolish nor very able, neither very virtuous nor very vicious, but slumbering in a peaceful and decent mediocrity, adopting without much difficulty the current opinions of the day, making no inquiry, exciting no scandal, causing no wonder, just holding on a level with their generation, and noiselessly conforming to the standard of morals and of knowledge common to the age and country in which they live.' For the roots of progress he had to turn from the social environment to the outstanding inner abilities of individuals. Progress rests finally on 'the discoveries of genius'. 'It is to them that we owe all we now have.' Their contributions are 'essentially cumulative'. The discoveries of the geniuses are more significant for progress in history than 'the actions of mankind at large' which he had elsewhere declared must be the basis for truth concerning history. These individuals and their discoveries have a distinctiveness of fundamental importance. They are in contrast with the phenomena of mankind in social relations with reference to which Buckle (in consideration of social statistics) had insisted that uniformities (or laws) should be primarily sought in history.

Buckle's central contention was that the well-being of mankind depends mostly on intellectual knowledge. The influence of physical phenomena and of moral principles are inferior to it. They may cause 'great aberrations in short periods, but in long periods' they correct and balance themselves. Advances in religion, literature, legislation are the products of preceding intellectual achievements and are secondary agents in progress as aiding the wider diffusion of intellectual changes. He maintained that in history there has been an antagonism between thinkers and military leaders. An increase of knowledge must result in a decrease of war. Writing of his own times, Buckle remarked: 'Russia is a warlike country, not because its inhabitants are immoral, but because they are unintellectual.' He raised the further question: What makes knowledge and the increase of it possible? His answer was: the accumulation of wealth, by which he meant a surplus of food and other necessities of physical life making possible the freedom of some from engaging in their production. Only thus can some men give themselves to the pursuit of knowledge. Without wealth in this sense there can be no advance in knowledge. 'Of all the great social improvements the accumulation of wealth must be the first.' However, over and above the obtaining of knowledge by the 'leisured' few, there must be a dissemination of it for social advance.

III

A treatment of history quite different from those so far described was given by Friedrich Nietzsche (1844-1900). As Dr G. A. Morgan remarks: 'a historical setting and mission is at the heart of Nietzsche's philosophy.' He challenged the purely rationalistic conception of Hegelian Idealism. 'History is not the work of reason; it is full of accident and irrationality, and "whoever does not comprehend how brutal and meaningless history is, will also not understand at all the impulse to make history meaningful".' But if history is 'meaningless' what can be the significance of the phrase 'the impulse to make history meaningful'? Nietzsche at times appeared to consider it 'aimless' in the sense that infra-human life might be described. 'The powers in history are doubtless discernible if one strips off all moral and religious teleology. They must be those powers which also operate in the entire phenomenon of organic existence. The plainest declarations (are) in the vegetable kingdom.' From another point of view, he insisted on the idea of 'eternal recurrence', which he declared to be the fundamental conception of his *Thus Spake Zarathustra*. That idea, however, indicates primarily the cyclic character of cosmic processes. Writing so much in aphoristic form and with such diverse references to so many sides of human life, Nietzsche gave the impression of inconsistency and of never having brought his thought into a coherent system. Hence there have been divergent views as to his real intentions. Some have maintained that he conceived mankind in history as continuing the processes described in the biological theory of evolution of his time. Through conflict and struggle a stage beyond the present condition of man is to be attained, to which he gave the name, Superman. Though what he wrote in defence of egoism shows that he was especially concerned with the individual, his distinction of a 'master race' and a 'slave race' has implications beyond particular individuals.

In contrast with the onward evolution have been the periods of decadence in human history. Neitzsche considered traditional morality and religion to be at the heart of much of this decadence. 'All history is indeed the experimental reputation of the fact that the priest (including those priests in disguise, philosophers) has become master not only within a limited religious community but everywhere, and that the morality of decadence, the will to nothing, has passed as morality *per se*, is to be found in this: that altruism is considered an absolute value, but egoism meets with hostility everywhere.' 'Soul', 'Spirit', 'Free Will', 'God'—ancillary concepts of morality, are 'lies'. The prehistoric ages were 'premoral'; the historical period to the present has been and is 'moral'; in the future there will be an attitude 'beyond morality'. This last involves the 'transvaluation of all values'. That is the 'formula for mankind's act of highest self-recognition'. Yet in explaining why he used the name of Zarathustra, who was pre-eminently a moralist, he said: 'To tell the truth and to shoot straight: those are Persian virtues.' 'Truthfulness', 'integrity', 'honesty' were values Nietzsche did not propose to change; and he also referred approvingly to 'eternal justice'. What he fought against was the morality of 'self-renunciation', which he regarded as the ethical essence of Christian teaching in history. Sometimes he wrote as though he thought that actually the fundamental in history has been constituted of struggles of 'the Will to power'. But the precise meaning of the phrase 'the Will to power' is difficult to ascertain. In periods of decadence, including the time in which he lived, men were 'soft, stale, over-specialized', their energies finding 'easier satisfaction in imagination than in action'. The religious myths on which the culture is based are undermined, and with emancipation from the moral ideas associated with them, an attitude of nihilism leads to the destruction of the culture. There has been a cycle of cultures in history, rising and declining, and 'the future too will follow a cyclic pattern'. 'Humanity must live in cycles, sole form of duration. Not culture as long as possible; but as short and high as possible.' 'The destiny of men is arranged for happy moments—every life has such—but not for happy ages.' With his gaze specifically on the future Nietzsche protested against any exaggerated attention to 'past' history that would tend to encourage a conservative continuity of the modes of life of the past. Concern with history as record of the past is not to weaken the spontaneity of the present.

Nietzsche was a *litterateur* rather than specifically a philosopher or a historian, and the same must be said of Max Nordau (1849-1923). In *The Interpretation of History*, he discussed diverse views on the nature of history but with a failure on his part to avoid inconsistencies and to arrive at a clear general view. 'The claim of written history to be a science is unfounded.' Its interest 'rests on the love of story-telling innate in mankind'. It is 'an artificial product of the ruling classes' used 'to cast a glamour, half-tender, half-reverential, awe over institutions that have lost any reasonable justification'. Nevertheless, 'there can be no worthier task for the human mind' than the philosophy of history, 'the attempt to give a rational explanation of historical events'. However, the customary philosophy of history assumes the existence of God with a purpose in history and does not endeavour to prove such a purpose from historical facts. It 'merely waves the torch of religion across the darkness it pretends to light up'. On the other hand, materialistic philosophy of history does not do justice to 'the whole living man'. Under the influence of Comte, Nordau sometimes tended to identify the historical with the sociological. 'Sociology is history without proper names; history is sociology made concrete and individual.' But he turned from this to the psychological and to specific emphasis on the individual person. 'The real thing is the psychology of the individual.' An accurate idea of the inner structure of the historical life of mankind as a whole can only be obtained by a study of individual characteristics, modes of thought and reactions, in a word of individual biology and psychology. 'The history of mankind is composed of the actions of individual men . . .' While giving a hedonist description of the individual's wish to live: 'he lives and will live because life gives him pleasure', at the end of his exposition he declared that only one ideal can stand the cold examination of knowledge: 'goodness and self-less love'. The State was originated and is sustained by compulsion. 'It was invented by selfishness and carried on by force as the machinery of parisitism.' Allied with the parisitism of the State has been that of the Priests. 'Externally history is a melodrama on the theme of parisitism.' 'Progress is assuredly movement toward a goal, but this goal is not mystical, has not been conceived by a supernatural spirit or determined by supernatural will; it is throughout earthly, concrete, immanent, the same for all; it is self-preservation.' Nordau virtually ruled out the metaphysical, but if the question of the nature of the 'self' to be 'preserved' were discussed adequately it might lead to the philosophical and theological ideas he scorned in his earlier pages. Certainly history contains no answers to 'the question of eternity' if it has no inner spiritual significance with a metaphysical basis.

A forceful consideration of the nature and meaning of history was published in 1872 by the anthropologist William Winwood Reade (1838-1875), under the title *The Martyrdom of Man*. Reade was best known as an explorer of 'darkest'

Africa. His work purports to be a form of 'universal history'. Its scope extends from ancient times in Asia, Africa and Europe up to the nineteenth century of Europe. The breadth of its survey and the fluency of its literary style ensured for it an extensive circulation in many editions. At the beginning of its final chapter, Reade gave a brief statement of what he regarded as the evolution of the solar system and of living organisms up to man. Turning then to the history of mankind, his fundamental concern was the nature of progress through wars and religions, the struggles for liberty, the advance of intelligence and the growth of knowledge. His central idea was that it has been through 'martyrdom' that succeeding generations have risen to higher standards of life. By his record of actual history, he tried to show that 'the progress of the human race' has been assisted by wars, however destructive, religions, however superstitious, slavery, however objectionable to later minds, and even by ignorance.

The impression that *The Martyrdom of Man* leaves most strongly on the mind is of the suffering in human history. Seen in the 'book of Nature' 'life is one long tragedy'. 'How many hearts yearning for affection are blighted in solitude and coldness! How many women seated by their lonely firesides are musing on the days that ought to have been! ... O cold, cruel, miserable life, how long are your pains, how brief are your delights!' He asked: 'Why is it ordained that bad should be the raw material of good?' The nature and extent of human suffering led him to reject belief in a personal deity as creator. 'Those who believe in a God of love must close their eyes to the phenomena of life or garble the universe to suit their theory.' The good and the evil of the world would have to be due to Him, all its cruelty and sin. Nevertheless, Reade did not consider his position atheistic. 'We teach that there is a God ... so great that He cannot be defined by man.' However, in that 'He does not deign to have personal relations with us human atoms that are called men,' He has no direct significance in and for human history. Reade restricted his view to Nature taken in its widest sense. In so doing the metaphysical implications of his thought are as ambiguous as those of our contemporary exponents of Naturalism. Through some of the exposition, it seems as though he regarded mind as emerging in evolution from non-mental causes. But in a definite statement he declared it to be always present. 'Mind is a property of matter. Matter is inhabited by mind.' Considered as within Nature human history is solely terrestrial. Though he did not indicate what effects 'the illusion of immortality' has had in the course of human history, he ended his last chapter with the declaration: 'The soul must be sacrificed; the hope of immortality must die. A sweet and charming illusion must be taken from the human race, as youth and beauty vanish never to return.' Man's vision is to be limited to the terrestrial, in which Reade insisted that there is progress, and in this we must place our hope. It is not likely that we shall soon rise above all evils. For long years to come war will 'be required to prepare the way for freedom and progress in the East, and in Europe itself it is not probable that war will absolutely cease until science discovers some destroying force so simple in its administration, so horrible in its effects, that all art, all gallantry, will be at an end, and battles will be massacres which the feelings of mankind will be unable to endure.' 'It is science alone which can ameliorate the condition of the human race.' 'Giving up faith in immortality it is the future of the human race to which men must look forward in history.' 'Life is full of hope and consolation.' 'Our own prosperity is founded on the agonies of the past.' 'Is it therefore unjust that we should suffer for the benefit of those who are to come?'

A quarter of a century later, the eminent biologist and medical scientist, Élie Metchnikoff (1845-1916), in his volume *The Nature of Man* (1903) suggested how men should look on history. A Russian, he taught in German and Russian universities and in 1888 became a professor in the Pasteur Institute in Paris. Mankind, he maintained, 'must be persuaded that science is all powerful'. His attitude was indicated by his subtitle: 'Studies in Optimistic Philosophy'. Man desires happiness: but 'What is happiness?' 'Is it the feeling of well-being experienced by the individual himself, or is it the judgment of others on his sensations?' The opinions both of the individual himself and of others may be fallacious. He nowhere gave a definite statement of what he understood happiness to be, though he left little doubt as to his general idea of it. Maintaining that science has shown that man is not of supernatural origin, he adopted the view of Naturalism that he is physically and psychically a product of the processes of Nature. Man is not a creation of the divine, but 'a miscarriage of an ape, endowed with profound intelligence and capable of great progress'. Metchnikoff was painfully aware of the imperfections and disharmonies of natural organisms, both infra-human and human. He described in detail many of these in man. The 'greatest disharmony' for man is his 'love of life and fear of death'. 'Instinctive love of life and fear of death, which is only a manifestation of the former, are of an importance in the study of human nature impossible to over-estimate.' To obtain happiness in face of this fundamental disharmony, in the past and widely in the present among the less enlightened, men have resorted to religion and philosophy. With an interesting survey of religion, and a narrower consideration of philosophy, Metchnikoff concluded that both are unsatisfactory. He took the religious attitude to be essentially faith in a future spiritual life in which the disharmony will be transcended. He maintained that from the standpoint of science any such faith must be rejected. 'The idea of a future life is supported by not a single fact—and there is much evidence against it.' With the advance of knowledge 'complete annihilation at death is the conception accepted by the vast majority of enlightened persons'. He doubted that a future life as frequently conceived would be of real happiness, and quoted Haeckel: 'However gloriously we may depict this eternal life in paradise, in the end it would be a fearful burden to the best of men.' Philosophical remedies for the disharmony are as ineffective as the religious. Ultimately philosophy teaches men to resign themselves to the prospect of annihilation.

Metchnikoff's 'optimistic philosophy' was based on science. He admitted that scientists have had many failures in the past, as they have in the present. 'If science does no more than to destroy faith and to teach that the whole living world is moving towards a knowledge of inevitable old age and death, it becomes necessary to ask if the perilous march of science should not be stopped.' Yet, though science destroys religious faith, it alone can point to an over-coming of the fundamental disharmony of human life. The scientific solution of the problem is the dominant theme of the book. Its exposition involved him in detailed consideration of the fear of death. Old age, as those in the past have experienced it, and most in the present know it, is essentially 'morbid' in character. It is not 'a true physiological process', but is due to detrimental factors alien to the real nature of the organism. Metchnikoff declared to be 'absolutely correct' and 'proved by a number of facts' Rousseau's statement that 'Life becomes dearer to us as its joys pass away. The old cling to it more closely than the young.' Because of abnormalities, death, the 'absolute extinction of consciousness' 'comes before man has finished his physiological development and when the instinct of life is still strong'. Science is eventually to relieve man of these abnormalities. With the 'instinct of life' fully satisfied, there would come an 'instinct of death'. Death would be accepted as the 'normal end' of life—if 'before attaining it, a normal life' has been lived, 'a life filled all through with the feeling that comes from the accomplishment of function'. The way we are to look on history thus becomes clear. History is fundamentally of individuals. The meaning of the history of each individual is in the experience of satisfaction in the performance of the functions which constitute living. There is to be no thought or anticipation of a meaning beyond death. Death itself is to have meaning as the 'normal end' of an entirely satisfactory life. To the sciences already concerned in aiding men to such a life, Metchnikoff added that of gerontology, that of the 'normal' (as distinct from the prevailing abnormal) processes of becoming old. 'True progress consists in the elimination of the disharmonies of human nature, and in the cultivation of physiological old age followed by natural death.' He admitted that his generation could not achieve physiological old age and normal death. The social aspects of history have an instrumental value primarily in co-operation in trying to achieve those goals.

Metchnikoff gave no adequate consideration to the question

of the detailed contents of the satisfactory life. He never definitely raised that question. But something may be inferred from some of his more incidental comments. What he vaguely called 'luxury' must be lessened, thus lessening the evils that come with luxury. 'Progress would consist in simplifying many sides of the life of civilized people.' In accordance with this attitude, he criticized Herbert Spencer, whose view of evolution and history as including increasing differentiation is exemplified in the multiplication of different kinds of things to eat and drink. Metchnikoff, as though with a dogmatic assumption that such differentiation led only to the deleterious, appears to have meant that we are to get gastronomic enjoyment, if any, only from foods required for proper nourishment. But history includes an increase of richness of values of all kinds with such differentiation. It is difficult to see that Metchnikoff, from his standpoint of Naturalism, could give these any more recognition than those of foods thus rejected. He gave quite inadequate attention to the 'profound intelligence' and the capacity for 'great progress' which he admitted in man. But he made quite clear that for him the meaning in history is to be conceived as a harmonious life for each, with death accepted without fear as its natural end.

The eighteenth-century doctrine of the perfectibility of man, the Hegelian conception of a synthetic dialectic process, and later the theory of evolution, were grounds for a widespread belief in history as a realm of human progress. The nature of the first World War induced some to doubt it. The idea was definitely challenged by Oswald Spengler (1880-1936) in his work *The Decline of the West* (1919; 1922). Spengler's position was metaphysically indefinite. He was Naturalistic specifically in that analogies fundamental to his general conception of history were physical and biological. Further, he had no place for God as real or any implications of a continued spiritual life for individuals after death. History for him was limited to the mundane. He endeavoured to give a general theory of history and in relation with this to present the detailed grounds for his contention of the decline of western culture. It is with the former that we are concerned. The essentials of his view may be learned from the following quotation: 'I see, in place of that empty figment of one linear history which can only be kept up by shutting one's eyes to the overwhelming multitude of the facts, the drama of a *number* of mighty Cultures, each springing with primitive strength from the soil of a mother-region to which it remains bound throughout its whole life-cycle; each stamping its material, its mankind, in *its own* image; each having *its own* idea, *its own* passions, *its own* life, will, and feeling, *its own* death. Here, indeed, are colours, lights, movements, that no intellectual eye has yet discovered. Here, the Cultures, peoples, languages, truths, gods, landscapes, bloom and age as the oak and the stone-pines, the blossoms, twigs, and leaves: but there is no ageing "Mankind". Each Culture has its own new possibilities of self-expression which arise, ripen, decay, and never return. There is not *one* sculpture, *one* painting, *one* mathematics, *one* physics, but many, each in its deepest essence different from the others, each limited in duration and self-contained, just as each species of plant has its peculiar blossom or fruit, its special type of growth and decline. These Cultures, sublimated life-essences, grow with the same superb aimlessness as the flowers of the field. They belong, like the plants and the animals, to the living Nature of Goethe, and not to the dead Nature of Newton. I see world-history as a picture of endless formations and transformations, of the marvellous waxing and waning of organic forms. The professional historian, on the contrary, sees it as a sort of tapeworm industrially adding on to itself one epoch after another.'

Spengler's terminology was unusual and may be misunderstood. But he appeared to suggest that a Culture is the expression of a 'gigantic' being—as though a group mind—which realizes itself through particular human beings. The idea of such a 'gigantic' being may be due to a fallacy of composition. One result of it was a failure on Spengler's part to do justice to individuals as the creators and experients of culture. He said that different Cultures were so diverse that adherents to one could not understand the others. Yet he himself professed to describe a number of Cultures, and had to admit that some Cultures had their initial development under influences from earlier ones. Concentrating his attention on the differences of Cultures, he failed to recognize the greater extent of their similarities. His biological analogies misled him. The different races and groups of mankind of different regions were not so many species analogous with species of plants. Human beings, as H. G. Wells insisted, are of the same species and there is a biological basis for their modes of life being essentially alike in fundamentals. The histories of groups may have some characteristics suggested by the biological analogy of birth, youth, maturity, old age, and death, or the physical analogy of spring, summer, autumn, winter, but the validity of taking such analogies as though expressing a fundamental principle of all history is to be challenged. Spengler's accounts of the different Cultures have been subjected to detailed criticisms. They are not important for our present purpose. But one final comment may be made. His contention that the extent of 'mechanization' in contemporary western civilization is a sign of its decline may well be rejected. For contemporary mechanization sets free human thought and energies for advance to a greater richness of experience, and is itself in large measure instrumental for particular values beyond those of other Cultures.

IV

The kind of empirical, non-Idealist, conception of history most widespread in the latter half of the nineteenth and the first quarter of the twentieth century may be best illustrated by writings of H. G. Wells (1866-1947), especially his *The Outline of History* (1920), which had a wide circulation in Britain and the United States. In a number of works published previously to it, *Mankind in the Making* (1903); *A Modern Utopia; New Worlds for Old* (1908), he had shown his deep-rooted and wide interest in social welfare and human progress. His interest in writing his *Outline of History* was to describe the factors leading to progress and to show some of the chief things which had hindered it. With an optimistic temperament, he placed more emphasis on the former. At the head of his Introduction, Wells quoted Ratzell: 'A philosophy of history of the human race worthy of the name, must be charged with conviction that all existence is one—a single conception sustained from beginning to end upon one identical law.' Wells stated the purpose of his own volume as 'an attempt to tell, truly and clearly, in one continuous narrative, the whole story of life and mankind as far as it is known today'. The work was not Philosophy of History as at present conceived, but as often previously thought of as Universal History. Nevertheless it indicated definite attitudes towards history and at least some of the author's views as to its meaning. He maintained that until the last two centuries there was no 'history' apart from 'merely priestly chronicles'. The peoples of earlier ages had no historical perspective. Even for the modern student of history it is difficult to sustain the proper sense of time intervals. The first nine chapters described, along the lines of the accepted natural science of his day, the processes, evolutionary and other, leading to 'the first true man', of the later Palaeolithic Age. Wells considered living organisms to have originated in the slime of ditches and sea beaches. Mind, for him the dominant factor in history, he simply accepted as having emerged in the processes of evolution. Though he gave due recognition to the continuities of history, he did not treat it as though a development along a single line but described different periods of peoples living their lives in the main independently of others. Instead of concerning himself with the ideas of diverse types of civilization, he sought similar processes in the histories of unrelated races and different periods. For him, the nature of man, as man, involved unity and similarity of greater consequence than differences of civilizations of particular times and localities. He insisted that the groups of mankind are not biological 'species' (the interbreeding of which leads to the sterile, as e.g. the mule). They are varieties capable of coalescence. In this there is a basis for the harmonization of mankind. But 'concurrently for thousands of years there have been two sets of forces at work, one tending to separate men into a multitude of local varieties and another to remix and blend these varieties together before a separate series has been established.

Wells described a civilization as a 'settlement of men upon an area continuously cultivated and possessed, who live in buildings continuously inhabited with a common rule and a common city or citadel'. In the course of history there has been a breaking into such settled communities by nomadic groups, and that with eventual benefits and human advance. Within the settled communities there arose the art of writing and along with it the ideas of science, of a universal righteousness, and of world polity. These ideas have arisen among different peoples at different times. 'The rest of the history of mankind is very largely the history of those three ideas of science, of a universal righteousness, and of a human commonwealth, spreading out from the minds of the rare and exceptional persons and peoples in which they first originated into the general consciousness of the race and giving first a new colour, then a new spirit, and then a new direction in human affairs.' Rejecting any notion that human history is predominantly a result of physical forces and conditions, he declared: 'All human history is fundamentally a history of ideas.' 'All the things that men and nations do are the outcome of instinctive motives reacting upon the ideas which talk and books and newspapers and schoolmasters and so forth put into people's heads. Physical necessities, pestilences, changes of climate, and the like outer things may deflect and distort the growth of history, but its living root is thought.' Though the invention of printing made for the possibility of a common sharing in knowledge, it was not until the provision of great supplies of paper that it has become actual. The importance of paper in living history cannot be over-estimated. Wells himself urged: 'It is scarcely too much to say that paper made the revival of Europe possible.'

The works of the professional historians upon which Wells relied gave little attention to 'the common man'. In a few passages Wells revealed some awareness of the question of what the meaning of history has been and is for the common man. Even after writing was invented the common man 'went on cultivating his patch, loving his wife and children, beating his dog and tending his beasts, grumbling at hard times, fearing the magic of the priests and the power of the gods, desiring little more than to be left alone by the powers above him. So he was in 10,000 B.C., so he was, unchanged in nature and outlook, in the time of Alexander the Great; so, over the greater part of the world, he remains today.' 'The real life of the ordinary man is his everyday life, his little circle of affections, fears, hungers, lusts, and imaginative impulses. It is only when his attention is directed to political affairs as something vitally affecting this personal circle, that he brings his reluctant mind to bear upon them.' Throughout most history settled peoples have been 'communities of obedience'. Most men have not shaken themselves 'loose from the desire for leading and protection' by their rulers. Yet 'Common men cannot shirk world politics and at the same time enjoy private freedom' but 'it has taken them countless generations to learn this'.

Along with the development of knowledge and of political government, Wells acknowledged the rôle of religion in history. 'Religion is something that has grown up with and through human association, and God has been and is still being discovered by man.' 'The beginnings of civilization and the appearance of temples are simultaneous in history. The two things belong together. The beginning of cities is the temple stage of history.' Though in their appropriate places he introduced accounts of other religions, as, for example, Buddhism, he paid more, and repeated attention to Christianity and Islām. 'It is in the fact that both Christianity and Islām in their distinctive ways, did at least promise for the first time in human experience . . . to give a common moral education for a mass of people, and to supply them with a common history of the past and a common idea of a human purpose and destiny that their enormous historical importance lies.' 'The history of Europe from the fifth century onward to the fifteenth is very largely the history of the failure of this great idea of a world government to realize itself in practice.' The inheritance of a complex dogmatic theology encumbered the Church. It had too much theology and not enough religion. Yet, 'through all its variations and corruptions Christianity has never completely lost the suggestion of a devotion to God's command that makes the personal pomps of monarchs and rulers seem like the insolence of an over-dressed servant and the splendours and gratifications of wealth like the waste of robbers. No man living in a community which such a religion as Christianity or Islām has touched can be altogether a slave; there is an ineradicable quality in these religions that compels men to judge their masters and to realize their own responsibility for the world.' 'And though much has been written foolishly about the antagonism of science and religion, there is indeed no such antagonism. What all these world religions declare by inspiration and insight, history as it grows clearer and science as its range extends display, as a reasonable and demonstrable fact, that men form one universal brotherhood, that they spring from one common origin, that their individual lives, their nations and races, interbreed and blend and go on to merge at last in one common human destiny upon this little planet amidst the stars. And the psychologist can now stand beside the preacher and assure us that there is no reasoned peace of heart, no balance and safety in the soul, until a man losing his life has found it, and has schooled and disciplined his interests and will beyond greeds, rivalries, fears, instincts and narrow affections.' 'The history of our race and personal religious experience run so closely parallel as to seem to a modern observer almost the same thing: both tell of a being at first scattered and blind and utterly confused, feeling its way slowly to the serenity and salvation of an ordered and coherent purpose. That, in the simplest, is the outline of history; whether one have a religious purpose or disavow a religious purpose altogether, the lines of the outline remain the same.'

Despite this acknowledgment of religion in history, it may be asked if Wells's account of religion was adequate. His conception of it was predominantly social, as ideally the universal brotherhood of man. The inadequacy of that conception actually involves a misrepresentation of the nature of religion as found in history. Wells rarely used the term 'God'. He had, indeed, in *God, the Invisible King* (1917) described God as though 'personal', the leader, the captain of mankind in its warfare against evil and its struggle for the good. But as though embarrassed by that idea, he made no use of it in *The Outline of History* or in any later writings. Wells's attitude was essentially Naturalistic. The religions go beyond any

Naturalism in their implications, which Wells ignored, as to the origin of life and minds. He failed to acknowledge that 'temples', to which he referred, have been for the worship of, for communion with, God as other than Nature and mankind. They have not been merely places for human assembly with the motive of cultivating social feelings, and social co-operation. Religions have been concerned with God and a continued existence beyond the terrestrial in ways for which Wells had no appreciation. Something that is essential in this is covered by the comment of Antonia Vallentin: 'Of all the human states of mind the one most shut off from Wells, most foreign to him, was that of mystical rapture.'

The Outline of History was published after the first World War. In it Wells still retained something of his earlier optimism, but he manifested serious doubts of its validity. 'We are beginning to understand something of what the world might be, something of what our race might become, were it not for our still raw humanity . . . Make men and women only sufficiently jealous or fearful, or drunken and angry, and the hot red eyes even of cavemen will glare out at us today. We have writing and teaching, science and power, we have tamed the beasts and schooled the lightning, but we are still only shambling towards the light. We have tamed and bred the beasts; but we have still to tame and breed ourselves.' In his final chapter he placed more emphasis on the moral. Knowledge has to be backed by moral force. 'History has still to become a record of human dignity.' The life of man 'must to the end remain a high and terrible enterprise'. For its future advance he advocated a comprehensive education for all sides of life for all individuals. Though he declared that 'Human history becomes a race between education and catastrophe,' he yet believed then that 'the world . . . progresses and will progress.' Wells lived through the second World War, and in works, fictional and other, urged his ideas of world federal government and universal education. Nevertheless, despite flickers of his earlier optimistic temperament, he tended to pessimism. He seemed no longer to be able to view history as a rising spiral. In 1938 (?9), in a lecture in Australia, he declared that the human race had reached its zenith and was sinking through successive disasters to final extinction. In his *Mind at the End of its Tether* (1946) nothing remained of his earlier hopeful attitude: the human species appeared confronted with final disaster. But this loss of faith of Wells as an old man should not be taken as evidence of a general rejection of the kind of conception of history for which he had stood. Others shared his doubts, and many still do, but much of contemporary life is still inspired with faith in the kind of progress he had described in *The Outline of History*.

CHAPTER IX

ATTITUDES OF HISTORIANS AND THE APPROACH TO PHILOSOPHY OF HISTORY

I

PHILOSOPHY of history is a subject for the philosopher rather than for the historian. In pursuing it, the philosopher should consider what historians have said of history as actual and as record. Today it is primarily modern historians who require attention. Yet the philosophical student of the nature and significance of history will not exaggerate the importance of views on history in any period, even his own. Despite the contention, sometimes made, that there have been 'real' historians only within the last two centuries, it may be acknowledged that there have been historians of merit since the days of ancient Greece and Rome. The freedom for and the facilities for historical research were, however, greatly enhanced in the nineteenth century and opportunities for it have continued to increase. The most important feature of modern historical study is not its methods but its vast scope. Almost all periods of the histories of people of the Occident and the Orient have been given some attention. While many historians have concerned themselves with specific aspects or parts of history or approached it from particular points of view and with diverse attitudes, there is increasing appreciation of comprehensive synthetic treatments of all sides of historical life.

Historians like J. G. Droysen (1808-1884) and H. von Treitschke (1834-1896) concentrated on patriotic nationalistic writings. Von Treitschke wrote: 'Only a stout heart which feels the joys and sorrows of the Fatherland as its own can give veracity to a historical narrative.' J. R. Seeley (1834-1895) and E. A. Freeman (1823-1892) devoted themselves mainly to the history of past politics; K. von Savigny (1779-1861) and H. Maine (1822-1888) to the historical development of law; H. Milman (1791-1865) and A. Harnack (1851-1930) to ecclesiastical history. Wider studies of particular periods and regions were carried on by J. Burckhart (1816-1897) and G. G. Coulton (1858-1947). The former in *The Civilization of the Renaissance in Italy* (1860), taking for his theme 'the thought and conduct, religion and art, scholarship and speculation—the reconstruction of the mental and moral atmosphere' of the period of the Renaissance in Italy, concerned himself more with the culture of the higher classes. The latter, though he had special interests in the religious life of Europe in the Middle Ages, in his *Mediaeval Panorama* (1938) described 'the English scene from the Conquest to the Reformation' for all sides of life, of peasants, artisans, merchants, priests and nobility. Within recent years many attempts have been made to survey external movements and inner feelings and ideas in the history of civilization. In France, H. Berr 1863-1942) inaugurated a series of historical studies under the general title of *L'Évolution de l'Humanité*, volumes of which were incorporated in the English *The History of Civilization*. The composition of a history of civilization is extremely difficult, especially with regard to the arrangement of the very varied data. Yet it has come to be appreciated that for an understanding of the significance of history, for proper perspectives and an adequate conception of what history is in its fullness, that history is essential. Only with such a basis can a tenible philosophy of history be developed.

There has been much discussion whether the historian, as historian, may go beyond an investigation and description of the facts to the passing of judgments on them and giving an interpretation of them in terms of conceptions of the meaning of life. Many historians have tried to find a pragmatic use in what they discovered. Some have even considered such possible use to be the main motive of their study. It is interesting that there has been more concern with, and more divergence of opinion relative to the ethical than the intellectual and the aesthetic, as to the appropriateness or otherwise of passing judgments. Lord Bolingbroke (1689-1751), describing history as 'philosophy teaching by examples', maintained that it leads to a knowledge of 'certain general principles and rules of life and conduct which always must be true because they conform with the invariable nature of things'. The historian will form a 'general system of ethics and politics on the surest foundations, on the trial of those principles and rules in all ages and on the confirmation of them by universal experience'. From such a standpoint, history has special significance with reference to morality. Joseph Priestley (1733-1804) advocated the study of history as 'strengthening virtue', for 'in history vice never appears tempting'. 'History enables us to form just ideas of the dignity and weakness of human nature.' William E. H. Lecky (1838-1903), who made a special study in the history of morals, while showing that there is 'perpetual change in the standard enacted and also in the relative value attached to particular virtues' maintained that 'what may be termed the primary elements of morals are unaltered'. In the last sentence of his book he wrote: 'There are certain eternal moral landmarks which can never be removed.' Lord Acton (1834-1902) strongly insisted on attention to ethical implications in history. In applying the moral code with 'inflexible integrity', he found 'the secret of the authority, the dignity, and the utility of history'. He said that the essence of history might be regarded as the striving for moral freedom, remarking to James Bryce that a history of liberty 'might be made the central thread of all history' showing 'through all events and in all ages the play of those moral forces, now creating, now destroying, always transmuting, which had moulded and remoulded human institutions and had given to the human spirit its ceaselessly changing forms of energy'. In a communication to the contributors to *The Cambridge Modern History*, in 1898, Acton indicated his conception of universal history: 'By Universal History, I understand that which is distinct from the combined history of all countries, which is not a rope of sand, but a continuous development, and is not a burden on the memory, but an illumination of the soul. It moves in a succession to which the nations are subsidiary. Their story will be told, not for their own sake, but in reference and subordination to a higher series according to the time and degree in which they contribute to the common fortunes of mankind.'

This predominantly ethical view of the task of the historian was challenged by Mandell Creighton (1843-1901) who protested against making history a branch of moral science. It was criticized by Henry Lea (1825-1909) on the ground of the relativity of the ideas of right and wrong to time and place. He urged that conduct must be considered with reference to the contemporary and local ethical standards. But his criticism failed to distinguish between the variable modes of conduct relative to circumstances and the persistent moral values. Lea implied the latter when in his conclusion he assumed that we can judge an ethical conception to be 'distorted'. He said that it is in accordance with scientific method 'To represent him (i.e. Philip II of Spain) as the inevitable product of a distorted ethical conception.' There was a reiteration of the ethical point of view by the American historian, W. R. Thayer (1859-1923), who wrote: 'The spirit of righteousness may take different forms in externalizing itself, but it does not change. So the loyalty of man to man, friendliness to one's neighbour, self-sacrifice, are abiding elements of human nature in the same way that iron and gold and oxygen are elements in the chemical world.'

The approach to the study of history from any standpoint of subjective bias was condemned by Leopold von Ranke (1795-1886), widely regarded as the foremost historian of his period. Though severely criticized by some of his fellow countrymen, a number of non-German historians were inspired by his works and followed his methods. He insisted on unprejudiced historical research with 'tranquil objectivity', relying on sources contemporary to the period surveyed. Though he made some profession of being free from *a priori* philosophy, he was under the influence of Hegel, trying to represent each age as expressing a fundamental general idea, leading, as new ideas arose and became synthesized, to an increasingly comprehensive life. Von Ranke made the study of history his chief aim in life. In his first work, *Histories of the Roman and German Peoples* (1824), he wrote that as a historian he wished 'simply to relate the facts as they actually occurred'. For this purpose he turned to a wide and detailed study of contemporary documents of the periods he was treating. He insisted that the ultimate aim of historians is universal history, and that only with an all comprehensive vision could studies of details be properly pursued. The ideal he himself aspired to, was 'to look at the world, past and present . . . to see with unbiased eyes the progress of universal history.' But the study of universal history necessitates careful enquiries into details. He emphasized the recognition of the uniqueness, the peculiarities, of different races, peoples, and times. With the concatenation of universal history full justice must be done to the individuality of great men in their particular nations. History is predominantly 'the work of certain minds, fulfilling more or less certain conditions and each having a certain sphere of influence'. But great men have arisen out of widespread movements of their time and environment. There is some justification for the view that von Ranke's interests were largely political, but he made constant references to civilization. Though his works were specifically concerned with particular periods, countries and individuals, he aimed at suggesting their intrinsic significance as making contributions to the growth of civilization. Somewhat repelled by Sir Walter Scott's historical novels, he said that historical truth is 'far more beautiful and far more interesting than romantic fiction'. History has to 'record the actions and sufferings of that multiple being which we are, at once savage, powerful, good, noble, calm, soiled and pure, to follow it from its birth and in its shaping'. His attitude was basically ethical, and he maintained that 'moral influences regulate the greatness and decline of nations'. Acknowledging the place of religion in history, he saw that it did not offer a solution to all our problems. Thus, for example, 'God uses wars for purposes which we do not know.' He was not a propagandist for Christian ideas of history. He declared: 'I am a historian first, then a Christian.'

Von Ranke's French contemporary, F. P. G. Guizot (1787-1874) devoted himself to special studies of civilization. His best known works were *The History of Civilization in Europe*

(1828) and *The History of Civilization in France* (1830). Philosophy of history, he wrote, 'consists in showing the relations of events with each other . . . the causes and effects of events'. He himself was especially interested in social and individual ideals. He asked: Is civilization good or evil? Some decry it 'as teeming with mischief to man'; others laud it 'as the means by which he will attain the highest dignity and excellence'. Is there a general civilization of the whole human race? Is the destiny of mankind to achieve a universal civilization through the efforts of succeeding generations? Guizot felt assured that that is man's destiny on earth. Civilization is still in its infancy. Many are so impressed with the obvious social aspects of civilization that they do not give due recognition to what is directed to the individual's satisfaction rather than to his social conditions. Yet there is much of that kind of satisfaction in religion, literature and the fine arts. Civilization is not comprised solely in what contributes to social well-being and happiness. It includes the development of the individual mind. Civilization reveals itself in 'the melioration of the social system and the expansion of the mind and faculties of man'. Near the beginning of the two works mentioned, he quoted from an unnamed writer: 'Human societies are born, live and die upon earth; there they accomplish their destinies. But they contain not the whole man. After his engagement to society there still remains to him the more noble part of his nature; those high faculties by which he elevates to God, to a future life, and to the unknown blessings of an invisible world. We, individuals, each with a separate and distinct existence, with an identical person, we, truly endowed with immortality, we have a higher destiny than that of states.' Guizot said that the questions involved in that statement haunt us 'at the close of the history of civilization'.[1]

Guizot emphasized the progress of men towards liberty. The Protestant Reformation was a step in the emancipation of the mind. The political revolutions in England, America, and France had overcome absolute temporal power. But in the period following those revolutions he saw a tendency to

---

[1] The kind of answers he gave them are implied in his views on religion, discussed previously in our Chapter IV.

political centralization and thus to some curtailing of liberty. One general result was not seriously affected: freedom of enquiry, 'one of the greatest facts of modern society'. In general, though not with equal pace or to the same extent, there has been progressive development of the two sides of civilization, individual and social. Guizot emphasized the fact of the wealth of values in modern Occidental civilization. There is a struggle for the unity of its constituents, but unity is only approached, never fully attained. 'In reflecting on his destiny, man recognizes in it three different sources, and divides, so to say, into three classes the facts which make up the whole. He is conscious of being subject to events which are the consequence of laws, general, permanent, and independent of his will, but which by his intelligence he observes and comprehends. By the act of his free will he also creates events, of which he knows himself as the author, and these have their consequences and enter into the tissue of his life. Lastly, he passes through events, in his view neither the result of those general laws from which nothing can withdraw him, nor acts of his own liberty, events of which he perceives neither the cause, nor the reason, nor the author.' He may put these last down to chance (which 'explains nothing') or to God.

In some accord with Guizot's general view, A. C. de Tocqueville (1805-1859) also considered that there was in the past and is in the present a continuous advance towards social equality. Such conceptions were challenged by their contemporary, C. A. Sainte-Beuve (1804-1869), who warned: 'History seen from a distance undergoes a singular metamorphosis: it produces the illusion—most dangerous of all—that it is rational. The follies, the ambitions, the thousand strange accidents which compose it, all these disappear. Every accident becomes a necessity. Guizot's history is far too logical to be true.' Nevertheless, since Guizot's time many historians have maintained that there has been a wide general advance of civilization. The American historian, D. J. Hill (1850-1932), contended that there is 'in the nature of man a scale of values by which progress or decadence in art, industry, economics, politics, literature and philosophy may be estimated'.

INTERPRETATIONS OF HISTORY

With the progress made in the sciences of the physical world in the nineteenth century, it is not surprising that some should conceive the possibility of a 'science of history' with the use of methods similar to those of the physical sciences. It has already been seen in Chapter VIII that something of this kind was what Buckle hoped to achieve. Addressing the Royal Historical Society in London in 1874, G. G. Zerffi (1821-1892) talked of subjecting 'all the phenomena of history by a strictly scientific method to the laws of causation', and declared that the scientific study of history is impossible, if chance, predestination or free will are assumed. In a later paper on 'The Science of History', he wrote: 'The most important duty of a historian is to show to conviction that the facts could not have happened differently, and that if the same causes were at work, they would inevitably again produce the same effects.' The American historian, G. B. Adams (1851-1925), accepted the idea of a Science of History analogous with the physical sciences. He asked: 'Are the objective facts with which the historian deals, the past actions of the race, determined in their occurrence by forces acting according to fixed laws, and similar in character and method of operation to the forces which are at work in the sphere of the natural and physical sciences?' He answered: 'I am convinced that in this sense history is a science.' The American advocates of what they called 'The New History' had considerable sympathy with this view. Stressing the modern advances in the sciences of psychology, ethnology, anthropology, sociology and politics, they have urged that history is essentially a co-ordination of the results of these. That these sciences are important for the study of history is unquestionable, but even taken together they do not constitute history as the historian is concerned with it. F. J. Teggart (1870-1946) claimed that this 'New' history differed from the old merely in respect to the selection of the factual data considered. Even thus it is not so new as its advocates supposed. As R. H. Shryock (1893-   ) has pointed out: 'The wider interest in social and cultural history was always maintained throughout the eighteenth and nineteenth centuries.' The work of J. R. Green (1837-1883), especially his *Short History of the English People* (1874), was an outstanding example. J. B. Bury (1861-1927) in his inaugural lecture at Cambridge in 1903 entitled 'The Science of History' did not take 'scientific' to mean the adoption of the methods and concepts used in the physical sciences. History is to be scientific through systematic and minute analysis of the sources, with an adequate perspective having regard to the future as well as the past, and an appreciation of the unity and continuity of history.

There have been attempts to found a science of history more specifically on social psychology. H. A. Taine (1828-1893) endeavoured to discover the nature of history by the study of 'national psychology', especially as mirrored in art and literature. K. Lamprecht (1865-1915) definitely asserted: 'Modern science of history is in the first place science of social psychology.' To raise history to the status of a science, with the methods of the natural sciences, he advocated Culture History on the lines of collective psychology. In spite of these contentions, his own works in the main followed the traditional methods of historians. It may be doubted whether many historians have been much impressed by this conception of a 'science of history'. As G. L. Burr (1857-1938) said: 'the psychological betrays itself ever by the interest in the law or type, the historical by its eye to the individual', particular person, group, event, movement, anything with a proper name or can be treated under a proper noun. 'What history is, what history is for, must be asked of history itself' and not from the sciences which are its neighbours. Burr urged J. H. Robinson (1863-1936), a proponent of the 'New' history, to turn 'to what the historians have themselves said of history ... to Xenopol, with his clear distinction between the sciences which deal with the facts of repetition and those that deal with the facts of succession ... to Grotenveldt with his vindication of history as the study of values ... to Monod ... to Bury.' C. A. Beard (1874-1948) wrote that contemporary historiography 'has broken the tyranny of physics and biology' and called Spengler's biological analogy: 'A fantastic morphological assumption.' 'The historian is bound by his craft to recognize the nature and the limitations of the scientific method and to dispel the illusion that it can produce a science of history embracing the fullness of history or of any large phase, or past actuality.'

One fundamental question has impressed itself more and more on historians in recent times: as to the kind of general synthesis, if any, that can be found in history. F. M. Fling (1860-1934) insisted on the importance of that question thirty years ago. The essentially qualitative—as distinct from quantitative—character of the synthesis in history, and its nature as rational system and not universal repetition, was emphasized by D. J. Hill: 'The social life of man, the progress of civilization, the formation and development of political institutions, the rise and fall of empires, the relation between independent states—all these transformations belong to the sphere of qualitative change, defy mathematical calculation and demand a new instrument of comparison and comprehension.' 'Since history is the record of particular occurrences, no one of which has the property of universal necessity, and since—unlike the phenomena of Nature—the phenomena of human history can never be exactly repeated, they contain no data that warrant absolute generalizations and therefore disclose no necessary laws of action.' 'The function of the historian is not to deal with uniformities or with universal formulas, but with the variations of human conduct as measured by its success and its failure upon the scale of national endeavour.' Yet there has been considerable doubt as to the nature and extent of possible synthesis. The English historian, H. A. L. Fisher (1865-1940), confessed: 'One intellectual excitement has, however, been denied me. Men wiser and more learned than I have discerned in history a plot, a rhythm, a predetermined pattern. These harmonies are concealed from me. I can see only one emergency following upon another, as wave upon wave, only one great fact with respect to which, since it is unique, there can be no generalizations, only one safe rule for the historian: that he should recognize in the development of human destinies the play of the contingent and the unforeseen. This is not a doctrine of cynicism and despair. The fact of progress is written plain and large on the page of history: but progress is not a law of its nature. The ground gained by one generation may be lost by the next. The thoughts of men may flow into channels which lead to disaster and barbarism.' With definite recognition of some of the implications of this statement, A. J. Toynbee has made a strong case for the view that history has some definite patterns. His work is considered in our later pages.

II

'While historical science is extending its conquests in every direction,' remarked G. P. Gooch in 1913, 'the Philosophy of History lags behind.' That is still true. Some historians have so depreciated philosophy of history that it has been called their *bête noire*. Among philosophers it has been neglected more than any other subject. Some of its earlier forms may justify this attitude of historians. Earlier philosophies of Nature are similarly scorned by modern scientists. But as these are being replaced by critical philosophies of science, so also critical philosophies of history are being developed. As far back as 1880, the German historian Ernst Bernheim, in his *Historical Research and the Philosophy of History*, complained of the 'unnatural alienation' between these. He endeavoured to bring about their co-operation first by criticism of the predominant types of philosophy of history and secondly by a constructive indication of what philosophy of history should be on the basis of historical research and its methods. He classified earlier philosophies of history in two groups: (1) the Idealistic-philosophical; and (2) the Naturalistic-scientific. He showed that both are one-sided and inadequate in principle and in method. He welcomed the 'new' philosophy of history as taking up 'the problem as a whole' in relation with empirical historical research. History is not simply 'narrative' (erzählend), but a distinctive science with its own methods. It is not merely an indication of the unique (events, persons, groups, epochs), but a search for relationships of the unique within 'wholes' which are themselves unique. The 'universals' of repetition of natural-scientific method have a place in history, but its own 'universals' are systematic 'wholes'. Whatever be said of 'free will', the spontaneous, the contingent, the emergence of the new, must be acknowledged in history. He suggested that all the problems of philosophy of history could be brought under two enquiries: What are the factors in historical development? What is the 'value-result' of the course of history? Bernheim's criticism may be considered of more significance than his constructive suggestions. Yet, as pointing to the transition to the modern form of philosophy of history, his suggestion of these two kinds of problems is of the highest value.

No one could affirm that the modern form of philosophy of history is fully developed, but its character is already evident from a number of works which have been leading up to it. Many, but not all, of the most distinctive early contributions were by German philosophers. In 1883, Wilhelm Dilthey (1833-1911) in his *Introduction to the Sciences of Mind*, drew attention to the differences between the methods appropriate for the study of the facts of history and those used for physical nature. In his lecture, 'History and the Natural Sciences', W. Windelband (1848-1915) restated and elaborated the same conceptions as Dilthey's. Georg Simmel (1858-1918) in *The Problem of the Philosophy of History* (1907) asked primarily: 'How is history possible?' He raised this question in a manner similar to the way Kant asked: 'How is knowledge possible?' Concentrating on the epistemological problems of the possibility of history as record, he did not make clear that a fundamental for philosophy of history is to enquire into the ultimate bases of actual history. Yet it is actual history, rather than history as record, which is itself only one aspect of that history, with which philosophy of history is concerned.

In 1887, the Italian scholar, Antonio Labriola (1943-1904) had clearly pointed to some of the directions to be taken, but his book, *The Problems of the Philosophy of History*, did not become widely known. Philosophy of history is not 'Universal History' written from the standpoint of preconceived philosophical ideas. It is primarily an investigation of the methods, the principles, and the systems of historical sciences. History cannot be considered as on a parallel with the natural sciences. The latter need make no reference to the spatial and temporal determinations of the objects with which they deal, but for history such particular configurations are fundamental. As distinguished from the genetic view of psychology, we need an epi-genetic theory of civilization in history. He warned against the forcing of particular ideas of unity on to the facts of history, a failing common among conceptualists. We should not presuppose any kind of unity. Similarly he challenged the validity of applying the idea of progress in a general way to the totality of human achievements, and insisted on the necessity for analysis and discrimination between different currents in history. That will make more clear the actual retrogressions as well as the progress in history. But Labriola himself later thought he found the main principle of history in the sequences and interrelations of economic conditions in what, in accord with Marx and Engels, he called 'Historical Materialism'.

The Rumanian historian A. D. Xenopol (1847-1920), though he definitely stated that his work was not itself a philosophy of history, insisted on some important aspects of history significant for it. His chief emphasis was on history as concerned with the 'facts of succession' as distinguished from those sciences predominantly occupied with the 'facts of repetition'. Historical succession cannot be described with 'universal laws' such as may be formulated for the repetitive processes of Nature. Its sequences are rather 'series' to be expressed by comprehensive ideas with their distinctive significance. The series are never repeated in identical fashion, and are dissimilar in their temporal and spatial relations. Admitting that the successive facts of history are causally related, Xenopol discussed the nature of causality in history. Among its causes he recognized states of consciousness of individuals and of groups. 'This state of consciousness constitutes the force without which no other cause can act.' But to attribute causality in history to such force alone, or to the antecedent phenomena alone, are both alike 'inexact'. He gave considerable attention to the 'unconscious forces' present in history. 'One sees how, on how many sides, the unconscious penetrates in the march of events.' A 'fundamental thought' for history is that it is only after an event has occurred that it is possible to consider it as the effect of a cause.

Though his treatment of the subject was inadequate, Xenopol raised the problem of the relation of values to history. In this he was chiefly concerned with urging the elimination or the reduction to a minimum of moral judgments from historical writing. He failed to appreciate the wider and deeper implications of the problem of values for a philosophy of history. But that problem received careful detailed consideration in the works of the Danish historian A. Grotenfelt (1863-1942). In *The Estimation of Value in History* (1903), he argued that when the historian embarks on the highest tasks of his science he cannot entirely avoid the great questions of philosophy, including those of valuation. In a later work he surveyed values and valuation as found empirically in history in the common consciousness of peoples, in the work of historians, and in philosophies of history. He concluded that though history has to do *immediately* only with 'relative temporal realities and values', 'absolute', 'supra-temporal' values must be admitted. We must conceive the ideals in actual history as stages towards, as symbols of, these absolute values. He expressed his own 'belief' that the 'point' from which one may pass from temporal values to supra-temporal lies 'in the pure, personal, inner feeling (Gesinnung) of the individual'.

The most thoroughgoing pioneer studies for a modern philosopher of history were those of Heinrich Rickert (1863-1936) carried on contemporaneously with the almost equally important ones of Ernst Troeltsch (1865-1927). Only his central theses can be referred to here. Taking the starting-point for a philosophy of history to be the logic of the historical sciences, Rickert devoted his chief works to it. Every object of knowledge can be viewed 'universally', with regard to the characteristics it shares in common with others of the same class; and 'individually' with regard to what may be predicated of it alone. While history requires some generalizations, its logical method is primarily 'individualizing', for it has to treat of a person, a nation, or other group, an age or other period of time, in its peculiarity as individual. The 'universal' of history is not the same as the abstract universal of the natural sciences, but a 'whole' in which 'particulars' have their significance. 'The "universal" of historical association is nothing other than the historical whole itself; not a system of universal concepts, for all comes into consideration in history always in its particularity, its uniqueness and individuality.' Evolution in history implies the emerging of something new, and therefore is different from the repetition, the persistent uniformities, implied in 'laws' as formulated in the natural sciences. Causal connections are to be sought in history, but Rickert pointed out that all *actual* causes are particulars, to be distinguished from the *conceptual* generalizations of 'laws'. Human freedom is not to be regarded as involving 'causeless action'. The second main emphasis in his works is on values and valuation. In history, what has no relation to values has no meaning to us. Every historian who is not a mere specialist has something of this aspect of philosophy of history in deciding what he holds to be more or less important. But the attitudes of historians are often one-sided in contrast with the all-sidedness of an adequate philosophy of history, which implies a system of values. Is it possible, and if so how, to arrive at a system of values which would enable us to grasp the meaning of the whole course of history? The historian finds general conceptions of values in history, but no merely empirical or relativist view of values is adequate. Thought needs, and we somehow apprehend, ideal norms and standards 'transcending' the historical facts, which we judge with reference to them. Thus, Rickert, with Windelband and Troeltsch, passed to the affirmation of absolute transcendent values and carried over to history the method of Kant's critical philosophy. In so doing all these writers so emphasized the concepts of transcendent norms that they failed to apply to actual value experiences as particulars their individualizing method of the philosophy of history. Rickert seems also to have felt some difficulty concerning a basis for the objectivity of such transcendent values. For he rejected any passing from the actual persons, groups and events of history to an Absolute beyond them, declaring that the concept of a *Transcendent Reality* is 'unfruitful' and 'completely empty' for philosophy of history, that indeed, with it the realm of history loses all its meaning. He may be judged not to have attained a clear idea as to the objectivity of 'transcendent values' in relation with actual history. Further, pre-eminent as was his pioneer work in the field, Rickert did not produce a comprehensive systematic philosophy of history.

Most of these German philosophers, engaged in logical analysis and the nature of valuation, did not give very much attention to the problem of general synthesis. That problem was the main concern in the work of H. Berr (1863-1942). In *La Synthèse en Histoire* (1911) he brought together some fundamental ideas and methods adopted in *La Revue de Synthèse historique* which he had edited since 1900. He made adverse criticisms of some earlier forms of philosophy of history, singling out for specific rejection the kind illustrated by him with a quotation from Fichte: 'The philosopher, who as philosopher, occupies himself with history, follows the course *a priori* of the plan of the world, which plan is clear for him *without any need of help from history*; and if he makes any use of history it is not to ask from it any demonstration of what may be ... it is only to confirm by examples and to utilize in the real world of history that which has already been comprehended without resource to its aid.' On the other hand, Berr urged that works by professional historians restricted to the careful survey and recording of facts, with all the paraphernalia of references and documentation, were not adequate. For scientific knowledge there must be 'synthesis', and his volume was devoted to a discussion of the nature of 'historical synthesis'. He described his work as a 'logical treatise' concerned with the preliminaries of a philosophy of history rather than the exposition of a system. He criticized treatments (mostly German) that represented history as concerned solely with the unique and particular in contrast with the attention of the natural sciences to uniformities and repetitions; and those (mostly French) that endeavoured to describe history with general sociological principles. He protested against the disdain of some historians for all philosophy of history, insisting that it considers problems that historians must face, and gives some suggestions with regard to them. He discussed almost all of the literature on the subject available at the time, but curiously made no reference to his fellow-countryman, Renouvier, with whom he was in much agreement in fundamentals.

Berr, with some though not complete justification, charged Rickert and those allied with him with making a divorce in thought between 'Nature' and 'History'. The unique events in history are not a mere chaos: they come into consideration of the historian only in a continuity or development. With development, besides change, there is an element of permanence. History is in Nature, and Nature is in History. Though specific characteristics of each may be distinguished, their constant relations must be acknowledged. The future work of historians will be rightly directed 'only with a deepening of the notion of cause. The search for causes in history has always been made gropingly by empiricists, has been conceived in a simple fashion by philosophers, and has not been definitely organized by logicians.' In his chapter 'Causality in History', he emphasized the importance of recognition of different kinds of causes. 'The chief problem of synthesis in history' consists in the relation between 'laws' (as of Nature) and 'contingencies' and 'reasons' (the term he substituted for the usual 'final causes'). Berr discussed contingencies as forms of chance and of individuality. For history there is an element of chance even with relation to laws, for 'when' and 'where' they are found in operation depends on something existing at a particular time and place. Chance is evident in a multiplicity of ways, illustrated by the suggestion that history might have been changed if Cleopatra's nose had been bigger. But Berr insisted that chance events must be considered in relation with their whole context and if that is done it will be seen that history has in no way been dominated by chance. The contingency of individuality is present in individual persons, groups, geographical environments, and in time periods. But these all have some uniformities with which their uniqueness is related. While some historians have exaggerated the rôle of chance, others have overemphasized individuality in history except that which is related either with 'the order of laws' or 'the order of reasons'. It is on the latter that Berr placed most emphasis, in that it involves the psychical. Psychology is an auxiliary of history (as record), for history (as actual) 'is the birth and the development of the soul (psyche)'. Further, the basis is in the individual person. 'We always fall back on the individual.' 'The crowd does not think; a tribe, a people, in a state of crisis does not think, does not create thought, it uses the thought it has acquired.' 'It is the individual who creates.' But it was of the essence of Berr's conception of synthesis in history, that the thought and creation of individuals always has a relation with the laws (of the physical world), with society and the 'laws of reason' (reflective logic related with the ends sought).

III

Berr did not himself attempt a universal historical synthesis. He organized others in a task of writing sections for it. The result of any such co-operative undertaking must inevitably be less unified than one by a single historian. With its range, its detail, its penetration into causal relationships, its comprehension of unities, its tracing of geneses, growth and decays, and its consideration of the fundamental nature and meaning of history, *The Study of History*[1] by Arnold J. Toynbee is the nearest approach to a universal history which man has yet achieved. With its consideration the task of the present volume is justifiably concluded. In the space here available even a brief summary is impossible. It is unnecessary, for we are concerned specifically with his ideas on the nature and interpretation of history.

Toynbee does not write of history with the pose of an impartial spectator but as conscious of himself as a participant in it. He tells of occasions when he seemed to have 'a momentary communion with the actors in particular historic events'. In one 'ineffable' experience he 'was directly aware of the passage of history gently flowing through him in a mighty current and of his own life welling like a wave on the flow of this vast tide' (X. 139). Though the intrinsic nature of history may have to be thus inwardly felt, the results of study of it require conceptual formation. For Toynbee, history is one of innumerable angles of vision of reality. Noting and

[1] A. J. Toynbee: *The Study of History*, Oxford University Press, London and New York; I-III 1934; 2nd ed. 1935; IV-VI 1939; VII-X 1954.

criticizing H. A. L. Fisher's disavowal of finding any patterns or rhythms in history, he maintains that there is now sufficient data for reliable conclusions as to the characteristics of history. He rejects Oswald Spengler's biological analogies and his account of history as dominated by omnipotent necessity with a law of disintegration and dissolution.

For proper perspectives the wholes studied must go beyond nations to include the wider unities of civilized societies. His classification of twenty-one of these, useful for his purpose, has no claim to 'absolute or universal' validity. The change from primitive to civilized societies is 'a transition from a static condition to a dynamic activity' (I. 195). But, he says that 'of even the most advanced and progressive civilization' the humanity of an 'overwhelming majority of ordinary people' is 'virtually primitive humanity' (III. 243). Nevertheless, the proletariat, 'in civilized societies but not fully of them' play a most important rôle in history, especially in religion. Detailed accounts of the different civilizations do not concern us here. With reference to their growth and disintegration the concepts of 'Challenge' and 'Response' are of special significance. Growth and disintegration are both dependent upon the modes and the extent of responses, their success or failure, to challenges of the physical and social environment. History has not been determined simply by physical conditions. Toynbee places emphasis on the inwardly generated responses. Success or failure may depend on the severity of the challenges relative to the capacities and power of those responding. 'There are challenges of a salutary severity that stimulate the human subject of the ordeal to a creative response, but there are also challenges of an overwhelming severity to which the human victim succumbs ... The most stimulating challenge is to be found in a mean between deficiency of severity and excess of it' (II. 393). There is a definite distinction between the processes of growth and disintegration. In growth there is 'a challenge evoking a successful response generating a fresh challenge, evoking another successful response, and so on, pending a breakdown'. In disintegration there is 'a challenge evoking an unsuccessful response, generating another attempt resulting in another failure, and so on, pending dissolution' (VI. 281). The challenges of the physical environment had much to do with the geneses of the different civilizations. A healthy civilization has never been one of static rest. 'The single finite movement from a disturbance to a restoration of equilibrium is not enough if genesis is to be followed by growth. To convert the movement into a repetitive, recurrent rhythm, there must be an élan which carries the challenged party through equilibrium into an over-balance which exposes him to fresh challenges and thereby inspires him to make a fresh response in the form of a further equilibrium ending in a further over-balance—and so on in a progression which is potentially infinite' (III. 119; see also 128). Ease is inimical to civilization. Physical nature in some measure prevents it. Men have to make constant efforts to retain against Nature's counterattacks what they have gained from it.

History has not been concerned merely with adaptation to Nature: it has also been an adaptation of Nature for cultural ends. 'All races are capable of civilization' (I. 238). But though differences of races are natural phenomena, the differences of civilizations cannot be traced solely to them. Geographic expansion is not a criterion of the growth of civilization. Toynbee is inclined to consider it predominantly otherwise. 'The correlation between geographical expansion and social disintegration holds good as any rate *on the whole*' (III. 150; see also 134). Though that *may* have been the case in the past, Toynbee surely does not mean to imply that the hope for a world-wide civilization in the future is to be ruled out. There may be static techniques in an advancing civilization or developing techniques in a declining one. In an advancing civilization new techniques may set the human mind free for other aims. In this connection and otherwise, Toynbee introduces the term 'Etherealization' for 'a transferring of energy or shift of emphasis from some lower sphere of being or sphere of action to a higher sphere'. The range and diversity of etherealization is very great. Action in the external field comes to count for less and that in the internal field for more (III. 193).

There are some periods and conditions of comparative rest

and consolidation, and others of increased activity and advance. Toynbee uses the Chinese terms *Yin* and *Yang* to refer to these. The Yin state involves the integration of custom and the Yang the differentiation of civilization: aspects of a 'rhythmical pulsation which runs through all the universe' (III. 376; see also I. 196; 207). Some periods of disturbance and severe challenges he designates as 'Times of Troubles'. In these men have tried to get away from the problems of the present by directing attention to the past or to the future or by striving for detachment from the mundane. Archaism, Futurism, Detachment try to solve a spiritual problem raised by a disturbance or a breakdown of the flow of the previous-growing civilization. 'Futurism and Archaism are both alike attempts to break with an irksome present by taking a flying leap out of it into another reach of the stream of time without abandoning the plane of mundane life on earth' (VI. 97). Both fail. Detachment—as typified in the Greek and Indic forms Toynbee discusses—is essentially 'a way of knowledge' with effort to attain emancipation from feeling. 'It does not provide a solution of the problem it sets out to solve.' There is a fourth possibility: Transfiguration, with relation to which 'Withdrawal and Return' have significance. For after a temporary withdrawal from the mundane to concentrate on the spiritual, there is a return with the aim of its transfiguration as contrasted with attempts permanently to escape from it.

Toynbee found that civilizations have not had complete meaning in themselves and so they ceased to be for him 'intelligible fields' of study. He passed on to the consideration of universal states, of wider range than civilizations but including them. Universal states 'come into existence in order to put a stop to wars and to substitute co-operation for bloodshed' (VII. 55). They embody a rally 'from the long unhalted rout of a Time of Troubles' (VII. 43), bring a sense of unity on the political plane, and continue the impression made by their founders and successors. Considering them as the goal of human endeavour, their citizens idolize them and regard them as though immortal. But history has invariably shown that a universal state is not the real goal of human strivings. It has brought only ephemeral peace. Nevertheless there have been benefits from universal states of the greatest significance in history, through their systems of communications, colonies, languages, laws, calendars, civil services, money, and to a less extent because not completely carried through, citizenship. Toynbee maintains that though universal states have at times persecuted and tried to suppress religions their chief beneficiaries have been universal churches. The nature of universal states is merely humanistic and as such they are inadequate to meet the problems of history. 'The only society that is capable of embracing the whole of Mankind is a superhuman *Civitas Dei*, and the conception of a society that embraces all Mankind and yet nothing but Mankind is an academic chimaera' (VI. 10).

Universal churches are a higher species of society than civilizations or universal states. Toynbee recognizes four of them: Hinduism, Māhāyāna Buddhism, Christianity, and Islām. He treats them as in some sense spiritually equivalent, none being complete or perfect, but each with distinguishing aspects of man's spiritual striving. They express the diversity of human nature, each satisfying some 'widely experienced human need' (VII. 442). They have been 'created by the internal proletariats of societies in decline' (I. 99). They arose in Times of Troubles. Their 'distinguishing mark' is 'that they all had as a member the One True God' however they regarded the Godhead. 'This human fellowship with the One True God, which had been approached in the primitive and been attained in the higher religions, gave to these certain vital virtues that were not to be found in either primitive societies or civilizations. It gave power to overcome the discord which was one of the inveterate evils of Human Society; it offered a solution of the problem of the meaning of history; it inspired an ideal of conduct which could be an effectively potent spiritual stimulus for the superhuman effort of making Human Life possible in This World; and it availed to exorcize the peril that was inherent in mimesis when this was oriented not towards the One True God, but towards one of Man's fellow human creatures' (VII. 507).

From his survey of history Toynbee cannot admit any claim for any religion that it 'is an exclusive and definitive revelation of Spiritual Truth' (VII. 428, n. 2). His expression regarding such a view is very strong. 'In denying that other religions may be God's chosen and *sufficient* (italics mine: A.G.W.) channels for revealing Himself to some human souls, it seems to me to be guilty of blasphemy.' If such denial is involved in Christianity, he cannot call himself a Christian. His view of history is not the traditionally orthodox Christian one as expounded, for example, by Augustine, von Schlegel, and Reinhold Niebuhr.[1] At times his language suggests acceptance of the Christian doctrine of divine incarnation. 'As Saint Athanasius had divined, God had to come down to man's level in order to raise Man to His' (VII. 514). Man's Creator 'manifested His power as Love Incarnate' (VII. 565). He talks of 'the love that had moved God to become Man in order to become Man's Saviour' (VII. 536). 'And now, as we stand and gaze with our eyes fixed upon the further shore, a single figure rises from the flood and straightway fills the whole horizon. There is the Saviour . . .'(VII. 278). He says that the uniqueness of the divine event is the essence of the New Testament story. But is this story record of actual historical fact or a form of poetry? He himself asks: 'Is God to be prohibited by a human veto from revealing Himself through *Dichtung*, if He will, as well as through *Wahrheit*?' (VI. Annex. 538). But with his thought on all four of the universal churches, he surmises that 'in the next chapter of a henceforth oecumenical human history, the four higher religions sprung from the ruins of civilizations of the second generation were destined to have an intimate spiritual encounter with one another, and whatever the outcome of this great imminent spiritual event might prove to be, it was evidently likely to inaugurate a new era in human life in This World' (VIII. 628).

Toynbee's final interpretation of history is fundamentally religious. It is necessary to bring together some of his statements as to the spiritual life. In an Annex (VII. 701-715), he discusses the antithetical character of 'the circumstances favourable to spiritual and to secular progress'. In a survey that appears to be inadequate to justify the conclusion, he

[1] This seems confirmed by his publication of a criticism of his position from the orthodox standpoint by Mr M. Wight: VIII, Annex iii pp. 737-748.

writes of the antithesis as 'a law for religion'. There are, however, 'breaches' of it 'for spiritual life in a wider sense' may cover 'aesthetic and non-religious cultural experiences and activities' (VII. 702-3; 547). Two conclusions are suggested to him: (1) 'that there is an intrinsic incompatibility between the quest for the Beatific Vision, which is the goal of Religion and the pursuit of material power in any of its forms'; and (2) 'that the secular vein of spiritual activity is a middle term between Religion on the one hand and the pursuit of material power on the other' (VII. 710). Of secular cultural experiences, he deals with Music, Poetry (Literature) and Visual Arts, but not with the intellectual achievements in Natural Science. The key idea of 'Challenge' and 'Response' is to be applied to religion. There is a challenge to decision in the antithesis of the spiritual to the material taken as an end in itself. The freedom of the individual to make vital decisions is a fundamental character of reality as revealed in history. Though Toynbee talks of freedom as 'relative', the general implication of his exposition is that intrinsically it is absolute: the relativity is as to the alternatives varying from occasion to occasion of its exercise. He gives full recognition to this basic factor of history that so many philosophers, historians, and theologians ignore, minimize, or deny. The challenge between good and evil, life and death, 'from God may evoke in human souls creative responses that are genuinely free human acts' (IX. 382). God challenges man by setting before him 'an ideal of spiritual perfection, which man has perfect freedom to accept or reject. The Law of Love leaves Man as free to be a sinner as to be a saint' (IX. 405). The sinner has opportunities to learn through suffering, to repent, and to seek the aid of God's grace. The channel for man's communion with God is not the intellect but the 'sub-conscious'. The religions have made use of intellectual forms obtained from beyond themselves and often become bound by them. 'The Christian Church as an institution has remained enmeshed in a Hellenistic theology of its own weaving' (VII. 484 n. 1). Toynbee is opposed to any attempt to express religion in our day in terms of contemporary thought. Without such, and freed from entanglements of the past, it must presumably be without intellectual formulation. That suggests that the spiritual life (as religious) is to be solely a mystical experience of the Beatific Vision in so far as that is attained (VII. 475 n. 1).

Though Toynbee says that the true concern of history 'is with the lives of societies in both their internal and external aspects' (I. 46); and his exposition is of civilized societies, universal states and universal churches, the individuality of particular persons seems to be fundamental in his interpretation of history. Though individual persons are obviously never for their whole lives in complete isolation, human souls are unique. 'All spiritual reality and therefore all spiritual value, resides in persons' (VII. 562). 'The society is not and cannot be anything more than a medium of communication through which the individual human beings interact with one another. It is human individuals and not human societies that make human history' (III. 231). Society is just 'a particular kind of relation between human beings' (III. 223). This is in accord with one of his main contentions, expounded in many ways throughout his volumes, that no kind of human society as such has complete significance in itself. Creation is due 'either to creative individuals or at most creative minorities' (III. 239), and 'there are, of course, creative individuals at the back of creative minorities' (III. 365 n.). The stress on inwardness, especially in his basic interpretation of history, implies the reality of the individual. 'It is through the inward development of Personality that individual human beings are able to perform those creative acts in their outward fields of action that cause the growth of human societies' (III. 233). The criterion of growth is 'to be found in progress towards self-determination'. No organization of society as such could be 'a substitute for the spiritual redemption of souls' (IX. 347). The view that individual souls (including those of the past) exist and have existed 'for the sake of society and not for their own sake or for God's' is 'repugnant' and 'inconceivable' when 'we are thinking in terms of the history of Religion' in which 'the progress of individual souls through This World towards God . . . is the end in which the supreme value is found' (VII. 564). 'If we believe that the true end of Man is "to glorify God and fully to enjoy Him for ever" we must believe that this glorious opportunity of attaining to communion with God and beholding the Beatific Vision has been open to every creature that had ever been raised by God to the spiritual stature of humanity' (VII. 565). It is interesting that Toynbee gives no detailed discussion of the hope of immortality or the belief in reincarnation in this connection.

In the tenth volume there is a section entitled 'The Quest for a Meaning behind the Facts of History' (X. 126-144). It is composed mainly of quotations from religious and poetic works classic in history. There are also many passages elsewhere in his work indicating his convictions as to the ultimate significance of history. 'The historical angle of vision shows us the physical cosmos moving centrifugally in a four dimensional frame of Space-Time; it shows us Life on our own planet moving evolutionarily in a five dimensional frame of Life-Space-Time; and it shows us human souls raised to a sixth dimension by the gift of the Spirit, moving through a fateful exercise of their spiritual freedom either towards their Creator or away from Him' (X. 2). 'The meaning behind the facts of History . . . is a revelation of God and a hope of communion with Him; but in this quest for a Beatific Vision that is visible to a Communion of Saints we are ever in danger of being diverted from our search for God to a glorification of Man . . .' (X. 126). God is always present and active in history. 'The experience which only poetry can convey, of the unity of the Spirit in the bond of peace is the revelation of a fellowship which is not the work of men but is an act of God . . .' (X. 140).

In his relatively brief consideration of evil Toynbee seems to point beyond history to a supra-temporal condition. In flashes of illumination 'a human understanding may divine that the service performed for God by Evil as an instrument of creation is a reality in God's creative work in Time which is transcended in those higher spheres that are entered by a concrete Doctor Marianus in the last act of the second part of Goethe's *Faust*; and this intuition is shared with Christianity by Buddhism if the conception of *Nirvāna* is to be interpreted as implying the extinction, not of Life itself, but of the tragically creative experiences of Life-in-Time' (IX. 402). So, in another place he writes: 'A human being who, in this life, *breaks the bonds of Time and Space* (italics mine, A.G.W.) by entering into communion with God is transfigured, if the communion becomes habitual, from a savage into a saint' (VII. 514).

The author thanks Dr Toynbee and the Oxford University Press for permission to make the quotations from *The Study of History*.

INDEX

Acton, Lord, 233
Adams, G. B., 238
Altmeyer, J. J., 181
Ambrose, 85
Ancillon, F., 178-9
Aristotle, 73-4
Arnold, M., 130
Augustine, 85, 118-23

Bacon, F., 146, 152, 154
Bakunin, M., 205-6
Beard, C., 239
Bernheim, E., 241-2
Berr, H., 232, 246-8
Bodin, J., 151
Bolingbroke, Lord, 233
Bossuet, 124, 158, 159
Brown, J., 161
Bryce, J., 233
Buckle, T. H., 210-14, 238
Bunyan, J., 126-7
Burckhardt, J., 145, 232
Burke, E., 176
Burr, G. L., 239
Bury, J., 124, 158, 239
Butterfield, H., 137-9

Calvin, J., 125
Carlyle, T., 187, 190-2
Chan, W-T., 28n, 36, 37
Chrysippus, 78
Chuangtze, 21-5, 40
Chu Hsi, 35-6
Cicero, 79-80
Comte, A., 203, 206, 207-8, 210, 217
de Condorcet, 160, 207
Confucius, 26-30, 40, 132, 175
Coulton, C. G., 232
Cournot, A., 209-10
Creighton, M., 234

Croce, B., 154, 155, 157, 197-202

Das Gupta, J. N., 59n
Damiani, P., 123
Dante, 123
Descartes, R., 148, 152
Dewey, J., 39
Dhalla, M. N., 95-8
Dilthey, W., 242
Domitian, 82
Droysen, J. G., 231

Emerson, R. W., 187-90
Empedocles, 67
Epictetus, 82
Epicurus, 77
Eucken, R., 196-7

Fichte, J. G., 173, 182-3
Fisher, H. A. L., 240, 249
Fling, F. M., 240
Freeman, E. A., 232
Friedlander, D., 104
Fries, J. F. 173
Fung Yu-lan, 24, 31, 34

Gautama, the Buddha, 52-4, 132
Gibbon, E., 170-1
Godolphin, A., 69
Gooch, G. P., 241
Green, J. R., 238
Grotenfelt, A., 239, 244
Grotius, 152
Guizot, F. P. G., 130, 235-7

Haeckel, E., 220
Han Fei Tze, 34
Harnack, A., 232
Hegel, G. W. F., 173, 179, 183-6, 199, 201, 204, 206
Heraclitus, 61

258

INDEX

Herbart, G. F., 173
Herbert of Cherbury, 168, 170
Herder, J. G., 165-7
Hemocrates, 69
Herodotus, 68-9
Hesiod, 66-7
Hill, D. J., 237, 240
Hobbes, T., 148-50
Hume, D., 162-3
Hsun Tze, 32

Inge, W. R., 85-9
Iqbal, M., 110-113

Jesus, 114-17, 124, 130, 132, 175
Job, 101-2

K'ang Yu-wei, 18, 37
Kant, I., 171-4
Kaye, J., 160, 162
Ibn Khaldun, 109-10
Krause, K. C. F., 179-81
Kropotkin, P., 206
Kuo Hsiang, 24

Labriola, A., 200, 242-3
Lamprecht, K., 239
Lanson, G., 158
Laotze, 19
Law, W., 161
Lea, H., 234
Lecky, W. E. H., 233
Leibnitz, G. F., 150-1, 159
Leo X, Pope, 145
Lessing, G. E., 145
Lin Yutang, 25, 40-2
Livy, 80
Lotze, H., 181n, 192-4
Lucretius, 77
Luther, M., 125

Machiavelli, 143-4, 150, 163
Madhvacharya, 59

Mahavira, 51
Maimonides, 103
Maine, H., 232
Mandeville, B., 160-2
Mani, 93
Marcus Aurelius, 79, 82-5
Marx, K., 200, 204-5, 206, 243
Mazdak, 83
Mencius, 30-2
Metchnikoff, E., 219-22
Milman, H., 232
Montefiore, C., 105
Montesquieu, 157, 159
Morgan, G. A., 214
Mo-Ti, 17, 30, 31
Muhammed, 106-7

Niebuhr, R., 133-7
Nietzsche, F., 113, 214-16
Nordau, M., 216

Paine, T., 174-7
Parmenides, 67
Parsvanatha, 51
Pericles, 66, 70
Pico della Mirandola, 145
Plato, 70-3, 152, 154
Plotinus, 85-9
Polybius, 74-6, 144
Porphyry, 87
Poteat, H. M., 74n
Priestley, J., 233

Quinet, E., 167

Radhakrishnan, S., 62-4
Ramanuja, 59
von Ranke, L., 234
Reade, W. W., 217-19
Renouvier, C., 194-6
Rickert, H., 244-6
Ritschl, A., 130
Robertson, J. G., 192

259

Robinson, J. H., 239
Rousseau, 159-60
Ruggiero, T., 198

Sainte-Beuve, C. A., 237
Sankaracharya, 56-60
von Savigny, K., 232
Savonarola, 143
Schelling, F. W. J., 173, 179, 181
von Schlegel, F., 127-30
Schopenhauer, A., 173, 186-7
Schweitzer, A., 132
Seeley, J. R., 130, 231
Shryock, R. H., 238
Simmel, G., 242
Smith, A., 161, 163-5
Spencer, H., 222
Spengler, O., 222-4, 239, 249

Tacitus, 70, 152
Taine, H., 239
Teggart, F. J., 238
Thayer, W. R., 234
Thucydides, 69

Tindal, M., 169-70
de Tocqueville, A. C., 237
Toynbee, A. J., 241, 248-57
von Treitschke, H., 231
Troeltsch, E., 244-5
Tsou Yen, 18
Turgot, R. J., 159

Vatsyayana, 50
Virgil, 76-7
Vico, G., 152-7
Voltaire, 158-9

Waley, A., 28
Wang Yang-ming, 36-7, 38
Warde-Fowler, W., 74n, 76, 77
Wells, H. G., 224-30
Windelband, W., 242, 245

Xenopol, A. D., 239, 243

Zarathustra, 90-4, 132
Zen, 87
Zerffi, G. G., 238